Tradition and Rhetoric in the Pastoral Epistles

Studies in Biblical Literature

Hemchand Gossai
General Editor

Vol. 3

PETER LANG
New York • Washington, D.C./Baltimore • Boston
Bern • Frankfurt am Main • Berlin • Vienna • Paris

Mark Harding

Tradition and Rhetoric in the Pastoral Epistles

PETER LANG
New York • Washington, D.C./Baltimore • Boston
Bern • Frankfurt am Main • Berlin • Vienna • Paris

Library of Congress Cataloging-in-Publication Data

Harding, Mark.
Tradition and rhetoric in the Pastoral epistles / Mark Harding.
p. cm. — (Studies in biblical literature; vol. 3)
Includes bibliographical references and index.
1. Bible, N.T. Pastoral epistles—Criticism, interpretation, etc.
I. Title. II. Series.
BS2735.2.H37 227'.83066—dc21 97-12463
ISBN 0-8204-3767-0
ISSN 1089-0645

Die Deutsche Bibliothek-CIP-Einheitsaufnahme

Harding, Mark:
Tradition and rhetoric in the pastoral epistles / Mark Harding.
–New York; Washington, D.C./Baltimore; Boston; Bern;
Frankfurt am Main; Berlin; Vienna; Paris: Lang.
(Studies in biblical literature; Vol. 3)
ISBN 0-8204-3767-0 Gb.

Cover design by James F. Brisson.

The paper in this book meets the guidelines for permanence and durability
of the Committee on Production Guidelines for Book Longevity
of the Council of Library Resources.

Printed in the United States of America.

to Sue
and our children
David, Philip, Mary-Ann and Jane

CONTENTS

EDITOR'S PREFACE

More than ever the horizons in biblical literature are being expanded beyond that which is immediately imagined; important new methodological, theological, and hermeneutical directions are being explored, often resulting in significant contributions to the world of biblical scholarship. It is an exciting time for the academy as engagement in biblical studies continues to make advances.

This series seeks to make available to scholars and institutions scholarship of a high order, which will make a significant contribution to ongoing biblical discourse. This series includes ventures in established and innovative methodologies in both general and particular areas of biblical study. For every volume considered for this series we ask the question as to whether it will push the horizons of biblical scholarship. The answer must be *yes* for this inclusion.

In this volume, Mark Harding has explored in great depth and with meticulous care the authorship and persuasive strategies of the Pastoral Epistles. While much has been written about these letters, the author has not only provided a substantial overview of the relevant literature but has taken the discussion to higher levels. Guided by the Pauline scholarship of J. Christiaan Beker, Dean Harding investigates persuasive strategies which the author of the Pastoral Epistles employs to commend the Pauline tradition, and to actualize the Pauline heritage and give it new voice.

In his wide ranging examination, Dean Harding explores extensively both the tradition of writing letters of moral exhortation and the theory and practice of oratory in the Greco-Roman world. This is an eminently readable and well argued thesis, and the author's conclusions will certainly expand the horizons of this area. Any future scholarly examination of the Pastoral Epistles will do well to reckon with this volume. The horizon has been expanded.

Hemchand Gossai
General Editor

ABBREVIATIONS

ABR	*Australian Biblical Review*
Acts Pet.	*Acts of Peter*
ad Alex.	*Rhetorica ad Alexandrum*
ad Her.	*Rhetorica ad Herennium*
AET	Abraham J. Malherbe, *Ancient Epistolary Theorists* (Atlanta: Scholars Press, 1988)
AnBib	Analecta Biblica
ANF	A. Roberts and J. Donaldson (eds.), *The Ante-Nicene Fathers* (reprint, 10 vols.; Grand Rapids: Eerdmans, 1986)
ANRW	W. Haase and H. Temporini (eds.), *Aufstieg und Niedergang der römischen Welt* (Berlin/New York: de Gruyter, 1972–)
Bar.	Baruch
2 Bar.	*2 Baruch*
Bib. Ant.	Pseudo-Philo, *Biblical Antiquities*
BJRL	*Bulletin of the John Rylands Library*
CBQ	*Catholic Biblical Quarterly*
CD	Cairo (Genizah text of the) *Damascus (Document)*
1 Clem.	*1 Clement*
de Inv.	Cicero, *de Inventione*
Did.	*Didache*
Eccl. Hist.	Eusebius, *Ecclesiastical History*
Ep. Clem.	*Epistula Clementis* (Pseudo-Clementine literature)
Ep. Jer.	Epistle of Jeremiah
EvQ	*Evangelical Quarterly*
FRLANT	Forschungen zur Religion und Literatur des Alten und Neuen Testaments
Herm. Vis.	*Hermas, Visions*
HUCA	*Hebrew Union College Annual*
Ign. *Eph.*	Ignatius, *Letter to the Ephesians*
Ign. *Magn.*	Ignatius, *Letter to the Magnesians*
Ign. *Pol.*	Ignatius, *Letter to Polycarp*
Ign. *Smyrn.*	Ignatius, *Letter to the Smyrnaens*
Ign. *Trall.*	Ignatius, *Letter to the Trallians*
Int	*Interpretation*
JAAR	*Journal of the American Academy of Religion*
JAC	*Jahrbuch für Antike und Christentum*
JBL	*Journal of Biblical Literature*
JEThS	*Journal of the Evangelical Theological Society*

JRelS	*Journal of Religious Studies*
JSNTSS	Journal for the Study of the New Testament Supplement Series
JSNT	*Journal for the Study of the New Testament*
JSOT	*Journal for the Study of the Old Testament*
JThS	*Journal of Theological Studies*
Jub.	*Jubilees*
LAE	*Light from the Ancient East*
LCL	Loeb Classical Library
LTP	*Laval théologique et philosophique*
2 Macc.	2 Maccabees
4 Macc.	4 Maccabees
Mart. Pol.	*Martyrdom of Polycarp*
MM	J. H. Moulton and G. Milligan, *The Vocabulary of the Greek Testament* (Reprint; Grand Rapids, Mich.: Eerdmans, 1983)
NovT	*Novum Testamentum*
NPF	P. Schaff and H. Wace (eds.), *Nicene and Post-Nicene Fathers* (Revised Edition; Grand Rapids: Eerdmans, 1989)
NTA	E. Hennecke and W. Schneemelcher (eds.) *New Testament Apocrypha* (Revised Edition; Louisville: Westminster/John Knox, 1992)
NTOA	Novum Testamentum et Orbis Antiquus
NTS	*New Testament Studies*
ÖBS	Österreichische biblische Studien
OTP	J. H. Charlesworth (ed.), *The Old Testament Pseudepigrapha* (2 vols; Garden City, N.Y.: Doubleday, 1983–85)
P. Oxy.	B. P. Grenfell and A. S. Hunt *et al.* (eds.), *The Oxyrhynchus Papyri* (London: Egypt Exploration Society, 1898–)
P. Tebt.	A. S. Hunt and J. Gilbart Smyly *et al.* (eds.), *Tebtunis Papyri* (London: Humphrey Milord, 1902–33)
Pol. *Phil.*	Polycarp, *Letter to the Philippians*
Prot. Jas.	*Protevangelium of James*
PSB	*Princeton Seminary Bulletin*
1QapGen	*Genesis Apocryphon* of Qumran Cave 1
1QH	*Thanksgiving Hymns* from Qumran Cave 1
4QAmram	Testament of Amram from Qumran Cave 4
RB	*Revue Biblique*
RThR	*Reformed Theological Review*
SBL	Society of Biblical Literature
SBLDS	Society of Biblical Literature Dissertation Series
SE	*Studia Evangelica*
Sir.	Sirach
SNTSMS	Society for New Testament Studies Monograph Series
T. Abr.	*Testament of Abraham*

T. Sol.	*Testament of Solomon*
T. 12 Patr.	*Testaments of the Twelve Patriarchs*
TDNT	G. Kittel (ed.), *Theological Dictionary of the New Testament* (trans. G. W. Bromiley; Grand Rapids, Mich.: Eerdmans, 1964–76)
ThZ	*Theologische Zeitschrift*
Tob.	Tobit
TynB	*Tyndale Bulletin*
WUNT	*Wissenschaftliche Untersuchungen zum Neuen Testament*
ZNW	*Zeitschrift für die neutestamentliche Wissenschaft*

INTRODUCTION

While engaged in the doctoral program in New Testament at Princeton Theological Seminary during 1989–1993, I encountered persuasive arguments for the pseudonymity of the Pastoral Epistles (PE). These arguments have to do not only with historical and linguistic matters and points of theological contrast between the undisputed Pauline letters and the PE but also with the manner in which the author addressed the audience of the letters. Under the guidance of J. Christiaan Beker, then Richard J. Dearborn Professor of New Testament Theology at the Seminary, I resolved to undertake a thorough investigation of the PE in my doctoral dissertation. This book is a modified version of that research conducted under Chris Beker's liberating tutelage.

Much of the scholarly investigation of the PE since ca. 1800 has concentrated on demonstrating that Paul did or did not write them. Initially this enquiry was conducted on the level of the historical and linguistic investigation of the PE as documents of the early Christian era. The examination of the theology of the PE served to shed further light on the historical circumstances of their writing and their place in the history and development of the Pauline trajectory in early Christianity.

The present consensus, though I use that term advisedly, holds that the PE are deutero-Pauline and pseudonymous.[1] I believe that in broad terms the arguments of the nineteenth century scholars Ferdinand Christian Baur and Heinrich Julius Holtzmann against Pauline authorship have not been rebutted in essence. Nevertheless, there are staunch defenders of the Pauline authorship of the PE. Many of these are attempting to preserve a particular construal of biblical authority. They judge the contention that there might be pseudonymous books in the canon to be incompatible with their notion of revealed truth. Pseudonymity is simply equated with deception and fraud. God could not be the "author" of such works. Other scholars maintain a discreet and veiled conviction that Paul was their author.[2]

This book will not mount a defence of the view that the PE are pseudonymous. However, it is my conviction that pseudonymity best accounts for the theological, and, to a lesser extent, the linguistic differences between the PE and the undisputed Pauline letters. However, the contention that there are pseudepigrapha in the Bible suggests to many conservative Christian scholars that its authority and inspiration are thereby compromised. To these I commend the direction outlined by David G. Meade on this issue.[3] He accounts for the pseudonymity of the letters on the grounds that the author was claiming his letters as the actualization (*Vergegenwärtigung*) of authoritative Pauline tradition. This continues a pattern observable in the prophetic, wisdom, and apocalyptic literature of the Hebrew Bible and the early Jewish era, and, indeed, in the NT itself, of pseudonymous authors contemporizing the body of tradition associated with an inspired prophetic figure or comprising an authoritative literary deposit. Attribution of the PE to Paul, argues Meade, "is primarily an assertion of authoritative tradition, not of literary origins."[4] The author was convinced of the continuity between his actualization of Pauline tradition and the originator of the tradition, and saw himself as the spokesman of the apostle.[5] From a confessional point of view, the PE, it can be affirmed, are both canonical and inspired. The letters are a testimony to the (divinely superintended) dialogue between "inspired" community and the body of tradition originating with an inspired individual, Paul. The fruit of that engagement, Meade observes, is canon.[6]

Scholarship, influenced by historical-critical presuppositions, has understandably expended much energy arguing the case for or against Pauline authorship since the PE claim to be written by Paul. As far as one can tell the early (orthodox) church, from the late second century at least, saw no cause to contest that claim. Both sides in the debate have subjected the letters to a comparison with what we know from the other letters of Paul, Acts, and other documents emanating from the early Christian movement. I must confess to a sense of unease with the outcome of much of the application of this methodology. In a number of instances the PE have been so contrasted with the Pauline letters and the theological distinctives often regarded as genuinely Pauline that the PE have been accorded little appreciation.[7] By the same token, one suspects that in other comparative studies the differences between the Pauline correspondence and the PE have been drastically minimized.

In recent times a number of monographs have appeared which have sought to account for and trace the ways in which Pauline tradition has been transmitted and adapted in the PE. These studies, almost exclusively theological and comparative in their orientation, I class as exercises in "tradition history" (*Traditionsgeschichte*). Although comparative, they have also focused attention on the author of the PE as a theologian in his own right.[8] By and large they have avoided negative value judgments of his achievement. Rather, they have sought to lay bare the precise contours of the resulting adaptation, or even modification, of the Pauline heritage. This book devotes a significant amount of attention to a number of German scholars who have examined the PE from this point of view, and whose insights deserve to be more widely known in English-speaking biblical scholarship.

In the last few years J. Christiaan Beker has contended for a theological and hermeneutical approach to the Pauline correspondence which he has applied to the post-Pauline deposit, including the PE, by the use of a comparative method. One of the strengths of his approach is the clarity with which he tackles the task of identifying what are essential and non-negotiable Pauline theological distinctives. Beker conducts his research into the deutero- (Ephesians, Colossians, 2 Thessalonians, and the PE) and post-Pauline literature (Luke-Acts) by comparing these documents with the contours of Paul as theologian he has elucidated from the seven undisputed letters. Consequently, Beker underscores the probability that the Paul of the undisputed letters could have not been the author of the deutero-Pauline letters. Nevertheless, I will argue that the strengths and limitations of his work are those shared by other scholars writing *traditionsgeschichtliche* analyses of the PE.

Still other monographs have been appearing since the early 1980's and, in the case of Robert J. Karris' dissertation on the PE,[9] early in the previous decade. These have made their focus either the social context of the PE or the way in which the Pastor addresses his audience. I have in mind not only Karris' dissertation but also the monographs of David C. Verner, Lewis R. Donelson, Benjamin Fiore, Margaret Y. MacDonald, and Reggie M. Kidd, not to mention the work of Klaus Berger in the broader field of NT scholarship.[10] In these studies attention is given, not so much to the Pastor's interpretation and re-casting of the theological distinctives of the Pauline heritage, but to the possible influences from his social and cultural context on his manner of writing. These studies are indebted to comparatively new, and related, directions in NT scholarship, namely, the application of methodologies derived from the field of social science and the analysis of classical and Greco-Roman rhetoric.[11] These approaches allow the possibility of the appreciation of the Pastor, not just as a theologian of the Pauline tradition, but as a creative and persuasive *communicator* of the Pauline heritage in his social context.

While there are studies of aspects of the rhetoric of the PE, none, to my knowledge, attempts an extensive analysis of these letters from the rhetorical point of view. While the investigation of the theological formulations of the PE, as compared to Paul in the undisputed letters and in the Pauline corpus as a whole, is valuable and necessary, the enterprise results in a potentially limited and one-dimensional appreciation of the PE. This book seeks to show that there are illuminating insights to be gained from the study of the rhetorical strategies employed by the Pastor. Comparison of these, where relevant, with those adopted by Paul will promote a new awareness of the creativity of both writers in commending their message to their respective audiences.

Consequently, I intend to demonstrate the literateness of the PE as letters and as persuasive communications of the received Pauline heritage when set alongside the backgrounds of the tradition of epistolary moral exhortation and the conventions of oratory. I will be seeking, therefore, to align the PE with other expressions of moral exhortation and pastoral guidance in the Greco-Roman, Jewish, and early Christian contexts.

The book has three chapters with a conclusion. Chapter one surveys four major approaches to the PE, including contributors to the *traditionsgeschichtliche* perspective, and investigates some of the major interpretive positions that scholars have adopted since Baur—Beker included. Chapter two investigates the Pastor's use of the strategies that were available to and selected by him in presenting his interpretation and communication of the message of Paul in such a form that the PE might be recognized as continuous both with the Pauline letter deposit and the venerable tradition of letters of moral exhortation. The form of the Pauline letter, I will argue, is the medium for the Pastor's actualization of his interpretation of Paul. Chapter three examines the rhetorical strategies commended in the rhetorical handbooks and principally applied to speeches. I will seek to identify the major strategies employed in this tradition of rhetoric, and to show how the PE evidence the use of these. The conclusion surveys the results of my research into the epistolary and rhetorical strategies utilised in the PE before proposing the outline of a new understanding and appreciation of them.

NOTES

1 See, e.g., the recent commentaries, monographs and extended discussions by J. L. Houlden, *The Pastoral Epistles* (Penguin Books, 1976); V. Hasler, *Die Briefe an Timotheus und Titus* (Zürich: Theologischer Verlag, 1978); Robert J. Karris, *The Pastoral Epistles* (Wilmington; Glazier, 1979); A. J. Hultgren, *I – II Timothy, Titus* (Minneapolis: Augsburg, 1984); U. Borse, *1. und 2. Timotheusbrief, Titusbrief* (Stuttgart: Verlag Katholisches Bibelwerk, 1985); R. F. Collins, *Letters That Paul Did Not Write: The Epistle to the Hebrews and the Pauline Pseudepigrapha* (Wilmington: Glazier, 1988); J. Roloff, *Der erste Brief an Timotheus* (Zürich: Benziger Verlag, 1988); N. Brox, *Die Pastoralbriefe* (Regensburg: Pustet Verlag, 1969 repr. 1989); F. Young, *The Theology of the Pastoral Epistles* (Cambridge: Cambridge University Press, 1994) and L. Oberlinner, *Die Pastoralbriefe* (3 vols.; Freiburg/Basel/Wien: Herder, 1994–96). Recent contenders for Pauline authorship are G. D. Fee, *1 and 2 Timothy* (San Francisco: Harper & Row, 1984); T. C. Oden, *First and Second Timothy and Titus* (Louisville: John Knox, 1989); D. Guthrie, *The Pastoral Epistles* (Rev. ed.; Grand Rapids: Eerdmans, 1990) and G. W. Knight III, *The Pastoral Epistles* (Grand Rapids: Eerdmans, 1992). Recently, Luke Timothy Johnson (*The Writings of the New Testament* [Philadelphia: Fortress, 1986], 387–9 has argued that 2 Timothy has an excellent claim to be a genuine letter of Paul. In his more recent *Letters to Paul's Delegates: 1 Timothy, 2 Timothy, Titus* (Valley Forge: Trinity Press International, 1996) Johnson argues that there are no plausible reasons why Paul could not have written each of the PE. J. Murphy-O'Connor ("2 Timothy Contrasted with 1 Timothy and Titus," *RB* 98 [1991], 403–18) has mounted a case for the different authorship of 2 Timothy, leaving open the possibility of Pauline authorship.

2 I judge Philip H. Towner, *The Goal of Our Instruction* (Sheffield: JSOT Press, 1989) to fall into this category. In his more recent *1–2 Timothy & Titus* (IVP New

Testament Commentary Series; Downers Grove: IVP, 1994), 30–35 Towner contends that either an amanuensis wrote the letters (thus explaining the differences between the PE and the remainder of the Pauline corpus), or that Paul himself did. With respect to the latter, Towner argues that since the majority of the letters in the corpus are co-authored the PE might be in Paul's own hand and, therefore, represent his own style.

3 David G. Meade, *Pseudonymity and Canon* (Tübingen: Mohr, 1986). See also James D. G. Dunn, "The Problem of Pseudonymity" in *The Living Word* (Philadelphia: Fortress, 1988), 65–85.

4 Meade, *Pseudonymity and Canon*, 139.

5 Meade, *Pseudonymity and Canon*, 199.

6 Meade, *Pseudonymity and Canon*, 213–4; cf. Brevard S. Childs, *The New Testament as Canon: An Introduction* (London: SCM, 1984), 21–24.

7 See, e.g., the discussion of the PE in S. Schulz, *Die Mitte der Schrift* (Stuttgart/Berlin: Kreuz Verlag, 1976), 100–09.

8 I persist in using masculine pronouns in referring to the author of the PE. Given the injunction of 1 Tim. 2.11–15, I infer that no woman could have written these letters, even a woman who agreed with the stance taken in this passage. I prefer to refer to the author of the PE as the "Pastor."

9 Robert J. Karris, "The Function and Sitz im Leben of the Paraenetic Elements in the Pastoral Epistles," Th.D. Dissertation; Harvard University, 1971. Karris seeks (a) to shed light on the "Problems of locating some 75% of the material in the Pastorals in time, place, and thought world" (xi), and (b) to investigate the paraenesis of the PE with respect to their use of polemic against opponents, and "their leitmotif of teaching" (xi).

10 David C. Verner, *The Household of God* (SBLDS 71; Chico: Scholars Press, 1983); Lewis R. Donelson, *Pseudepigraphy and Ethical Argument in the Pastoral Epistles* (WUNT 39; Tübingen: Mohr, 1986); Benjamin Fiore, *The Function of Personal Example in the Socratic and Pastoral Epistles* (AnBib 105; Rome: Pontifical Biblical Institute Press, 1986); Margaret Y. MacDonald, *The Pauline Churches: A socio-historical study of institutionalization in the Pauline and Deutero-Pauline writings* (SNTSMS 60; Cambridge: University Press, 1988); Reggie M. Kidd, *Wealth and Beneficence in the Pastoral Epistles* (SBLDS 122; Atlanta: Scholars Press, 1990); Klaus Berger, *Formgeschichte des Neuen Testaments* (Heidelberg: Quelle & Meyer, 1984) and "Hellenistische Gattungen and Neues Testament, *ANRW* II.23.2 (1984), 1034–1432, 1831–85.

11 My interest does not lie in the field of rhetorical ornamentation, but rather in the rhetoric of the letter genre and the persuasive strategies to be encountered in the

rhetoricians' discussion of the genre of rhetoric (forensic, deliberative, and epideictic), and the use of the three major "proofs," namely, reason, ethos and pathos. Aristotle discusses ornament in his *Rhetoric* in 3.1–12. For studies of ornamentation and its implication for persuasion and effect in the NT materials, see C. G. Wilke, *Die neutestamentliche Rhetorik: Ein Seitenstück zur Grammatik des neutestamentlichen Sprachidioms* (Leipzig: Arnold, 1843) and J. Weiss, "Beiträge zur Paulinischen Rhetorik", in *Theologische Studien: Herrn Wirk. Oberkonsistoriahlrath Professor D. Bernhard Weiss zu seinem 70. Geburtstage dargebracht* (Göttingen: Vandenhoeck & Ruprecht, 1897), 165–247.

CHAPTER ONE

FOUR APPROACHES TO THE PASTORAL EPISTLES

The first extant attestation of the PE clearly identified as letters of Paul occurs in Irenaeus (ca. 180 C.E.).[1] 1 Tim. 2.1–2 is attested (without ascription of authorship) in the contemporaneous or slightly earlier writings of Athenagoras and Theophilus.[2] Allusions to the wording of passages of the PE and possible citations of them may be found in the Apostolic Fathers.[3]

The authority of the letters was not universally acknowledged in the second century. According to Tertullian, Marcion (fl. ca. 140 C.E.), though he knew the PE, excluded them from his canon on the basis that Paul did not write to individuals.[4] Clement of Alexandria mentions "heretics"—"false" Gnostics—who, perceiving themselves under condemnation in 1 Tim. 6.20–21, rejected the letters to Timothy.[5] Jerome writes in the "Preface" of his commentary on Titus that while Marcion and Basilides rejected Titus, Tatian (d. ca. 170 C.E.), who rejected the letters to Timothy, did accept Titus.[6] However, not only Irenaeus, Tertullian, and Clement of Alexandria but the author of the Muratorian Canon, as well as the later Fathers, had no doubt that the letters were penned by Paul.[7] Nevertheless, the fact remains that by contrast with the other letters of the Pauline corpus the PE are only unambiguously attested and explicitly acknowledged as authored by Paul late in the second century.

In the modern era, it was not until the early nineteenth century that scholars expressed doubts about the authenticity of the PE.[8] F. E. D. Schleiermacher (1807) was the first to argue that 1 Timothy was not a genuine Pauline letter, though he indicates that doubts had been raised by J. E. C. Schmidt a few years earlier in 1804.[9] Schleiermacher based his arguments on the grounds of the letter's vocabulary and style, as well as its theology, doubting also that the personal notices were genuine.[10] He also argued that 1 Timothy was a composite of the other PE since, he observed, much of the paraenesis of the three letters overlaps. Nevertheless, Schleiermacher accepted the authenticity of Titus and 2 Timothy. Just a few years later, J. G. Eichhorn (1812) argued for the stylistic unity of the PE and for the pseudonymity of each letter.[11]

The work of Ferdinand Christian Baur (1835) and Heinrich Julius Holtzmann (1880) effectively consolidated the view that the PE are pseudonymous. Both scholars assess the PE from a comparative point of view; they compare the PE with the Pauline corpus. Both argue from a perception of what is or is not genuinely Pauline with respect to the style and theology of the letters, the ecclesiastical situation of the PE as compared to that glimpsed in the genuine letters, and the identity of the false teachers. In short, both scholars subjected the PE to rigorous historical-critical scrutiny.

A. The Achievement of Baur and Holtzmann

Ferdinand Christian Baur (1792–1860)

Baur devoted much attention to the reconstruction of the historical situation of the PE. Consequently, the identity of the false teachers assumes a high priority in his monograph. He argues that the PE stem from the mid-second century C.E. Making use of Schleiermacher's own observations with respect to 1 Timothy, Baur's arguments for the non-Pauline authorship of all three PE are as follows:

1. the style and vocabulary of the PE are not what one would expect of Paul,
2. the personal notices and the situation of PE cannot be fitted into the life of Paul as we know it from the Pauline letters, and
3. the author fails to provide demonstration of his theological positions based on logical argument.

With respect to 3 Baur argues that the author of PE does not theologize like Paul. The author lacks the clear Pauline commitment to arguing from a theological position, and hands down arbitrary decrees.[12]

In the Foreword he asks whether or not the NT knows anything of the second century C.E., a point Schleiermacher was willing to argue in the affirmative for 1 Timothy only. Baur was prepared to research the question of historical milieu of the PE more rigorously. The aim of chapter one and, to a lesser extent, chapter two of Baur's book is to demonstrate that the PE evidence a consistent and thoroughgoing attack on the positions espoused by mid-second century Gnostics and by Marcion as we know their views from the extant works of Irenaeus and Tertullian. Baur argues that intimations of Gnostic thinking attacked in the PE also apply to Marcion, in whose theology, Baur argues, are the elements of a Gnostic system.[13] With respect to the Jewish law nothing of Paul's polemic of the letters to the Romans and Galatians is to be encountered in the PE. Indeed, the author of 1 Timothy sees the issue differently from Paul since he argues in 1.9–10 that the law is indeed able to restrain sinful behavior.[14]

Baur argues that Marcion's lost work, the "Antitheses" (ἀντιθέσεις), is mentioned by name in 1 Tim. 6.10, a passage which also includes a warning to avoid "what is falsely called 'knowledge'" (ἡ ψευδώνυμος γνώσις).[15] Moreover, the PE attack Gnostic and Marcionite elitism and dualism, as well as the attempt to forbid marriage and wine (see 1 Tim. 4.3; 5.23).[16] Marcion, Baur argues, denied the resurrection of the body for believers, an issue Baur saw reflected in 2 Tim. 2.17–18.[17] Marcion's positive evaluation of the ministry of women is castigated in 1 Tim. 2.9–15.[18] Marcion and the Gnostics argued that conventional marriage, with its expectation of child-bearing, amounted to immorality (πορνεία).[19] The Pastor, on the other hand, believes that women will be saved by shouldering the duties and responsibilities of the married state (1 Tim. 2.15). Certainly, they have no rightful access to the positions of leadership in the congregation. The Pastor has no hesitation in claiming categorically that the apostle Paul did not sanction the exercise of such authority.

However, Baur is unable to adduce a persuasive reason why the false teachers, who appear to be espousers of Jewish opinions and upholders of Jewish traditions (see 1 Tim. 1.7; Titus 1.10, 14), should be so closely identified with Marcion and his followers. The judgment that Marcion was anti-Jewish has militated against scholarly acceptance of Baur's arguments of the anti-Marcionite *Tendenz* of the PE.[20]

Notwithstanding the difficulty of accepting fully Baur's identification of the false teachers, the remainder of Baur's monograph is dedicated to demonstrating that the PE espouse a theology, Christology, and ecclesiology much more in keeping with the second century C.E. than with Paul. He sees the author engaged in the struggle to maintain Paul for the church, particularly in light of the fact that Marcion claimed to be the authentic interpreter and mediator of Paul's heritage.[21]

At the outset, Baur states that there is very little of Paul's teaching in the PE. Had they not claimed Paul for their author no one would argue that they were written by Paul. As it is, Baur is fully persuaded that the letters originate in the struggle against second century C.E. "heretics." He shows that he is aware of the significance of persuasive strategies in the PE centered on the presentation of "Paul." Thus, his imprisonment and impending death (see 2 Timothy) are decisive for the question of ecclesiastical ordering since 2 Timothy is a testament, Paul's last word on the matter. "Wie natürlich war es," Baur writes:

> den Apostel in einer solchen Lage schreiben zu lassen, was man sich als den Gegenstand seiner ihn auch damals beschäftigenden Sorge für die christlichen Gemeinden denken mußte! Welchen tiefen, rührenden Eindruck mußte alles machen, was der Apostel in einem solchen Moment, in der nahen Erwartung seines Märtyrertodes, anordnete und einschärfte![22]

Chapters 4 and 5 are devoted to further detailed arguments for the post-apostolic dating of the PE. The terminology of the PE, e.g., the use of θεοσέβεια and εὐσέβεια, belongs to the post-apostolic era, as does the rite of laying on of hands in ordination.[23] The description of Jesus Christ as one raised from the dead and descended from David "according to my gospel" (2 Tim. 2.8) alludes not to Rom. 1.5 but the Gospel of Luke, the Gospel to which Marcion subscribed while rejecting the other three, though he did not accept Luke 1–2.[24] Baur makes much of the supposed Roman origins of the PE. Luke's Gospel was known as "Paul's Gospel," and that Gospel was favored at Rome. The statements—"Luke alone is with me"/"Bring Mark"—suggest to Baur the developing synthesizing of the Pauline and Petrine parties of the later NT writings (*contra* the earlier historical antithesis of Peter and Paul evidenced in Galatians 2).[25] Acts is also a testament of the process towards synthesis. Finally, Baur seeks to strengthen his argument for the late dating of the PE by contending that the PE are dependent on

Polycarp (see also n. 3 above), and that Marcion's canon lacks the PE because, quite obviously, the letters, as polemical engagements with Marcion, had not yet been written.[26]

Heinrich Julius Holtzmann (1832–1910)

While Baur stressed the mid-second century C.E. dating of the PE and identified the false teaching as a gnosticizing Marcionism, Holtzmann examined in more detail than scholars hitherto the relationship of the PE to Paul, especially in matters relating to their theology. As far as identifying the false teachers and dating the PE, Holtzmann is prepared only to identify them as Gnostics who are provided with Jewish pedigrees by the author of the PE as part of the pseudonymous technique employed by the author.[27] After all, if the opponents of the historical Paul were Jews it stood to reason that the authority of the pseudonymous author of the PE was likewise challenged by Jewish opponents. He dated the PE to the first half of the second century.

Holtzmann's comparative study of Paul and the PE is thorough in all respects. The vocabulary, style, ecclesiastical situation, and theology of the PE are subjected to intense scrutiny in an endeavor to demonstrate once and for all that a Paulinist, not Paul himself, was the author of the letters. As far as vocabulary and style are concerned, Holtzmann notes that the PE's use of words has much more in common with Luke-Acts and the Epistle to the Hebrews.[28] Certain terms commonly used in the Pauline corpus such as σῶμα (71 times in the undisputed Paulines), δικαίωμα, παράδοσις, περιπατεῖν, ταπεινός, and χαρίζεσθαι do not occur in the PE.[29] Whole word-families encountered in the Pauline corpus, such as ἐλευθ-, φρον-, πρασσ-, ἐνεργ-, and περισσ-, are also missing.[30] Moreover, the PE use terms like ἐπιφάνεια and εὐσέβεια which are not used in the Pauline corpus.[31]

On the matter of style, Holtzmann observes considerable differences between the undisputed Paulines and the PE. Of particular note is the absence in the PE of certain conjunctions, particles, and prepositions common to Paul.[32] Holtzmann notes that γάρ, a pointer to the dialogical nature of Paul's theological discourse, is found in Galatians more often than in the PE.[33] He also detects a certain latinizing of the Greek style of the PE.[34]

Nevertheless, there is also evidence of considerable literary dependence of the PE on the Pauline corpus and Luke-Acts.[35] Holtzmann argues that the author of the PE actually had Paul's letter to the Philippians in front of him.[36] Baur and Schleiermacher had also remarked upon the literary affinity of the PE and the undisputed Paulines. A. E. Barnett mounts a compelling argument for the knowledge and use of a ten-letter Pauline corpus by the Pastor, showing the evidence of "practically certain" instances of literary dependence—especially on Romans (six instances), 1 Corinthians, and Philippians (twice each).[37] With less degree of certainty, Barnett contends that the remaining seven letters of the Pauline corpus are alluded to in the PE.[38] The Pastor, he suggests, was motivated—as was the author of Ephesians, whose letter, Barnett surmises, was written as the preface commending the publication of a nine-letter Pauline corpus (ten letters counting Ephesians)—by the desire to present the message of Paul for the whole church for "guidance in church discipline and doctrine."[39] The conjecture that the PE are concerned to mediate the Paul of the ten-letter corpus, not just the undisputed letters, helps to explain the contours of the actualization of Pauline tradition in the PE.[40]

Holtzmann devotes much space to an examination of the theological concepts of the PE compared to those of Paul in the undisputed Paulines. He begins his discussion by noting that while the general thought-world (*Begriffswelt*) underlying the PE is unquestioningly Pauline ("fragelos paulinisch ist"), the Paulinism of the PE, in keeping with their more developed ecclesiastical situation, is to be characterized as tempered by catholic concerns and ecclesiastical interests.[41]

Clearly Pauline thinking has undergone considerable change and modification. Much of the theological flavor of the PE is dictated by the encounter with Gnosticism and heresy. With its high view of the whole scriptural deposit, 2 Tim. 3.15–16 represents the author's attempt to counter the esoteric oral tradition of the Gnostics and their selective canonizing of parts of scripture.[42] The coupling of "God" and "Christ" as Savior(s) is intended to counter the Gnostic doctrine of God.[43] On the other hand, Paul's opinion that the letter of the law causes sin to awaken and renders one "dead" (see, e.g., Rom. 7.6; 2 Cor. 3.6) is at odds with the PE.[44] The PE's doctrine of the epiphany, used of the first and second coming of Christ, also seems odd if Paul were the author.[45] He, of course, does not use this terminology. Moreover, Paul's thinking is more oriented to the *imminence* of the second coming, the parousia.

In contrast to its centrality in Paul, the salvific efficacy of the cross is only incidentally referred to in the PE where one finds considerable stress on the life and immortality that characterizes the life of the saved.[46] Comparing the concept of the atonement in the Pauline letters with the PE, Holtzmann remarks that for the author of the PE the σωτηρία effected by Christ in his death is not related so much to "guilt" (*Schuldbewußtein*) with respect to the law of Moses but much more to the immorality of one's previous life-style.[47] Thanks to moral renewal (*sittliche Erneuerung*), the life of the believer can now be characterized by piety and good deeds (καλὰ ἔργα).[48] For Paul, however, the law and its curse are integral to understanding just what Christ did achieve in his death on behalf of believers. The believer, languishing under the condemnation of the law and knowing its dread curse, is freed by the death of Christ for new life in the Spirit (see, especially, Romans 8). However, for the author of the PE the meaning of the death of Christ appears not to be located in redemption from the curse of the law. Rather, the author concentrates on the moral shape of the new life of the believer as contrasted with the old life of those without belief.[49]

Paul's doctrine of justification scarcely appears in the PE.[50] Only 1 Tim. 1.9 uses δίκαιος in Paul's sense, though the term is used in 2 Tim. 4.8 of God and in Tit. 1.8 of the moral rectitude of the candidate for the office of bishop. The verb δικαιοῦσθαι only occurs at 1 Tim. 3.16 (ἐδικαιώθη ἐν πνεύματι), but with Christ as the object and God as the implied subject. In Tit. 3.7 the use of δικαιοῦσθαι seems to denote the state of grace into which the believer is placed by virtue of his/her baptism, and not the inner change of heart or the new life-orientation in response to the preaching of the cross as in Paul.[51] By the same token, Holtzmann observes, the Pastor's use of "faith" (πίστις) more often than not denotes the content of right thinking commended by the author, i.e., orthodoxy, as opposed to heresy.[52]

The PE's ecclesiology echoes the post-Pauline situation. Comparing the use of ἐκκλησία in the PE with its use in Ephesians, Holtzmann argues that the concept of the church in the PE is cast in decidedly catholic terms.[53] He understands 2 Tim. 2.19 and 1 Tim. 3.15 to refer to the "church universal" and not, as in Paul, a local community of the elect.[54]

Finally, the eschatological concepts of the author reveal a vagueness and lack of clarity we certainly miss in the undisputed Paulines. The parousia to come has become one of the articles of the *regula fidei* received by the Pauline churches. In the author's purpose it serves to contribute to the picture of the grim future ("glänzender Hintergrund für das dunkle Zukunftsgemälde der letzten schweren Tage") which he is eager to impress upon his audience to prepare them for the struggle with the false teachers. The ecclesiastical situation prescribed by the author—no mere temporary arrangement—reaches into the distant future.[55] Where the author does speak of the Kingdom of God, it is not the hope of its imminent arrival on earth, but it is a kingdom *in* heaven for which Christ will save his people.

In the undisputed Pauline material, however, one encounters the hint of the expectation of the reign of Christ on earth (1 Cor. 15.25); a reign in which the "saints" will judge "the world" (1 Cor. 6.2). Until that time, believers possess a "commonwealth" (πολίτευμα) in the heavens (Phil. 3.20; cf. 1.23; 2 Cor. 5.8). Those who have died will be brought with Christ at his parousia to rule on earth (1 Thess. 4.14).[56] Paul, Holtzmann contends, locates his hope in the descent of Jesus *from* heaven (ἀπ' οὐρανοῦ, 1 Thess. 4.16) and, by implication, in the coming down from heaven of a kingdom which will be realized on earth.[57] Holtzmann argues that 2 Tim. 4.18, on the other hand, speaks of a kingdom *in* heaven (lit. "a heavenly kingdom," βασιλεία ἐπουράνιος).[58] According to the PE, he concludes, the βασιλεία begins after the death of the believer. With Paul, however, it begins after the general resurrection at the time of the parousia.[59]

The effect of Holtzmann's investigation is to leave one convinced that, while in general terms the PE are suggestive of certain Pauline qualities, comparative analysis reveals the non-Pauline nature of many of their specific theological formulations, and much of their vocabulary and style. At critical points Paul's thinking either does not come to light, or is more or less concealed from view, or has been modified. Moreover, the ecclesiastical situation presupposed in the letters appears much more developed than the much more charismatically charged *Kirchenordnung* one glimpses in the authentic Paulines.

On the terms of the debate set by Holtzmann, it is difficult to resist the conclusion expressed later by Bultmann that the Paulinism of the PE is a "jaded" Paulinism.[60] In Bultmann's analysis this extends not just to the theology of the PE but to the manner in which the author addresses his audience. Unlike Paul, the Pastor does not combat the false teaching within his purview by counter-argument. All debate with it is declined.[61] Moreover, the Christian life in the PE is the life of "piety," the pattern for which is provided by the *Haustafeln* and the virtue and vice catalogues. Consequently, Bultmann argues, a notably "bourgeois" ethic pervades the PE.[62] Elements of the Pauline tradition can be traced in the PE, but the parousia is delayed and the church is making a home for itself in the present.[63] Faith has become a virtue to be linked with other virtues; its content is synonymous with orthodox belief. The term has lost that distinctive Pauline character which placed it at the basis of Christian existence with respect to the believer looking away from self to Christ.[64]

I conclude that the scholarship of both Baur and Holtzmann and their twentieth century heirs with their persuasively argued account of the differences between Paul and the PE has rendered any insistence on the Pauline authorship of the PE problematical. Consequently, in German scholarship especially, there exists a persistent consensus on this question in twentieth century scholarship, the lines drawn up by scholars such as Jülicher and Bultmann operating within the parameters outlined so expertly by Baur and Holtzmann.[65] However, Holtzmann was by no means dismissive of the PE. It was not the case that nothing of the Pauline gospel had been retained. His study concluded with the important observation that salvation for the PE and for Paul was largely a matter of hope, not of present possession (as in the Fourth Gospel).

Holtzmann perceived that the Pastor was motivated by the need to safeguard the Pauline heritage against the inroads of errorists.[66] He was also aware of the function of the pseudonymous strategy used by the author. For this reason the personal notices are important for the author, who perceived that if his work was to be regarded as genuine it must, like the Pauline letters he knew, contain a modicum of *personalia*.[67] Moreover, the author knew that to secure his perception of how the church and its members must conduct themselves, he had to convey a convincing and persuasive anchoring of that vision. Consequently, he intended to write *Pauline* letters which commend "Paul's" gospel and ecclesiastical order to arm the church in its struggle with heretics.[68]

B. Defenders of Pauline Authorship

The Baur-Holtzmann reading of the PE as documents emanating from the post-Pauline era, which embody theological insights that can be contrasted rather than compared to the thinking of the undisputed Paulines, has not gone unchallenged. The most extensive commentary on the PE which argues for the Pauline authorship of all three letters is that of Ceslaus Spicq.[69] He acknowledges that the three PE have one and the same author, a point few scholars would doubt. The letters exhibit the same style and the same doctrine, and combat the same false teachers. They envisage that the same ecclesiastical order is to be imposed and maintained both at Ephesus and Crete, the Ephesian ecclesiastical order providing the model for the Cretan.[70] With respect to the dating, the identity of the false teachers, and the theological positions espoused by the PE, Spicq is committed to demonstrating their consistency with Paul's theological distinctives and with what we know of his life, or what might be fairly surmised as to its direction where there are gaps in our knowledge.

Spicq reads the PE as directives which the apostle, perceiving his impending death, had no opportunity to give orally to his collaborators Timothy and Titus.[71] Paul is not writing to congregations. Thus Spicq seeks to account for the genre of the PE and for their different tone from the other Pauline letters, a difference which he and other scholars readily acknowledge.[72]

Unlike many other commentators, Spicq is cognizant of the rhetorical craft and the question of the genre of the PE.[73] He thus anticipates the direction of the discussion that will follow in chapters 2 and 3 of this book. Spicq observes that the paraenesis of the PE most readily corresponds to the paraenetic exhortations of Isocrates' *To Nicocles*, which he classifies as a λόγος προτρεπτικός, a species of exhortation designed to persuade the audience/reader to a life-orientation of philosophical enterprise.[74] The PE, Spicq argues rightly, are nothing less than a collection of paraenetic addresses directed to his delegates regarding church leaders, the married, the old and the young, widows, and slaves and masters that they might be exhorted to observe the obligations appropriate to their situation in the church and in life.[75] The PE, he adds, also resemble the moral tractates of Plutarch. It should not be doubted that the PE are hortatory in essence. On the basis of the frequency of hortatory verbs and imperatives alone, it is demonstrable that the letters participate in this mode of address.[76]

Furthermore, Spicq contends that the juxtaposition of various subjects with paraenesis is to be regarded as an example of diatribe, a rhetorical strategy that has influenced the whole Pauline corpus.[77] Diatribes, Spicq observes, were designed to address moral or philosophical issues in a popular and dialogical style for the exhortation of the uninitiated. While Greek diatribes had their *Sitz im Leben* in the street preaching of the Cynics, Roman diatribes had a more sophisticated audience in mind. The PE, Spicq contends, are analogous to the latter, and find their closest analogy in the style of much of the correspondence of Seneca to Lucilius.[78] However, the PE have more in common with letters and discourses of moral exhortation than with the diatribe, especially if one seeks to maintain the integrity of the definition of the diatribal mode of address as a dialogical teaching strategy.

The identity of the heretics and the polemic used against them by the author of the PE receive attention in chapter 5 of the introduction to Spicq's Commentary. He is quick to point out that Paul does use invective against his opponents.[79] The heretics are certainly not second century Marcionites or Gnostics. Reference to Jannes and Jambres in 2 Tim. 3.8 evokes early Jewish *haggada*. The enigmatic Jewish "genealogies" (*toledoth*) of 1 Tim. 1.4 and Tit. 3.9 might be readily paralleled in early Jewish *haggadic* material, such as *Jubilees* and the *Genesis Apocryphon* (1QapGen).[80] Allusions to Gnostic ideas are entirely expected since Paul not only had to deal with the incursions of Jewish-Christians but incipient Gnosticism also (1 Cor. 4.18–20; 2 Cor. 10.4–5).[81] Spicq, like Holtzmann and others scholars, is not persuaded by Baur's contention that 1 Tim. 6.20 is an explicit reference to Marcion's *Antitheses*.[82] As to the identity of the heretics, Spicq writes:

> A Éphèse et en Crète, saint Paul a eu à faire avec un judéo-christianisme que l'on peut qualifier de pré-gnostique, en sens qu'on y discerne une tendance ou des symptômes qui exploseront trente-quarante ans plus tard.[83]

Chapter 8 of Spicq's introduction deals with the question of the authenticity of the PE. Against those who argue that the ecclesiastical situation presupposed in the PE is redolent of a second century provenance, Spicq contends that they are documents of naissant first century catholicism.[84] The ecclesiastical order of the PE is, he argues, not only the historical Paul's directive but is in full accord with the order we see developing in the undisputed letters and in Acts, and which has definite Jewish roots.[85]

Although there is no place for the PE from the career of Paul as we know it from Acts and the letters, the conclusion of Acts could be read to suggest that Paul had a further ministry.[86] This is a reasonable assumption, Spicq argues, which receives confirmation in Clement of Rome's statement to the effect that Paul gave his testimony before rulers after he had reached the "limit of the west."[87] Spicq takes this to mean that Paul did indeed evangelize Spain after being released from the imprisonment recorded in Acts 28, only to be imprisoned a second time and martyred in the last year or two of Nero's reign.[88] His return to the east, to which the PE alone bear witness, also occurred in this hiatus between the first and second imprisonments.[89]

If the PE were written by a pseudonymous author, why, Spicq asks, did not the writer attempt to harmonize his statements more with the letters?[90] As it is, the personal notes are believable and clear pointers to the authenticity of the PE.[91] To deny Pauline authorship implies that the author was a deceiver whose forgeries are not worthy of canonical status. The notices are without *Tendenzen*, precisely the sort of thing one would expect Paul to write on the analogy with the other letters.[92] Indeed, Harrison had already argued that the *personalia* were genuine Pauline fragments on the grounds of their Pauline vocabulary and style.[93]

These views are shared by George W. Knight III, a more recent commentator on the PE. It is not hard to perceive his sense of the theological offence implied by the idea of the pseudonymity of the PE.[94] He affirms the impression of the authenticity of the *personalia* noted above. He is clearly dissatisfied with the view that they were penned merely to supply the audience of the PE with models of how the godly church leader should live. Unpersuaded by David G. Meade, who argues that the *personalia* were included to give verisimilitude to the letters' claim to be actualizing Pauline tradition, Knight objects that such a view assumes that there are pseudepigrapha in the NT in the first place.[95] He equates pseudonymity with un-ethical deception, charging that the onus is on those who argue for the pseudonymity of the PE to prove their case. Moreover, contenders for pseudonymous authorship should give an account why the early church, which had definite scruples in these matters, would accept letters known to be falsely ascribed into the canon. One has only to recall Tertullian's account of the discovery of the orthodox presbyter's forgery of the *Acts of Paul* which includes a letter, the so-called *3 Corinthians*.[96]

Returning to Spicq's Commentary, he notes that the teaching of the PE witnesses both to significant Paulinisms and to the evolution of Paul's thinking. He observes the urgency of the situation the author was addressing and the need to consolidate and to leave a deposit for the sake of defending and maintaining what had already been preached and established in the churches.[97] If the PE silence women, e.g., it is because the Spirit has ceased to manifest itself in the egalitarian and random fashion operating in 1 Cor. 11–14.[98]

Spicq concedes that the sole valid argument against the authenticity of the PE is that of style. He observes that the author neither demonstrates nor argues his case, but prescribes and exhorts.[99] Undaunted, Spicq asks why the author (i.e., Paul) cannot be permitted to write in a different way to suit the occasion. The circumstances of his life and of the churches must be taken into account. And, of course, Spicq has a point if one is willing to concede, as I am not, that the PE could have been written in the mid to late 60's, that the "heretics" are actually mid first century C.E. Jewish-Christians with some proto-Gnostic leanings, and that Paul did have further ministry in the East (as is presupposed by the PE). Spicq argues that events and the subject at hand caused a change in the apostle's style of presentation.[100]

Moreover, the Paul of the PE takes into account the culture of his correspondents. They are, after all, more at home in the Greek milieu. Moreover, Titus is a Gentile, and Timothy grew up in a mixed home. For this reason, the vocabulary statistics of, e.g., Holtzmann, designed as they are to highlight the un-Pauline character of the PE, are in fact to be explained as evidence of Paul's genius for adaptability. Furthermore, in the midst of all the evidence of adaptability he notes the Paulinisms and the Pauline formulae. To account for the unusual and unexpected vocabulary, Spicq interposes a redactor who imposed his own distinctive style on the PE.[101] Paul, after all, was in prison. Thus, Spicq concludes that these letters were genuinely written by Paul because (i) they claim to be, (ii) the doctrine is Paul's, (iii) Pauline formulae are present in them, and (iv) the author's state of mind at the time of writing accounts for many of the distinctives of their content.

On the question of the theology of the PE, Spicq, unlike Holtzmann, is persuaded that the major theological concepts of Paul are to be found here.[102] We are dealing not with a faded Paulinism but the pure gospel, the gospel preached by the apostle. However, the results of Spicq's analysis of the theology of the PE when compared to the rest of the Pauline corpus cannot be but more positive than, say, Holtzmann's, because Spicq accepts the Pauline authorship of all ten letters with which he compares the PE.[103] It is conceivable that the Pastor has taken up the Pauline tradition as he has received it in a ten-letter corpus into his presentation of Paul. Any reading of the theology of the PE should not ignore the possibility that this is the case.

Spicq's survey of the theology of the PE begins with discussion of the PE's presentation of the persons of the Trinity. With respect to Jesus as the Christ, the PE in common with Paul, stress his descent from David and the underscoring of his fulfilment of messianic promises (2 Tim. 2.8; Rom. 1.2–3), though Spicq notes that the PE designate Jesus as Ἰησοῦς Χριστός or Χριστὸς Ἰησοῦς whereas the other Paulines employ the singular Ἰησοῦς or Χριστός. The stress on the humanity of Jesus (see 1 Tim. 2.5) is balanced by focus on his glorification. Parallels with the undisputed Paulines, e.g., the hymnic Phil. 2.5–11, are readily apparent. The ascription of the title Κύριος to Jesus is in conformity with the undisputed Paulines. By calling him θεὸς σωτήρ (Tit. 2.10), and even μέγας θεὸς σωτήρ (Tit. 2.13), Spicq argues that Paul is countering the propaganda of the claims made for Diana of Ephesus, as well as the imperial cult of Asia Minor.[104] The corresponding lack of explicit attention accorded the Holy Spirit causes Spicq no undue alarm.[105] This is, in part, because he aligns Pauline teaching with that of the PE, such as the mention of πνεῦμα δειλίας in 2 Tim. 1.7, as a reference to the holy πνεῦμα indwelling the baptized believer.

The soteriology of Tit. 3.3–8 accords completely with Pauline sentiment expressed, e.g., in Rom. 6.17 and 1 Cor. 6.9–11. That all are under the power of sin (Tit. 2.12) agrees nicely with Pauline thought expressed in Rom. 1.18–25.[106] That the sinner is not saved by works (Tit. 3.5) is manifestly Pauline in its emphasis. The PE's particular understanding of salvation, however, stresses not so much the event of the cross, but the ecclesial ramifications of the historical saving event.[107]

The understanding of the church with its hierarchical ordering and its conception as "une institution salutaire," has its origin in the Hebrew Bible.[108] The ministry of church leaders, as mandated in the PE, is precisely that which Paul believed would guarantee the continuation of his apostolic ministry, and, in particular, its kerygmatic and moral dynamic.[109] Appealing to the concept of a fixed "deposit" (παραθήκη), the apostle transmits prescriptions, which were already known beforehand, to his apostolic associates, namely, Timothy and Titus. The PE, therefore, prescribe no new teaching.[110] The παραθήκη is the sum of the Pauline kerygma. In the light of his impending death, the apostle is entirely justified in laying before his associates the responsibility of guarding it and passing it on.[111]

The question of the meaning of πίστις in the PE is the subject of much of section V of Spicq's treatment of their theology. The subjective sense, he concludes, is not uncharacteristic of the undisputed Paulines.[112] There exists sufficient evidence for Spicq to conclude that the PE and Paul are in agreement on the conception of "faith."[113]

With respect to the expectation of the parousia, the author motivates the faithful to zealous living by laying before them the hope of the return of Christ and the coming retribution (e.g., 1 Tim. 6.12; 2 Tim. 1.8; 2.5; 4.8).[114] On the question of hope, Spicq concludes that the author does express all that Paul means by the concept, especially in the light of its definite Christological focus.[115]

On the ethical values commended by the PE, Spicq concedes their Greek lineage. In the PE the reader encounters the Christianizing of the Athenian ideal, i.e., the disciple of Christ is one who trains like an athlete in the gymnasium.[116] This is the first time, Spicq writes, that Christian morality had been expressed in "concepts et en mots européens." He has in mind terms such as the εὐσεβ- and σωφρον- cognates which are not found among the other Pauline letters. The place of ethical values derived from Paul's reflection on the cross is replaced by ethical values common to the Greek philosophers.[117] Spicq argues that the PE are imbued with the spirit of Hellenistic philosophical ethics because Paul finds himself addressing a much more decidedly Gentile audience, one which has already broken with its Jewish origin. The reason for this, Spicq surmises, is the decisive sundering of the church from the synagogue by the time of the outbreak of the First Jewish Revolt of 66 C.E.[118] Issues arising out of the Jewish heritage of the church which had motivated Paul so profoundly in his earlier letters no longer needed to be addressed. Rather, Paul takes up the challenge of casting the gospel and prescriptions for the ethical orientation of the believer in Greek, no longer in Jewish, terms. Christianity, he asserts, is becoming the "religion of the world."[119]

While it is not my intention to offer a detailed critique of the defenders' thesis, it should be asked, nonetheless, whether the authorship of the PE is in fact better explained according to the Baur-Holtzmann critique. The difficulty of placing the letters in the context of the life and cultural context of Paul as we know them are not overcome by the defenders. Moreover, arguments from silence with respect to the apostle's putative second captivity following a renewed missionary enterprise and the pleading of the almost boundless versatility of the author with respect to the vocabulary and style of the PE are conspicuously present in the defenders' contending for Pauline authorship.

One might also object that issues concerning the theological ideas expressed by the author of the PE and the image of Paul that is conveyed in these letters are of more weight than Spicq and the other defenders allow. Is it acceptable to explain the differences by recourse to the thesis of the evolution of his thinking, or to the apostle's changing circumstances as do Spicq, Kelly, Jeremias, and Knight?[120] Indeed, many of the defenders of Pauline authorship are under necessity to do so, since they rule out pseudepigrapha in scripture on *a priori* grounds. Admittedly, we are dealing here with letters explicitly addressed to associates, not with letters addressed primarily to congregations. Paul is not bound to write the same way whenever he writes, though it might be demonstrated that the undisputed Paulines are homogeneous in vocabulary and style (whether secretaries were used or not).

Still, we should ask what kinds of letters Paul would have written to associates in the light of the imminence of his death, and what kinds of strategies he would have employed to ensure the continuation of his work. Surely we ought to expect that if Paul really is the author of the PE, and if this is his final opportunity to address his associates and "heirs," then matters such as those concerning faith, the law, the place of the cross—distinctives for which he fought so long and hard in the correspondence of just the previous decade—would be more clearly enunciated in Pauline terms.[121]

Spicq's confidence in the genius of Paul's adaptability is decidedly misplaced. Surely Paul would have contended vigorously for retention of the Jewish framework in which his gospel had been cast from the beginning of his ministry. Moreover, the Paul who had argued so passionately for "Jew first" would surely not have capitulated so mildly to anchoring his message to new moorings.[122]

Nevertheless, it is to be observed in analyzing the whole comparative enterprise of those scholars arguing for and against Pauline scholarship of the PE that the evidence used by one school of thought is by no means palpable of merely one interpretation. While it is my view that the case for the pseudonymity of the PE pioneered in the nineteenth century has proven remarkably resilient and remains persuasive, the persistence of the defence of Pauline authorship is also to be reckoned with and is to be accorded due respect.

C. STUDIES IN *TRADITIONSGESCHICHTE*

Baur and Holtzmann, together with their twentieth century heirs, have tended to highlight the contrasts between Paul and the PE. These scholars stress the late dating of the PE, the putative second century C.E. character of the heretics opposed, the non-Pauline theological distinctives and ecclesiastical focus, and the refusal of the author of the PE to engage his opponents in the same manner as Paul. The Pastor, they argue, prefers instead to prescribe an orthodoxy sanctioned by the apostle, and to warn against the false teachers rather than counter their teaching by reasoned argument.

However, there is a recent development among scholars who seek a more sympathetic account of the Pauline character of the literary, ecclesiological, and theological formulations of the PE. These scholars evaluate the PE and the deutero-Pauline deposit from the perception of the discipline of *Traditionsgeschichte*. By this term I mean that these scholars assess the PE as documents which seek to contemporize, or actualize, Pauline ideas for a new generation finding itself beset by issues, crises, and challenges which Paul did not address or envisage. These readings of the PE tend, therefore, to investigate the links between the PE and Pauline tradition as it comes to expression chiefly in the undisputed Pauline letters, while also acknowledging the contrasts between the two *corpora*. This program builds on the scholarly consensus that the PE are not by Paul. Therefore, most scholars participating in this enterprise argue that the PE are pseudonymous. The letters are redolent of adaptations and even modifications of Pauline ideas and *personalia* available to modern readers in the extant undisputed Pauline letters only. The PE emanate from a period at least a generation after Paul when the Pauline heritage was under attack.

Klaus Wegenast

The work of Klaus Wegenast on the understanding of tradition in Paul and the deutero-Paulines is a study not only of the character of tradition in the NT era, or more specifically, the Jewish and Hellenistic world of the first century, but an examination of the contrast in the understanding and function of tradition between Paul and the deutero-Pauline literature, especially the PE.[123]

Wegenast also contrasts Paul's conception of tradition with the Jewish understanding, though, he notes, attempts have been made to align Paul with early Judaism in this respect.[124] He rejects three other various current theories of Paul's relationship to tradition in favor of one based on his own exegetical study of the Pauline letters and the wider deutero-Pauline corpus (which for Wegenast comprises the PE as well as Ephesians and Colossians).[125]

He argues that it is crucial that the Paul of the undisputed letters regards his gospel as an "apocalypse," i.e., that it came by revelation and not by some merely human mediation.[126] The revelation he received has significant consequences as far as the possibility and means of salvation are concerned. For Paul, salvation is exclusively through Christ—crucified, dead, and raised. This matter is of supreme importance for understanding the encounter of Paul with the Galatians and the false teachers who stand behind them. The false teachers appeal to the law as the indispensable means by which the saving benefits of Christ become operative in the believer's life. As far as the false teachers are concerned, their teaching is hallowed by revelation mediated by Moses and by Jesus.[127] But for Paul, Wegenast argues, the law-free gospel he preaches is of a completely different order and cannot be understood in the terms so prized by his opponents.[128] Paul contrasts the teaching and the tradition of his opponents with his own even more direct revelation. Therefore, a different and contrasting role for tradition is to be perceived in the Pauline correspondence.

What is the relationship between gospel and tradition in the Pauline letters? Wegenast acknowledges that in Paul there are traces of confessional formulae and teaching that derive from the traditions of the audience. These, however, do not function as timeless principles or as summaries of a dogmatic nature.[129] This is an important observation in the task of assessing the PE's attitude to the Pauline tradition the author seeks to inculcate. For Paul, tradition functions in the communities as markers of their historical existence in the faith.

Paul's attitude toward tradition is exemplified in 1 Corinthians 15. Why does Paul use a traditional formula in v. 3? Wegenast's answer is that Paul understands the tradition he cites as the confirmation of his own revelation.[130] For this reason, Wegenast suggests, there is no appeal to tradition in Galatians because this would seem to call into question his definite claims to his gospel as revelation. With respect to his insistence on the unmediated revelation by which he received his gospel, Paul's position in 1 Cor. 15.8 is, however, consistent with that of Galatians.[131]

Paul is not bound to reproduce the exact "wording" (*Wortlaut*) of the traditions he has received. Moreover, the traditions he might cite are not binding, i.e., they are not set over his gospel, but are confirmatory. They amount to another way of expressing the significance of the Christ event. Furthermore, the tradition is no "deposit," no παραθήκη, in the sense understood by the author of the PE. Paul is in no way endeavoring to conform his gospel to tradition and confession, nor is he seeking to align the formulae he encounters with his own understanding of the gospel.[132] There is nothing approaching the early Jewish/Rabbinic principle of "fixed tradition" (*festgefügte Tradition*).[133] The tradition

Paul has received is not the norm for his understanding. Rather, Paul is free with regard to tradition and cites it for his own purposes. Before turning his attention to the deutero-Paulines, and the PE in particular, Wegenast concludes his discussion of Paul in a way that prepares for his contrastive investigation of the deutero-Pauline material. Paul shows, he observes,

> weder Interesse an formaler Konstanz der Überlieferungen . . . noch legt er Wert darauf, die von ihm vorgelegte Tradition durch Zeugenreihen oder durch sonstige Methoden zu sichern.[134]

Colossians and the literarily dependent Ephesians show the post-Pauline community confronting the tradition terminology of the Gnostics and mystics in their midst. Wegenast argues that the reminder to the Colossians—"as you received Christ . . ." (see Col. 2.6, ὡς οὖν παρελάβετε τὸν Χριστὸν Ἰησοῦν)—is an exhortation to heed the Lordship of Christ made manifest in their lives in the salvation he has wrought and, thereby, to recall the paraenesis in which they, as saved people, should now walk. This use of παραλαμβάνω, Wegenast contends, has been adapted from the false teachers whose tradition spoke of salvation through Christ coupled with ascetic practice.[135]

Wegenast argues that Michel, Ranft, Spicq, and Jeremias agree that the concept of tradition possessed by the author of the PE must derive from the Hellenistic synagogue.[136] Michel, e.g., appeals to the interest shown by the author in the succession and ordination of "elders." The language of the PE and the function of these officials suggest more than an accidental relationship between Jewish thinking about tradition and the PE. Wegenast, however, is not persuaded as to the Jewishness of the thinking of the PE at this point. His investigation of the precise nature of the concepts of the PE takes the following character.

The three PE are dedicated to fighting heresy, engaging with it polemically. The heretics, and there are several groups, might be characterized thus:

1. they espouse certain ascetic regulations, particularly with respect to marriage,
2. they espouse a law-oriented and pneumatic interpretation of the Hebrew Bible,

3. they believe that the resurrection of believers has already occurred and, significantly, that
4. they term their teaching "tradition" (παράδοσις).[137]

In this last respect, Wegenast argues, they are exactly like the second and third century C.E. Gnostics.[138] For this reason the author of the PE does not use παράδοσις, the term favored by Gnostics (at least those of the second and third centuries) and by Paul himself (see 1 Cor. 11.2; Gal. 1.14; cf. Col. 2.8; 2 Thess. 2.15; 3.6). Rather, the Pastor uses the term παραθήκη (1 Tim. 6.20; 2 Tim. 1.12, 14) to denote the Pauline tradition he is committed to guarding at all cost. In this regard the author stands over against the undisputed and the deutero-Pauline letters.

Paul, the sole apostle in the mind of the author, thus authorizes the struggles against the heretics.[139] As the bequeather of a παραθήκη, the apostle becomes the author of a tradition binding not just on "Timothy" and "Titus," but through them to the elders they sponsor and to their successors in turn. Ordination is, therefore, not merely to an office but to an office the chief task of which is to "guard the deposit" (1 Tim. 6.20). The PE present an image of Paul in which he is the bestower of legal formulation and the promulgator of edicts and decretals. The παραθήκη envisaged by the author of the PE, Wegenast argues, is nothing less than the whole Pauline proclamation.[140] It is the whole Pauline heritage. It must be guarded not only against every falsification but against every diminution (see 1 Tim. 6.14). In fact, diminution amounts to the same thing as falsification. The παραθήκη has become something fixed, something juridical.

The contrast with Paul is exceedingly marked—as strongly drawn by Wegenast as by Holtzmann or Bultmann. On the one hand, the revealed gospel Paul preached was the norm of every tradition. Paul used traditional formulae and the content of tradition he had received to suit the contingencies of the moment. Tradition is no judge of his apocalyptic gospel. In the PE, on the other hand, a dramatic change has taken place with respect to the function of tradition. Whereas Paul's gospel confirmed tradition,

> wird nun seine [Paul's] Verkündigung zur Norm über aller Predigt, ja steht für alle Predigt παραθήκη, die bewahrt werden muß, die eingeprägt und

> proklamiert wird.[141]

The consequence of this can be readily perceived in the later NT writings and in the early Fathers. Teaching authority is concentrated in the apostles.[142] The subsequent succession of bishops is closely plotted, as reported by Hegesippus (ca. 180 C.E.), and chronicled by Irenaeus and Eusebius.[143] Wegenast characterizes the concept of tradition that holds sway as

> die abgeschlossene, keiner weiteren Entwicklung fähige, allgemein bekannte apostolische Lehre, die als ursprüngliche Offenbarung wahr und damit normativ ist.[144]

The roots of this development can be traced to the PE.

Wegenast's conclusion signals the debt the early church owed to the Gnostics who forged a new concept of tradition at variance in significant ways with the prevailing Jewish idea from which it in turn had received its inspiration and its terminology. The teaching of the Gnostics emanated from the apostles who, in Gnostic writings, became its guarantors. In turn that teaching had its source in revelation. However, in contrast to the Jewish understanding of tradition, no stress was placed on the line of mediating tradents between apostolic and contemporary times. Nor did they (the Gnostics) and the PE emphasize the exact wording of received tradition as did the rabbis. Appealing to 1 Tim. 6.14, Wegenast argues that for the PE the securing of ecclesiastical order and the maintenance of the Pauline message and its content are the burdens of the officials. Their duty it is to guard the deposit and to keep the "commandment" undefiled and free from reproach until the appearing of the Lord Jesus.

Although Wegenast's study perpetuates the contrastive mode of the analysis of the PE and the undisputed Pauline letters, he does highlight in a significant way the forces at work in producing the response to the challenge posed by the Gnostics to the Pauline heritage as it was perceived by the Pastor. To safeguard the legacy of Paul, his strategy was to generate an image of Paul in the PE who sanctions the securing of that legacy by means both of a corpus of pastoral letters actualizing the Pauline tradition and a "deposit" comprising that actualization to be passed on without diminution to trustworthy men.

Norbert Brox

Brox is the first Roman Catholic scholar to write a major commentary on the PE advocating pseudonymous authorship.[145] He begins his analysis of the letters by noting that behind them stands the memory of Paul as one whose care for the churches (see 2 Cor. 11.28) is now the model of the ecclesiastical officials addressed in the PE and, according to 2 Tim. 2.2, of future generations of officials.[146] But he notes how the Paul of the PE places himself *above* not *alongside* the pastors.[147]

The image of Paul generated in the PE has been widely discussed in recent literature.[148] I have indicated above (n. 65) that Jülicher argued that the Paul of the PE addresses his fellow-workers with excessive and uncharacteristic formality. Taking this further Brox observes that even to trusted and respected co-workers, who supposedly share the full confidence of the apostle, the assumed author ("Paul") feels obliged to spell out clearly the qualifications apposite for deacons and overseers.[149] We have had reason already to note the PE's stress on Paul as legislator and as the model for ecclesiastical officials. Schleiermacher had already argued that the Paul of the PE issues arbitrary decrees.[150] Furthermore, the only apostle in the PE is Paul himself.[151] This sits uneasily in the context of the Pauline corpus where, e.g., in Galatians 1–2, 1 Cor. 12.29 and 15.7 (cf. Eph. 4.11) Paul clearly understands his apostleship as an office shared by others.

This matter of the image of Paul in the PE is one to which I shall return below in the discussion of Beker's *Heirs of Paul*. However, I do not find every characteristic of Brox's delineation of the PE's image of Paul persuasive. A case in point is the PE's description of Paul as κῆρυξ and διδάσκαλος ἐθνῶν in 1 Tim. 2.7, which Brox regards as part of the testimony about Paul in the PE. While not couched in the terms Paul uses of himself is, nevertheless, we are not far from the historical Paul in this passage, as C. K. Barrett argues.[152] Moreover, I do not find it convincing to argue for the pseudonymity of the PE on the grounds that they are "formal." Paul, as David G. Meade argues, already adopts what he calls a "patriarchal" attitude to his converts.[153] Moreover, in the tradition of paraenetic letters, a tradition in which the PE stand (as we shall see in the next chapter), superiors wrote to inferiors sometimes urging precepts without explicitly offering reasoned argument, yet without compromising the familial relationship that existed between the writer and the receiver.

The extent to which the theology of the PE contrasts with the theology of Paul in the undisputed letters is not lost on Brox. He observes how different the eschatology of the PE is to the Pauline letters. Though the second coming of Christ still exercises considerable pull for the author and his addressees, the hope of an imminent parousia has faded.[154] The gospel has now become encapsulated in sound, orthodox teaching; a dependable word ("verläßliches Wort").[155]

Brox makes the observation that nothing is left unclear and nothing left un-envisaged as far as ecclesiastical organization is concerned. To this end organization of the churches is a significant theme of the PE. Brox speaks of the PE's solidarity with the world. The PE breathe a sense of community, the church sharing the ethical values and religious terminology of the dominant culture. This is not what we would expect from the genuine Paulines with respect to the imminent in-breaking of the eschaton, or to believers' mode of relating to the structures of the world (cf. 1 Cor. 7.29–31).[156]

Nevertheless, Brox believes that the PE are not totally un-Pauline. He concludes with K. H. Schelkle that the PE represent what the author hoped would amount to an interpretation of the apostle—"Paul for a new day."[157] To this effect the author wants to meet the new challenges not without Paul—not jettisoning him—but to meet the crises head-on with the help of his words and authority.[158] To this extent, the PE ought to be perceived as oriented to Paul, the Paul of the corpus of ten letters, the author setting out to say precisely what he thought Paul would have said. No other document from the post-Pauline era is so closely oriented to Paul's own thought, as it was bequeathed to the church in the ten-letter Pauline corpus, than the PE.[159] 1 Timothy and Titus function as a re-affirmation and a re-application of his teaching as it was understood by the author. 2 Timothy, on the other hand, projects a potent image of Paul for the benefit of the church of God now facing a future without the apostle but who, in the PE, bequeaths his vision for the church at the point of his being executed.

Finally, Brox notes that the PE are witnesses to a lively interest in the transmission of Pauline tradition in the sub-apostolic church. That the PE do not actualize the whole Pauline heritage is evident in the literature of actualizations of that heritage in extra-biblical literature such as the *Acts of Paul*.[160] The PE, however, directed the later orthodox interpreters of Paul, such as Irenaeus, to an era much closer than theirs to the apostle. They found in the PE a compression and sharpening of the Pauline tradition extant in the ten letters with which the apostolic tradition of the Twelve in the four Gospels was harmonized to form the basis of orthodoxy.[161]

Jürgen Roloff

In his commentary on 1 Timothy, Jürgen Roloff also contends for the pseudonymous authorship of all three PE, rehearsing the familiar arguments of the lack of a situation in the life of Paul for the situation presupposed in the PE and the different vocabulary and style of the letters compared to the genuine Paulines.[162] However, he argues that the consideration of vocabulary and style are not definitive against Pauline authorship. The contrasting theological terminology, however, is quite another matter.[163] Roloff, like Brox, argues that the PE attempt an actualization of the Pauline tradition as it lay before the Pastor, chiefly in the ten-letter corpus.[164]

Why does the author write, asks Roloff? In company with other scholars, he surmises that false teaching, perhaps teaching that appeals to Pauline traditions, threatens the continuation of Paul's heritage in the churches. Consequently, the author places the Ephesian church under the obligation and mandate to maintain the Pauline deposit, with Timothy and Titus as the personal embodiments and actualizers of that tradition as its mouthpiece.[165] Paul himself is the blue-print (*Urbild*) of the ecclesiastical official.[166]

What claim does the author have to be a transmitter of authentic Pauline traditions? Roloff discusses this question at some length in his summary on 376–90. He identifies three items which reveal the author's dependence on Pauline tradition. These are:

1. The author knows the Pauline corpus.[167] He sharpens and

consolidates the authority of Paul for the church.

2. The author is no mere transposer or transliterator of Pauline traditions.[168] Rather, he undertakes the task of bringing Paul to speech by adapting and, in the process, transforming the historically conditioned Pauline corpus and its author Paul to address the third generation situation in a way that takes the contingency of that situation seriously.[169]

3. For that reason many of the central motifs of Paul's theology (e.g., justification) are present only in a superficial way. The church no longer finds itself in that dialogue with Judaism which absorbed Paul's attention. Paul's own understanding of concepts such as "faith," "righteousness," and "law" have become part of an unusable past for the author. Thus, in contrast to Paul, the Jewish Torah (νόμος, see 1 Tim. 1.8), "if used rightly," functions as a repository of the general norms of communal living, the ideals of which are achievable. The concept "faith" takes on increasingly the meaning of the content of religion, not the confidence of the believer before God arrested by the Word of God in Christ. Christology is no longer related to justification, but the author dwells on the epiphany of Jesus as the pre-eminent manifestation of God's will to save humankind (see, e.g., 1 Tim. 2.4–6). The cross is reduced to a mere cipher, part of the martyr-example bequeathed to the church by Christ. Struggle and suffering are no longer related to the groaning of the present order, but are combined with popular philosophy's concept of competition. The author's eschatological concerns see the extinguishing of the now–not-yet concept familiar in Paul. The present becomes not the arena for the overlap of the eschatological age and this age and the tensions this produces but the context in which the believer progresses towards the godliness which constitutes the eternal salvific state to come. The lack of attention to the role of the Spirit is the most clear deficiency of the PE. There is no reckoning of the Spirit operative among the members of the community. Instead the ordained (male) clergy are the possessors of the Spirit by virtue of their ordination. Unlike the situation in the undisputed Paulines, they perform the work of ministry in the worship of the church household.[170] On the one hand, this amounts to a devastating critique of the Pastor's grasp of Pauline theology, but on the other we have to

reckon with the changed situation of the church.

In conclusion Roloff observes that the PE testify to an exclusive Paulinism.[171] The author affirms the need of the church to be oriented to Paul's vision of the communal life.[172] Yet, the author espouses an ecumenical theology comprising synoptic-like Jesus traditions and pre-Pauline liturgical confessions. The literary embodiment of these amounts to what Roloff terms a "grosskirchliche Konzeption" legitimated, sanctioned, and now mandated by the "Paul" generated by the author of the PE.[173] Roloff rightly observes that for the author of the PE everything that strengthens the church and its ecclesiastical order, and which corresponds to the gospel and is considered orthodox (*rechtgläubig*), is counted "apostolic."[174]

Finally, Roloff addresses the value of the PE for the contemporary church. He takes a middle course between, on the one hand, the dismissiveness of scholars who adjudge the PE as a "fall" from the Paul of the undisputed letters and, on the other, the proponents of "early Catholicism" who regard the PE as a providential integration of Pauline distinctives within the wider currents of the gospel preached in the NT church.[175] Instead, Roloff argues that the PE have had a remarkably influential effect on the church since the third generation of believers. The author attempted to come to grips with the passage of history and the task of ensuring that Paul's gospel, as it was understood by the Pastor, was maintained in the church for present and future generations. As witnesses to the need to bring the heritage of the apostolic era to voice in changed historic circumstances, the PE serve as helpful models of the way this can be done.[176] The modern interpreter must ask not only whether the PE have translated the Pauline gospel faithfully but whether his/her own translation of the Pauline gospel is legitimate.

Peter Trummer

Peter Trummer declares at the outset of his investigation of the Pauline tradition in the PE that "the only appropriate exegesis of the PE begins from the recognition that they be perceived as embodying 'Paulustradition'."[177] Not surprisingly he also regards the PE as pseudonymous. In an extensive discussion of this matter, he, like some of the defenders of Pauline authorship, ventures to point out that the early church was very much alive to the problem posed by pseudepigrapha. The early Fathers, as shown, e.g., in the case of the exposing of the forgery of the so-called *3 Corinthians*, were persistently discriminating, although, it should be remembered, the inclusion of the Wisdom of Solomon—"written by friends of Solomon in his honour"—in the Muratorian Canon demonstrates the respect that might be accorded works that were written under an assumed name.[178]

Nevertheless, arguments for the Pauline authorship of the PE cannot be easily dismissed in the light of the early church's scruples. Consequently, Trummer argues that the author of the PE ascribed to Paul the tradition he had received in much the same way that the evangelists placed the traditions they had received about Jesus in his mouth.[179] The PE function as the extension of the apostle's personal authority—already encapsulated in the corpus of his own correspondence—for the post-Pauline era. Trummer regards the Pauline pseudepigrapha (Colossians, Ephesians, 2 Thessalonians, and the PE) as works embodying the claim to apostolic authority.[180] The recognition of the very distance (*Abstand*) of the PE from Paul provides the only basis for their proper interpretation. The fact that the PE were by and large accepted in the early church (certainly by the orthodox) testifies to the perception of the appropriateness of the author's translation of Paul for the needs of the day.

Following the thesis of earlier writers, such as Holtzmann, Harrison, and Barnett, Trummer argues that the point of reference (*Bezugspunkt*) of the Pauline pseudepigrapha is the existence and knowledge of the genuine Pauline letters.[181] With the death of Paul, the genuine letters in all their historical and contingent particularity were, by the production of Pauline pseudepigrapha and the publishing of a corpus of Pauline letters, broadened in their horizon. What Paul said to the churches he addressed, he now said to all believers, and, indeed, to believers of every era.[182] The formation of the corpus has a three-fold purpose, namely,

1. to maintain the word of the apostle (especially in the face of his use by heretics),
2. to promote the use and understanding of the Pauline corpus, and
3. to actualize and propagate the teaching contained in them by means of organizational structures.[183]

Trummer goes so far as to characterize the PE as embodiments of regulations for church order (*Kirchenordnungen*) rather than letters.[184] The image of Paul in the PE also plays a clearly delineated role. "Paul" is the example for his audience, the prototype (ὑποτύπωσις, 1 Tim. 1.16) of the redeemed, and the concrete and tangible example of the possibility of the transformation of humanity arrested by the grace of God.[185]

But, of course, the literary dependence of the PE on the Pauline corpus must not blind the interpreter to the real contrasts that exist between the genuine letters and the PE, particularly with respect to the theology of the PE.[186] However, he is not content to allow the contrast to dictate his analysis. The PE can be only understood against the background of the ten-letter corpus.

The theology of the PE must therefore be seen as the expression of Pauline tradition, a tradition that is polemically involved in resistance to false teaching. This teaching is posed by Gnostic opponents to the view of the Pauline heritage advocated by the author of the PE and his communities. As such, the polemic is dictated by the needs of the churches of the PE as post-Pauline institutions. Trummer proceeds to characterize the theological strategy of the author of the PE as an exercise in underscoring the function of Paul the apostle as the author perceives him operating in the genuine letters. The function is prolonged and maintained in and through the institutional church and its leaders.[187] Trummer notes that 1 Tim. 4.1–5 is probably the only sustained theological argument in the PE, though I would contend that 2.11–15 must also be considered.

The ecclesiology of the PE is a driving force behind the author's seeking to achieve his purpose to secure the Pauline heritage in the new and potentially dangerous situation in which the church finds itself. To this end, the leaders envisaged in the PE are exhorted to safeguard the "deposit" (παραθήκη), i.e., the whole Pauline tradition, understood as "commandment" (see 1 Tim. 6.14).[188] Trummer wants to allow for the possibility of the leaders modifying the traditions received by them—while at the same time acknowledging that they are responsible for maintaining the content of the "deposit"—as they face the challenge of applying the Pauline teaching to different circumstances, even introducing teaching from other sources in accord with the "deposit."

This is, after all, what the author of the PE has done with respect not only to the Pauline but to the non-Pauline traditions he has encountered.[189] However, in agreement with Wegenast, I suspect that the author of the PE regarded the content of the deposit as settled for all time: neither modification nor translation is necessary or envisaged.

Showing appreciation of the Pastor's use of the strategy of persuading by the use of paradigms, Trummer also emphasizes the PE's generation of an image of Paul, not only as one who suffers for the gospel but as one whose suffering is a model for the ecclesiastical officials who take on the burden of the preaching of the gospel and the guarding of the deposit. They can expect to suffer as Paul did (see, e.g., 2 Tim. 1.8).[190] On the ethics of the PE, a contentious issue for many detractors of the PE, Trummer makes the astute observation that the institutions of marriage and family have, as far as the theology of the PE are concerned, a significant role in the salvation of humankind.[191] Nevertheless, Trummer argues that the ethics of the PE are grounded in the kerygma and in the perception of the cross as the saving event.[192] The author is not merely interested in inculcating the norms of "christliche Bürgerlichkeit."

Trummer's analysis of the actualization of Pauline tradition in the PE is less contrastive than those of many other scholars. He finds more authentic Paulinism in the PE than either Roloff or Brox, thereby implying that the PE are more successful actualizations of Pauline theological and ethical distinctives than they are prepared to acknowledge.

Michael Wolter

In the introduction to his book on Pauline tradition in the PE Wolter establishes his approach to the letters.[193] They embody a tradition intended to be normative for the church.[194] Under the fictive authorship of Paul, the author sets out to re-present Pauline tradition for his own generation. The author commends the propagation of Pauline tradition, securing it through ecclesiastical officials. Timothy and Titus are types of the kind of leader to whom the burden and task of maintaining the Pauline deposit are entrusted.[195] The image of Paul in the PE shows signs, Wolter observes, of a developing hagiography.[196] This Paul, in contrast to the undisputed letters and the Acts of the Apostles, is portrayed as the only apostle, besides whom there will be no further expression of apostolic authority.[197] In the PE, Paul becomes the authoritative teacher of the church (*Kirchenlehrer*); the first link in an unbroken chain of tradition through his co-workers, Timothy and Titus, and the church leaders who succeeded them in the communities to which the PE were addressed.

The PE, Wolter contends, were written against the background of a crisis of identity as well as the struggle for self-perpetuation in which self-consciously Pauline communities were engaged in the post-Pauline era.[198] The author seeks to restore and institutionalize the Pauline tradition for that community, or, in other words, to make Paul the apostle speak afresh for the consolidation and perpetuation of his gospel and teaching. The writer belongs to the third generation of faithful men

> denen Timotheus zufolge 2 Tim 2,2 das apostolische Erbe weiterzugeben aufgefordert wird.[199]

Part B ("Paulus, der Garant des Heils," 27–130) focuses on the image of Paul in the PE, the stress in Wolter's discussion falling chiefly on the passage announcing Paul's apostolic calling in 1 Tim. 1.12–17. Here he is presented as the prototype of the saved person. The author not only establishes him in his apostolic service but, furthermore, depicts him as the chief of sinners with corresponding authority and primacy over the church (which functions, one might add, as the authentication of his apostolic call). Wolter contrasts 1 Tim. 1.15—with its twin claim of Paul's priority and authority—with the historical Paul's own perception of his calling in 1 Cor. 15.5 in which he speaks of his inferiority and posteriority, but for all that he is still an apostle. The Paul of the PE becomes the embodiment of the gospel of grace he preaches, and, like Abraham, the guarantor of salvation for believers. 1 Tim. 1.12–17 is the basis, therefore, of the author's claim for the exclusive authority of Paul in the church in the face of all other loyalties.[200] The author of the PE, Wolter continues, perceives Paul's apostleship after the manner of the calling of the prophets of the Hebrew Bible. Like them he too is called and sent by God. As in the prophets, faithfulness and truth are present and embodied in him.[201]

Accordingly, the PE understand the Pauline apostleship as the constitutive element of the divine saving purpose. In this respect there is a significant contrast between the Paul of the PE and that of the undisputed letters. Paul never bound his own conversion so closely with the gospel that his conversion took on soteriological implications for the Christian community.[202] In the PE, only in orientation to Paul is eschatological salvation secured for the church. Everything that stems from the apostle by way of teaching becomes normative by definition for the present and successive generations of believers. This teaching is encapsulated in the PE. Its perpetual validity is guaranteed by its integral association with the Paul of the PE. Wolter rightly questions whether the historical Paul regarded his own letters to have similar "timeless validity."

In the third and final section of part B, Wolter considers the consequences of Pauline priority for the persuasive strategies of the PE. Paul's priority, he argues, is integral to the PE's claim of authority. Wolter cites the rhetorical tradition for this view.[203] Other traditions in the NT evidence awareness of the same issue. The priority of Peter for the Petrine tradition (see Matt. 4.18–20; 16.16–20; cf. 1 Cor. 15.5; *Ep. Clem.* 1.3) and the role of the Beloved Disciple for the Johannine community are prominent examples. This has its counterpart in the pre-occupation with demonstrating how ancient one's ethnic ancestors were; a significant theme in Jewish and later Christian apologetic.[204] However, it might be fairly conjectured whether this strategy would have much to commend it if the false teachers also appealed to Pauline authority, as I think likely.

Consideration of the relationship between priority and authoritative tradition in the PE (114–30) brings Wolter to a closer examination of the function of the deposit in the PE than he has undertaken to this point. The deposit connotes all that is normative for the PE.[205] As far as its content is concerned, Wolter rehearses the arguments both for restricting it to the gospel and for extending it to cover the whole collection of teachings contained in the PE.[206] He tends towards the latter alternative, though he elsewhere expresses the view that 1 Timothy and Titus are the real vehicles of the deposit, 2 Timothy functioning as the "covering letter."[207] The deposit, Wolter concludes, is to be passed on to each generation unchanged, the deposit functioning as constitutive of and prescriptive for the Pauline character and identity of the community.[208]

Part C (131–248) concentrates on the literary form taken by the Pauline tradition in the PE. This is a matter that has not received significant attention in the scholarly analysis of the PE. The first section (131–56) opens with an examination of the PE from the standpoint of knowledge of paraenesis and ancient epistolary practice, the subject of chapter 2 of this book. The presence of paraenesis in other ancient genres and epistolary corpora is briefly noted, Wolter citing friendship letters (Pliny, *Letters*, 8.24), testaments (*T. 12 Patr.*), farewell addresses (Tobit 4), and pseudonymous collections (Socratic letters).[209] He argues that Ignatius' letter to Polycarp furnishes the best parallel to the genre of the PE.[210] The testamentary characteristics of 2 Timothy are extensively analyzed.[211] He also discusses briefly the epideictic characteristics of the PE, noting that the false teachers function as negative examples of the kind of life-style characterized by Paul *par excellence* and the church leaders. Of recent scholars of the PE, Wolter is the most aware of the rhetorical and paraenetic parallels in the classical and Greco-Roman tradition.

The final part of Wolter's study (Part D) investigates the PE as witness to a Pauline community and its opponents in the post-Pauline era. That the opponents possess Jewish and Gnostic characteristics seems assured. Their description in the PE suggests that they shared positions similar to the historical Paul on a number of issues.[212] While it is difficult, Wolter observes, to separate traditional polemic from actual description of the opponents in the PE, it is possible that they profess to stand in the Pauline tradition denying that claim with respect to the communities addressed in the PE.[213] The message of the PE for them is that they remain true to their heritage and maintain their hold on the salvation extended to believers in the gospel by remaining true to Paul, whose teaching, ecclesiastical vision, and example are set out conveniently in the PE. Every compromise of the "deposit" constitutes a betrayal of Paul and of the Christian identity of the community.[214]

D. J. Christiaan Beker on Paul and the PE

Paul the Theologian

J. Christiaan Beker's understanding of Paul is most fully expounded in his 1980 book *Paul the Apostle: The Triumph of God Life and*

Thought. The book makes a plausible case for reading Paul as an apocalypticist whose encounter with the risen Lord Jesus impelled him to become an apologist to contemporary Jews and a herald/preacher to the Gentiles of the faith he once sought to extirpate (Gal. 1.23).

Two strategies adopted by the apostle in his correspondence are the focus of Beker's investigation. These are:

1. Paul is committed to meaningful theological dialogue with the churches in his correspondence, and
2. Paul proceeded in his letters to interpret the significance of the Christ event in accord with the "indispensable" apocalyptic categories of his own world-view.[215]

The apostle, Beker argues, is consistently engaged in relating what he terms the "coherent" structure of Paul's interpretation of the Christ-event to the "contingent" theological life-situation, as Paul perceives it, of the churches he addresses in his letters and with whom he is in dialogue. The structure of his thought has its origin in the Jewish apocalyptic worldview espoused by Paul before his conversion. In general terms the basic co-ordinates of that worldview are:

1. the resurrection of Christ as an anticipation of the future resurrection of believers,
2. historical dualism or the existence of the kingdom of God over against the world, and
3. the imminent end of the world and the ushering in of the reign of God.[216]

What does Beker mean by "coherent?" Unfortunately, the term is never clearly defined in *Paul the Apostle*. He argues that the center of Paul's thinking must be viewed as a

> symbolic structure in which a primordial experience (Paul's call) is brought into language in a particular way.[217]

This language is that of Jewish apocalyptic; language now affirmed by the Christ-event. The center of Paul's thought is "coherent," Beker contends, because its elements cohere and are each consistent with an apocalyptic world-view now affirmed, though also modified, by the Christ-event.[218] Making for some terminological confusion, however,

Beker also seems to define "coherent" as the opposite of "contingent." On this understanding, "coherence" in Paul has to do with the apostle's basic convictions, the settled framework of his thinking, which he brings to speech in each situation.[219]

This process he explains in the following way. Drawing on a distinction between "primary" and "secondary" levels of language, Beker argues that concepts such as adoption, righteousness, reconciliation, "being in Christ" and the like—which from time to time have been individually nominated as the core of Paul's thought—are secondary "symbols." They function to bring to the surface Paul's "deep structure," i.e., his primary language, which is his coherent and apocalyptic understanding of the Christ-event "in its meaning for the apocalyptic consummation of history."[220] These symbols function as signifiers of the contingent interpretation of Paul's thought. Thus Paul is enabled to address the particular, contingent situations of his churches. While the totality of the symbols constitute Paul's symbolic structure, when they are used "in their particularity" they translate the meaning of the Christ-event for each contingent situation Paul addresses.[221]

Beker contends that the interaction between the coherence of his gospel and its contingent interpretations comprises his hermeneutic, i.e., his way of doing theology. These two aspects of Paul—the structure of his thought and his hermeneutic—are vital foci of his understanding of Paul and, by contrast, the deutero-Pauline literature, the PE included.

It was the very particularity of Paul's letters that was the stumbling block for the understanding Paul in the early church.[222] The church, Beker argues, diffused and blurred the particularity of the letters by positing their "universal 'catholic' relevance." This, of course, resulted in a harmonization of Paul, and, for that matter, other diverse, particular, and uncongenial NT voices. Thus, in the Acts of the Apostles he becomes both a witness to the doctrinal harmony arising from the fellowship of the Jerusalem apostles and a preacher of the same gospel they preached. Consequently, the search for the center of Paul's theology became an exercise in locating a doctrinal core—a dogmatic, timeless truth.[223]

To do justice to Paul's hermeneutic, Beker contends that the interpreter must honor what he describes as

> the singularity and specificity of the Pauline letters in their hermeneutical interaction with the coherent center of Paul's thought.

Paul's thought, he adds, exhibits

> a creative freedom that allows the gospel tradition to become living speech within the exigencies of the daily life of his churches.[224]

Thus the essence of Paul's thought is not a frozen message either imposed on the readers or accommodated to their situation. Rather, for Paul the παράδοσις he received always becomes interpreted παράδοσις—a "word on target"—for the original readers. It confirms his interpretation of the significance of the Christ-event. He was able to bring the gospel to speech in a variety of contingent circumstances without compromising the coherence of its message or denying the specificity of the occasion. Beker concludes that this hermeneutical interaction is Paul's chief legacy to theology.[225]

Beker's thesis regarding the commitment of the apostle to addressing the contingent situation of the churches is well-illustrated in his interpretation of the letters to the Galatians and Romans. If Paul appears inconsistent on the question of the law it is because he has radicalized his position *vis à vis* the Judaizers (his opponents in Galatians).[226] If he appears to allow a more positive role for the law in Romans it is because he is endeavoring to disabuse the Gentile audience in Rome of the idea that they possess in Christ some religious superiority over their Jewish brethren. Damage control in the wake of the Galatians' polemic amounts to a significant component of Beker's interpretation of the situation addressed in Romans. Nevertheless, Paul insists in both letters that Jew and Gentile share equality on the same basis of *sola fide* and *sola gratia*.[227] The eschatological unity of Jews and Gentiles, foreseen by the Hebrew prophets, is inaugurated by the response of both Jews and Gentiles to the kerygma of Christ crucified "for us," and the fellowship of both under the Lordship of Christ. This unity is jeopardized in Rome because of Gentile pride (Romans 14–15), and in Jerusalem (see Rom. 15.30–32) because of the disturbing radicality of Paul's law-free gospel.

Nevertheless, Paul does appear to suspend his creative, dialogical hermeneutic when the apocalyptic coordinates of his gospel are at stake. Herein lies much of the difficulty Paul has in addressing those Corinthians who do not espouse his apocalyptic world-view, and who persistently interpret Paul's teaching about the resurrection of Jesus as implying a consistent and thoroughgoing present elevation of believers in the present ("celebrating D Day as though it were V Day").[228] For Paul, however, Jesus' resurrection and his present status as exalted Lord anticipate the final triumph of God. His resurrection and exaltation are a preliminary manifestation of the general resurrection, which, in Paul's eyes, is yet to come. For the Corinthians, however, it is a present reality. The end-time triumph of God, Beker insists, must not be equated with the triumph of Christ over death,[229] nor, for that matter, should the Kingdom of God (proleptically present in the Christ-event) be identified with the church.[230] The Corinthians, informed by their philosophical heritage which treated the body as an irredeemable part of the transient material world, are in danger of transgressing the Pauline stress on the tension between the "now" and the "not yet." Driven by transforming enthusiasm in the Spirit, they appropriate the resurrection teaching by claiming for the present what God has ordained for the future (see 1 Cor. 1.5–7; 4.8; cf. 15.12).

The clash of Paul's apocalyptic worldview and Hellenistic categories is evidenced acutely in 1 Corinthians 15. In this passage, Paul responds to the Corinthians and their accommodation of the apocalyptic framework in which his gospel is packaged to their own worldview. The apostle, Beker acknowledges, will not

> tolerate a world-view that cannot express those elements inherent in the apocalyptic world-view and that to Paul seem inherent to the truth of the gospel.[231]

Beker suggests that Paul's strategy in 1 Corinthians 15 could be interpreted as an "imposition" of his worldview on his addressees, demanding their assent and submission to his worldview. Beker seeks to demonstrate that what is at stake for Paul in 1 Corinthians, and in ch. 15 in particular, is the interconnection of apocalyptic categories and "profound Christological, anthropological and ethical issues"—matters which are not appreciated by his addressees.[232] Spirit and body cannot be sundered as they apparently are in the minds of the Corinthian believers. Life in the body is ethically significant in the present because the resurrection of Jesus anticipates the provision of a resurrection-body.

Beker establishes within the flexible parameters of his coherence/contingency model a presentation of Paul's thought and thinking which not only sheds light on Paul, but, as we will see, makes the deutero-Paulines stand out by contrast. The commitment of Paul to contextual theology and to the expression of the significance of the Christ-event were the first casualties in the enlargement of the Pauline corpus. On the other hand, the Paul of the genuine letters regards the eschatological victory of God as an essential coordinate of his gospel, and the Christ-event as the proleptic manifestation in history of the new order of the divine righteousness to come. On the other hand, the deutero-Paulines, especially Ephesians and Colossians, make the former (i.e., the final victory of God) subordinate to the present reign of Christ. Such a priority, Beker concludes,

> results in an ecclesiology that is no longer geared to the cosmic future triumph of God over his creation.[233]

The final triumph of God has become secondary to the present reign of Christ in the church. All things have already been reconciled to God through Christ (Col. 1.19; Eph. 1.10). This tendency one perceives in Colossians and Ephesians to speak about the redemption as an already completed process is thus out of keeping with Paul's apocalyptic theocentric hope.[234]

Beker has written two further books on Paul—*Paul's Apocalyptic Gospel* (Philadelphia: Fortress, 1982) and *The Triumph of God* (Minneapolis: Augsburg/Fortress, 1990; German original published in 1988). These develop in a more popular and concise way the themes of his more extensive *Paul the Apostle*. He has also been alive to criticism of his earlier work and has sought to respond to it not only in the *Triumph of God* but in two articles,[235] and in the preface to the 1984 reprint of *Paul the Apostle*. Part of his response has been to explore the deutero-Pauline literature of the NT, as well as Acts. This he does in his 1991 book *Heirs of Paul: Paul's Legacy in the New Testament and in the Church Today* to which I now turn.

Heirs of Paul

A number of responses to *Paul the Apostle* criticize Beker's perceived dismissal of the deutero-Pauline letters as unworthy of Paul.[236] In *Heirs of Paul*, Beker sets out to address this impression.

He is convinced of the need for modern believers to continue to interact creatively with the Pauline gospel lest either through anachronistic and literalistic readings, or through "deconstructionism" (Beker's term), the church loses its right to claim that it (the church) validly and authentically preserves the Christian gospel in its Pauline colors. Beker urges his readers, therefore, to commit themselves to hearing and proclaiming the *viva vox* of Paul. The strategies adopted by the "heirs of Paul," i.e., the deutero-Pauline writers of the NT, including the author of Acts, are, as a consequence, valuable guides as to how that might be done, or done better, by our own generation.

The Preface states the two foci of the book. These are:

1. the problem of appropriating Paul in the church today, and
2. the guidelines and warning signals from Paul's NT interpreters for contemporary appropriation of Paul.

In the first and fifth of his 5 chapters ("The Problem of Paul's Legacy" and "Paul's Impact on the Post-Pauline Period and on the Church Today"), Beker encourages his readers to attempt a valid transmission of Paul's legacy. But this can only be done, he writes,

> when the claims of the original tradition (the *traditum*) are properly balanced by the claims of the adaptations that the transmission of the tradition necessitates (the *traditio*).[237]

The task is to transpose Paul's gospel from its first century moorings to the modern situation, a process which should be

> attentive to the claims of the original tradition and the claims of the new historical and socio-cultural situations, to which the tradition intends to speak in a live manner.[238]

In other words, unless new language is found by which to express the Pauline gospel for today, Paul's gospel remains a frozen deposit unable to come to voice and unable to become a "word on target" for the modern church. Unintelligibility is the end-product of such an encounter with the first century biblical text.

Beker expresses his dissatisfaction with the "fall from Paul" school. Such an approach ends up merely dismissing the deutero-Pauline literature by means of its excessively contrastive methodology. Acknowledging his debt to scholars such as Roloff and Brox, Beker proposes to apply a dual methodology with comparative and traditio-historical components to the problem of interpreting Paul for today in order to assess the appropriateness of the adaptation of the Pauline gospel by Paul's NT heirs. The comparative component examines the extent to which the heirs "were able to do justice to the claims of Paul's original gospel," while the traditio-historical component seeks to determine

> how these interpreters adapted Paul's gospel as a living and relevant voice to the new historical circumstances of their time.[239]

Such a way forward hopes to avoid the excesses of applying the comparative method exclusively.

In chapter 2 ("Basic Issues in the Transmission of Tradition") much of Beker's already published views on Paul are summarized. Paul's method of interpreting the gospel resists our attempts "to establish the 'fixed core' of his thought."[240] The content of his gospel is so determined by the contingent situations Paul addresses that an abstraction is impossible.

Chapter 3 ("A Comparative Analysis of Post-Pauline Writings") is the longest chapter (35–75), and the one that is most germane to my investigation of the PE. Beker proposes to set himself against the view that these writings represent a falling away from the true Paul.[241] Yet it is not easy to imagine a more devastating critique of this material short of dismissing it as unworthy of the apostle.

In the PE Paul's dynamic coherent language is "petrified." Paul is presented as a "static" and "dogmatic" person. He imposes doctrine. He engages in monologue. Dynamic and relational Pauline concepts (such as "righteousness") become terms of pragmatic moral injunction. Beker's three main co-ordinates of Paul's apocalyptic worldview have undergone radical transmutation in the PE. The imminence of the parousia has been replaced by a distant, yet certain, expectation of eschatological judgment of all, and by a belief in the equally distant second "epiphany" of Christ. The radical dualism of Paul has disappeared. The Kingdom of God plays no role in the PE. The Pastor amounts to an accommodationist as far as Roman societal structures are concerned. The hope of the resurrection has been eclipsed in the PE—the language of "rebirth" (Tit. 3.5) and "immortality" (2 Tim. 1.10) has moved to the forefront. Believers live under the watchful eye of the guardians of the Pauline deposit. Believers' sights are set on the eschatological judgment, assured that they are already being equipped in the present for salvation by the operation of divine grace, which amounts to a process of "rebirth" which began at baptism (see Tit. 3.4–7). Progress in divine education should be the focus of the believer. History continues. Therein lies the challenge for the Pastor: how best to ensure the Pauline heritage for successive generations until the appearance of the Lord.

The remainder of the chapter surveys the other documents of the deutero-Pauline deposit, including Acts, from the comparative point of view. Thus the author of Luke-Acts promotes a "culture-friendly" Paul, as does the author of the PE. Paul preaches the same message—one that accords with that preached by the Jerusalem apostles—wherever he travels. The Lukan Paul faithfully adheres to the teaching of the Jerusalem apostles. He is subordinate to the apostolic witness. He is a pillar of orthodoxy; a man of "glamor" and "strength," a veritable θεῖος ἀνήρ. In Colossians, Paul has assumed heroic status. We encounter Paul of "blessed memory," rather like the portrait of Paul in Acts. Yet the contingent/coherent interplay is present in this letter in a way absent from Acts and the PE. With respect to his hermeneutic, there is not all that much (if anything) in this document that betrays the author as a post-Paulinist. Ephesians, on the other hand, lacks contingent features, though it is an imaginative and creative reworking of Pauline ideas. This letter celebrates Paul as a "mystagogue." His insights into the mystery of God, like those of Qumran's Righteous Teacher, surpass those of the apostles and prophets. Instead of placing the church on an apocalyptic trajectory, the author portrays the church as the arena in which God's eschatological and ecumenical purposes are already realized. Ecclesiology swallows up eschatology. The author of 2

Thessalonians actually reduplicates Paul, not by creative re-working of the Pauline message the author had inherited, but by copying as much as possible from 1 Thessalonians.[242] While Paul's hermeneutical strategy is followed, the author has simply modulated Paul's gospel in 1 Thessalonians "in an almost literal way" to the author's own, but different, situation. The presence of the apocalyptic timetable in 2 Thessalonians 2 betrays the author's distance from the thinking of the historical Paul. The warmth of Paul's encounter with the Thessalonians recorded in the first letter changes to a more "impersonal and didactic" tone in the second.

The reason for this pallid assessment, particularly where the PE are concerned, is that Beker compares and contrasts the various post-Pauline documents with the *seven* undisputed letters. However, in the case of the PE, it is possible, as A. E. Barnett sought to show, that the Pastor had already before him a Pauline corpus of ten letters, and sought to bring to speech Paul and his teaching as it was at hand in that corpus for his own generation. On this view, the PE, therefore, are not an actualization of the *undisputed* Pauline corpus of seven letters, but of the whole Pauline corpus, i.e., the corpus of ten letters. If Barnett is correct, the PE cannot simply be compared to the undisputed letters to ascertain the success or otherwise of the Pastor's actualization of the Pauline heritage. Rather, we must reckon on the Pastor's attempt to bring to speech and mediate to the church of his day the Paul of the whole corpus—the Paul of a wider tradition. Nevertheless, Beker has underscored in a powerful way many of the reasons why Paul could not have written the PE (and, for that matter, the remainder of the deutero-Pauline letters).

Chapter 4 ("The Traditio-Historical Method") ostensibly exposes to scrutiny the contingencies operating on the authors which dictated the manner in which they appropriated the tradition. Given the rather poor performance of the deutero-Pauline authors in adapting Paul's ideas and hermeneutical strategies, not much light can be expected to be shed on their circumstances by Beker's application of the traditio-historical method, as he himself is fully aware. The deutero-Pauline letter writers suppress the contingent circumstances of their writing.[243] Beker regrets that they did not tackle the new circumstances by applying Paul's strategies, particularly his commitment to dialogical argument. Only Colossians, he concedes, does this. I conclude that we are better served by scholars such as Margaret MacDonald (*The Pauline Churches*) for an account of the social situation of the addressees of the post-Pauline correspondence, and by scholars in the succession of Baur who are committed to an analysis of the historical contingencies operating in the post-Pauline world.

The return from Beker's application of the traditio-historical method, therefore, is rather slim. The deutero-Pauline deposit shows how the translation of Paul should *not* be attempted. Beker concludes with the predictable observation that

> most of the post-Pauline authors fall short of translating Paul's gospel properly.[244]

However, it is scarcely fair to adjudge the post-Paulines inflexible and insensitive with respect to the contingent situations of their audiences in contrast to Paul's commitment to dialogical argument. Can they be evaluated fairly when they are subjected to the kind of test applied by Beker? Paul does not always use dialogical argument himself. He can lay out precepts. He is capable of what one might term a lack of sensitivity to the theological preferences of his audience, as in 1 Corinthians 15.[245] The contingent situation addressed in Paul's letter to the Romans is not exactly transparent, and Beker's own reading of the situation presupposed in the letter has been criticized.[246]

Moreover, the Pastor may be transmitting Paul as he had received him through the Pauline corpus. If so, then Paul had already been refracted through the lens of the other deutero-Paulines. Consequently, the Pastor, as a third generation Paulinist, may be actualizing a Paul whose message had already been translated by the authors of the deutero-Pauline letters of the second generation.

Ernst Käsemann's insight is worth mentioning here. He argues that the post-Pauline authors set about saving Paul the way they did because the historical Paul we encounter in the undisputed letters was basically unsaveable.[247] Paul, the angular and individual apostle of freedom, was basically unintelligible to subsequent eras of church history who knew him only through the fiction created by the post-Pauline authors. The author of the PE is especially significant because he saw Paul as the originator of a world-wide ecclesiastical order which was extraordinarily well-adapted to face the challenges of the second and succeeding generations.[248]

Beker's two books, *Paul the Apostle* and *Heirs of Paul*, are particularly thought-provoking and creative attempts to explicate the way Paul interacts theologically with his addressees. The following three observations represent my assessment of Beker's work on Paul and on the post-Pauline deposit, the PE in particular.

1. Beker is generally reticent about discussing issues related to the social and historical background of the Pauline letters. In his evaluation of *Paul the Apostle*, Beker himself admits his neglect of the socio-economic aspect of the first century C.E. milieu of the letters.[249]

Given the fact that he is committed to exposing the interplay between "coherence" and "contingency" in the letters, one might have expected a more precise discussion in *Paul the Apostle* of the concrete situation of the addressees as far as that can be revealed by the documents themselves and by attention to their historical and cultural background. The term "contingency" is therefore a slippery one as Beker uses it. He implies that he intends to address Paul's dialogue with the churches as participants in their culture. However, Beker's approach to the matter of Paul's commitment to addressing the contingent situation of his audiences amounts to a study of Paul's interaction with their theological questions and preferences. These are perceived in the abstract by Paul and presented by Beker as such. One should allow a place for the cultural and religious contingencies of the Pauline congregations to set Paul's dialogical agenda.

2. In arguing the "how" of exegesis, Beker frequently illuminates the contextualization of Paul's thinking. Beker presents a Paul whose chief contribution to theology is precisely this genius of making his gospel a "word on target," at least with respect to the theological perceptions he has of his audiences. However, as he fully acknowledges, there are occasions—1 Corinthians 15 is the chief example—where Paul cannot "translate" his message if that means jettisoning his apocalyptic worldview. In that chapter Paul's commitment to the apocalyptic framework of the gospel prevents accommodation to the theological preferences of the Corinthians. Furthermore, in 1 Corinthians 11 the moral and social shape of Christian

fellowship as Paul perceives it, indeed, as it was received by him, is also non-negotiable. "Maintain the traditions" (τὰς παραδόσεις κατέχετε), he exhorts his addressees (11.2). In such instances Paul suspends contextualization. Beker is right to argue that certain key ideas are normative for Paul. When these are challenged or misunderstood by his readers, they are re-imposed on them.

The PE convey precisely this image of Paul, namely, the image of the apostle whose kerygma has indissoluble implications for the life and worship of the Christian community. Just as Paul imposed on his congregations non-negotiable precepts, so does the Paul of the PE. It was an essential aspect of the image of Paul which the Pastor was committed to embodying in his letters. This raises the question whether the coherence/contingency hermeneutic works only in certain argumentative contexts, and not in others. It is certainly worthy of note that the PE show the receding of Jewish questions, such as the role of the law, the goal of salvation history, the place of the Jewish people in God's purposes, and the significance of the cross. These were precisely the arenas in which Paul's creative hermeneutic was manifested. These were the issues in which Paul was passionately involved with his addressees. In the PE, the Pastor invariably declines to argue the case against the false teachers. The thrust of the letters is mainly paraenetic. The time for engagement with the false teachers had passed.

3. Beker does not evaluate the influence of classical and Greco-Roman rhetoric on Paul. Galatians, e.g., presents the commentator with excellent opportunities to explore the possible influences of classical rhetoric on Paul's argumentative technique. 2 Cor. 11–12 also allow for further insight into Paul's knowledge of rhetorical conventions, although, it must be underscored, he plays down any claim to being *skilled* in the craft.[250] He claims that he eschewed rhetorical cleverness and artistry in preaching the gospel to the Corinthians (1 Cor. 2.1–5). Powerful discourse and rhetoric go hand in hand. It would seem, therefore, that Paul intentionally avoided the power that might be fostered through oratory in favor of the "plain speaking" of the gospel (see 1 Cor. 2.2). That ought not blind us, however, to the strategies and persuasive techniques that he manifestly, if subtly, does use.

SUMMARY

Baur and Holtzmann, as well as other scholars since, have persuasively argued the case for the non-Pauline authorship of the PE. They arrive at their conclusion by means of the application of a double methodology. They *compare* the theology, ethics, and ecclesiology of the PE with the presentation of these matters in the Christian literature of the early second century C.E.; and they *contrast* the PE with the Pauline corpus, especially the seven undisputed letters. In this way the non-Pauline authorship of the PE and the other deutero-Pauline letters has been more or less convincingly demonstrated.

Defenders of the Pauline authorship of the PE have long sought to interpret differently the same internal and external evidence. At back of the defensive strategy of many of the defenders lies an acute sense of the inappropriateness of the presence of pseudepigrapha in the NT canon. Pseudepigraphy is regarded as literary falsification or deception. Moreover, the early Church did express scruples about pseudepigrapha. In general, the defenders contend for the authenticity of the remaining canonical Pauline letters with which they compare the PE. By this strategy they attempt to show that the PE are more redolent of Pauline authorship than is thought by those who argue for the pseudonymous authorship.

Scholars who attempt *traditionsgeschichtliche* studies of the PE are concerned to trace and account for the contours of the actualization of Pauline tradition in the PE. Usually these scholars assume the results of the Baur-Holtzmann investigation of the pseudonymous authorship of the letters. Generally, however, these studies perpetuate the approach of comparing them with Pauline tradition and focusing on the concerns of theology, ethics, and ecclesiology. The recent book of Michael Wolter is an outstanding exception to this trend because he is aware of the Pastor as a utilizer of persuasive strategies.

Beker's analysis of the PE has the advantage of deriving logically and coherently from his earlier treatment of Paul. He too produces a comparative analysis of the PE; one which is consistent, however, with the analyses of those scholars who contrast the PE with the seven undisputed letters.

I am contending for an awareness not only of the Pastor's claim to be actualizing Pauline tradition but of the literary-rhetorical form in which that *Vergegenwärtigung* was embodied. This book is about the Pastor as a user of persuasive techniques derived from the traditions of epistolary moral exhortation and the rhetoric of persuasive speech. My contention is that the Pastor drew on rhetorical and epistolary conventions, as well as on the Pauline heritage, in order to commend his actualization of Pauline tradition for the needs of his own day.

Consequently, chapter 2 will investigate the PE as letters of moral exhortation. Chapter 3 will examine the PE from the standpoint of oral rhetoric as a contribution to awareness of the literateness of the PE.

NOTES

1 *Against Heresies*, 2.14.7 (1 Tim. 6.20); 3.14.1 (2 Tim. 4.10–11); 1.16.3 (Tit. 3.10). For texts, see *ANF* 1.378, 438, and 341 respectively.

2 Athenagoras, *A Plea for the Christians*, 37; Theophilus, *Letter to Autolycus*, 3.14. For texts, see *ANF* 2.148 and 115 respectively.

3 See the compendium compiled by A Committee of the Oxford Society of Historical Theology, *The New Testament in the Apostolic Fathers* (Oxford: Clarendon, 1905), 95–96 for plausible, though not conclusive, arguments for the priority of 1 Tim. 6.7, 10 over Pol. *Phil.* 4.1 (ca. 120 C.E.). The Committee also acknowledges a particularly close relationship between Ign. *Eph.* 14.1; 20.1; *Magn.* 8.1 and 1 Tim. 1.3–5 (71–72). For possible allusions to the PE in *1 Clement*, see also P. N. Harrison, *Problem of the Pastoral Epistles* (Oxford: University Press, 1921), 177–8. It is also possible that Pol. *Phil.* 4.1 and 1 Tim. 6.7, 10 are derived from popular wisdom. On this point see M. Dibelius and H. Conzelmann, *The Pastoral Epistles* (Philadelphia: Fortress, 1972), 1–2, 84–86. They argue that Ignatius' and Polycarp's supposed literary dependence on the PE cannot be proven. See further discussion in W. Bauer, *Orthodoxy and Heresy* (Philadelphia: Fortress, 1971), 223–4.

4 *Against Marcion*, 5.21 (*ANF* 3.473–4). Tertullian is at a loss to explain Marcion's

failure to include the PE since he knew that Marcion had accepted the presence of Philemon, a letter to an individual, in his canon. Tertullian can only suppose that he wanted to extend his "interpolating process even to the number of [St. Paul's] epistles." It is more likely that (i) Marcion did not know the PE, or (ii) if he did know them, objected to their doctrine, or (iii) that the PE had not yet been written. The last is Walter Bauer's position (see *Orthodoxy and Heresy*, 222–5). Epiphanius (ca. 315–403) notes in his *Panarion* that Marcion rejected the PE. See Philip R. Amidon, S.J. (trans. and ed.), *The Panarion of St. Epiphanius, Bishop of Salamis: Selected Passages* (New York: Oxford University Press, 1990), 42.9.4, 11.9–11. On the question of an alleged explicit anti-Gnostic thrust in the PE, J. N. D. Kelly's observation (*A Commentary on the Pastoral Epistles* [London: A. & C. Black, 1963], 4) that the *Gospel of Truth* (ca. 150 C.E.), ascribed to the Gnostic Valentinus, cites every book of the NT except the PE is wide of the mark. The *Gospel* actually paraphrases passages from many books of the NT, including Romans, 1 and 2 Corinthians, Ephesians and Colossians, but not the three Pastorals, Philippians, 1 and 2 Thessalonians, and Philemon.

5 *Stromata*, 2.11 (*ANF* 2.359).

6 See the paraphrase of Jerome's "Preface to Titus" in *NPF 2*, 6.498. See also Ferdinand Christian Baur, *Die sogenannten Pastoralbriefe des Apostels Paulus* (Stuttgart and Tübingen: J. G. Gotta'schen Verlagshandlung, 1835), 135; Jerome D. Quinn, *The Letter to Titus* (New York: Doubleday, 1990), 3.

7 See brief surveys in Ceslaus Spicq, *Les Épîtres Pastorales* (Paris: Gabalda, 1969), 1.176–9; W. W. Lock, *A Critical and Exegetical Commentary on the Pastoral Epistles* (Edinburgh: T. & T. Clark, 1924), xxv–xxvi. Lock notes that the PE are ascribed to Paul in the Syriac and Old Latin versions of the NT (xxv). Spicq, *Les Épîtres Pastorales*, 1.169, and Quinn, *Titus*, 3, also note the early attestation of Titus in the manuscript tradition. 𝔓32 (ca. 200 C.E.) comprises Tit. 1.11–15 and 2.3–8. However there is doubt that the early third century collection of letters, 𝔓46, would have had sufficient room to have contained the PE. See the discussion in Jerome D. Quinn, "P46—The Pauline Canon?" *CBQ* 36 (1974), 379–85. Quinn plausibly surmises that 𝔓46 represents a collection of Pauline letters (including Hebrews) written to churches, and would have included 2 Thess. (but not Philemon), while 𝔓32 represents a collection of Pauline letters written to individuals, namely, Philemon and the PE.

8 See the survey in Heinrich Julius Holtzmann, *Die Pastoralbriefe* (Leipzig: Verlag von Wilhelm Engelmann, 1880), 7–15.

9 See the note in Schleiermacher's *Über den ersten Brief Pauli an Timotheus* (Braunschweig/Leipzig: Gerhard Reuter, 1897), 11.

10 Baur, *Pastoralbriefe*, 3–4. See also Schleiermacher's summary of his objections in *Über den ersten Brief Pauli an Timotheus*, 7–14, 120–4.

11 See J. G. Eichhorn, *Einleitung in das Neuen Testament* (Leipzig: Weidmannischen Buchhandlung, 1812), 3.315–7 (stylistic unity). See 3.319–28 for Eichhorn's discussion of the arguments against Pauline authorship.

12 Baur, *Pastoralbriefe*, 3 in which he builds on Schleiermacher's observation of the argumentative strategy of 1 Timothy.

13 See Baur, *Pastoralbriefe*, 14–18 in which he argues that the antinomianism of Marcion is polemicized in the PE (*pace* Holtzmann, *Pastoralbriefe*, 128). The supposed Gnosticism of Marcion is by no means accepted by scholars. Adolf von Harnack would admit only Marcion's "loose connections" (Rudolph's phrase) to the Gnostic systems. However, see K. Rudolph, *Gnosis* (Trans. R. McL. Wilson; San Francisco: Harper & Row, 1987), 313–7, and see also his n. 140 (388). Rudolph is much more prepared to regard Marcion as one influenced by Gnostic ideas. The evidence of Irenaeus on this point is both ambiguous and tendentious. Marcion is presented as the successor of the heretic Cerdo, and a contemporary in Rome of the Gnostic Valentinus (see Irenaeus, *Against Heresies*, 1.27.1–2; 3.4.3; cf. Tertullian, *Against Marcion*, 1.2, 22; 4.17). In *Against Heresies*, 1.27.1 and 3.4.3 Cerdo's teaching, developed further by Marcion, is allegedly derived from Menander, a disciple of Simon Magus, the founder of all heresies including Gnosticism, as far as catholic thought was concerned. Yet Cerdo's teaching, what little can be gleaned of it, does not seem to stem from the same origin as Valentinus' decidedly Gnostic cosmology. See the discussion in R. Joseph Hoffmann, *Marcion: On the Restitution of Christianity* (Chico: Scholars Press, 1984), 39–44.

14 Note, e.g., the perceptive comments on the un-Pauline cast of 1 Tim. 1.7 in H. Räisänen, *Paul and the Law* (Philadelphia: Fortress, 1986), 119, 206–07.

15 *Pastoralbriefe*, 26–27.

16 *Pastoralbriefe*, 18–19, 24, 25.

17 *Pastoralbriefe*, 38–39.

18 See Tertullian, *Prescription against Heretics*, 41 (text in *ANF* 3.263) and *Against Marcion*, 5.8 for women ministering in heretical congregations. For the tradition that Paul commissioned women to teach, see *Acts of Paul*, 3.41 (text in W. Schneemelcher [ed.], *New Testament Apocrypha: Volume Two: Writings Relating to the Apostles; Apocalypses and Related Subjects* [Revised Edition; Louisville: Westminster/John Knox, 1992], 246) and the discussion in Dennis R. McDonald, *The Legend and the Apostle: The Battle for Paul in Story and Canon* (Philadelphia: Westminster, 1983), ch. 1.

19 *Pastoralbriefe*, 52–53. See also Irenaeus, *Against Heresies*, 1.24.2 (Saturninus); Tertullian, *Prescription against Heretics*, 33 (Marcion and Apelles); Clement of Alexandria, *Stromata*, 3.6 (heretics who boast in [false] sexual continence). Cf. *Acts of Paul*, 3.20.

20 See, e.g., Holtzmann, *Pastoralbriefe*, 127–8; Kelly, *Pastoral Epistles*, 151–2. See, however, the arguments for the pro-Jewish slant of Marcion's thinking in Hoffmann, *Marcion*, esp. 226–34, 287–93. Hoffmann argues that Tertullian's charge (*Against Marcion*, 3.6) against Marcion that he had formed an alliance with the "Jewish error" is to be taken as an actual, rather than polemical, indication of Marcion's intentional pro-Jewish sympathies and theological program.

21 Baur, *Pastoralbriefe*, 57; cf. 74–80.

22 Baur, *Pastoralbriefe*, 68.

23 Baur, *Pastoralbriefe*, 98.

24 Baur, *Pastoralbriefe*, 100.

25 Baur, *Pastoralbriefe*, 102.

26 Baur, *Pastoralbriefe*, 137, 138–40.

27 Cf. Bauer, *Orthodoxy and Heresy*, 88–89. As "Paul," Bauer writes, "he must deal with the 'teachers of the law' (1 Tim. 1.7) and the 'circumcision party' (Titus 1.10), but as a second century churchman, he opposes Gnosticism" (89).

28 See Holtzmann, *Pastoralbriefe*, 95–98. Holtzmann argues for the dependence of the author on Acts in the case of 2 Tim. 1.3 (χάριν ἔχω τῷ θεῷ ᾧ λατρεύω ἀπὸ προγόνων). Cf. Acts 24.14 (οὕτως λατρεύω τῷ πατρῴω θεῷ) as well as Rom. 1.9 (μάρτυς γάρ μού ἐστιν ὁ θεός, ᾧ λατρεύω . . .).

29 *Pastoralbriefe*, 98. Cf. Harrison, *Problem*, 26.

30 *Pastoralbriefe*, 98–99. See also Harrison, *Problem*, 31–38, esp. 33.

31 *Pastoralbriefe*, 99. Cf. Harrison, *Problem*, 20–24.

32 *Pastoralbriefe*, 100–01. Cf. Harrison, *Problem*, 34–38.

33 *Pastoralbriefe*, 101. Cf. Harrison, *Problem*, 42. Harrison notes that the PE lack the Pauline "impetus," and the "drive and surge of mighty thoughts never spoken before."

34 *Pastoralbriefe*, 109. Cf. Spicq, *Les Épîtres Pastorales*, 1.190–3.

35 See *Pastoralbriefe*, 109–18. The following examples are among those adduced by Holtzmann in support of his contention: (i) 1 Tim. 1.5 with its stress on the priority of love seems to be dependent on Rom. 13.9, (ii) 1 Tim. 1.12 recalls 1 Cor. 7.25 with its note of Paul having been considered faithful, (iii) the presentation of Paul as former persecutor of the church in 1 Tim. 1.12–17 owes much to Gal. 1.13–14, 1

Cor. 15.9 and Phil. 3.6—the theme of overflowing grace being common to 1 Tim. 1.14 and 1 Cor. 15.10, (iv) the teaching on the passive role of women in the congregation has affinity with 1 Cor. 14.34, especially with respect to women learning in silence (ἐν ἡσυχίᾳ, 1 Tim. 2.11–12; cf. the phrase αἱ γυναῖκες . . . σιγάτωσαν in 1 Cor. 14.34), (v) the use of ἔργον to denote ecclesiastical function in 1 Thess. 5.13 is paralleled by 1 Tim. 3.1, (vi) 2 Tim. 1.7 (οὐ γὰρ ἔδωκεν ἡμῖν ὁ θεὸς πνεῦμα δειλίας) bears affinity with Rom. 8.15 (οὐ γὰρ ἐλάβετε πνεῦμα δουλείας πάλιν εἰς φόβον), (vii) the phrase "seed of David" in 2 Tim. 2.8 can be paralleled in Rom. 1.3, (viii) the phrase "according to my gospel" occurring at 2 Tim. 2.8 also occurs at Rom. 2.16 and 16.25, (ix) the use of σπένδομαι in Phil. 2.17 has clear affinity with 2 Tim. 4.6, (x) the prologue of Titus (1.1–4) has marked literary affinities with Rom. 1.1–2. See also A. T. Hanson's discussion of the Pastor's usage of four passages in the Pauline corpus in his *The Pastoral Epistles* (London: Marshall, Morgan & Scott, 1982), 28–31.

36 See *Pastoralbriefe*, 115–6. Cf. Harrison, *Problem*, 6, 87–93.

37 *Paul Becomes a Literary Influence* (Chicago: University of Chicago Press, 1941), especially 251–77 with respect to the PE. See the convenient summary of the results of his literary analysis on 277.

38 *Paul Becomes a Literary Influence*, 277.

39 *Paul Becomes a Literary Influence*, 222. Cf. 251 in which Barnett, a good student of Baur on this matter, argues that the author of the PE sought to mount the rescue of the Pauline letters from the disfavor into which they had fallen towards the middle of the second century "as a result of their popularity among the Marcionites." Cf. K. L. Carroll, "The Expansion of the Pauline Corpus," *JBL* 72 (1953), 230–7. The theory of the function of Ephesians as a preface to the Pauline corpus was mooted earlier by E. J. Goodspeed. See, e.g., his *The Formation of the New Testament* (Chicago: University Press, 1926), ch. 3 (pps. 20–32).

40 See especially P. Trummer, *Die Paulustradition der Pastoralbriefe* (Frankfurt am Main/Bern/Las Vegas: Lang, 1978). Trummer's work is discussed in section C of this chapter.

41 *Pastoralbriefe*, 159. Cf. E. Käsemann, "Paul and Early Catholicism," in *New Testament Questions of Today* (Philadelphia: Fortress, 1969), 237–51. For Käsemann, the ecclesiastical polity that emerged in the early second century, and which is to be observed in the PE, is poles apart from that of the genuine Pauline letters. Nowhere is this more distinctly seen than in Paul's perception of Christian ministry. For Paul, Käsemann argues, every Christian is to be addressed as a charismatic. All have received the Spirit through baptism, all are Spirit-endowed for the purpose of building one another up in the "body." The implication for this view of the activity of the Spirit is that all are laymen in Paul's churches. There is no distinction between ordained ministers and the rest of the congregation as

receivers of ministry at their hands, or, worse, dependent on such a ministry for the reception of grace. Paul eschews every semblance in the services of the church of the *cultic* celebration. There are no holy times, places, celebrations, and functionaries in the life of the believers. See also his essay "Ministry and Community in the New Testament," in *Essays on New Testament Themes* (Philadelphia: Fortress, 1964), 63–94. See also John H. Schütz, *Paul and the Anatomy of Apostolic Authority* (SNTSMS 26; Cambridge: Cambridge University Press, 1975), 262–3, 278. For the sociological background of the growth of institutionalization in the Pauline corpus, see Margaret Y. MacDonald's *Pauline Churches*.

42 *Pastoralbriefe*, 161.

43 *Pastoralbriefe*, 166.

44 *Pastoralbriefe*, 163–4. See also n. 14 above.

45 *Pastoralbriefe*, 168–9. On the language of epiphany in the PE, see Jouette M. Bassler, "A Plethora of Epiphanies: Christology in the Pastoral Epistles," *PSB* 17 (1996), 310–25.

46 *Pastoralbriefe*, 169.

47 *Pastoralbriefe*, 169–70: "Die bedeutendste Abweichung vom paulinischen Typus liegt aber darin vor, dass jener λύτρωσις keine unmittelbar religiöse Beziehung auf das Gesetz und seinen Fluch, sondern lediglich eine solche auf das sittliche Leben der Erlösten gegeben wird."

48 *Pastoralbriefe*, 170. Cf. H. von Lips, *Glaube—Gemeinde—Amt* (Göttingen: Vandenhoeck & Ruprecht, 1979), 75–76 in which he argues that the Pastor perceived no antithesis between πίστις and ἔργα (νόμου) as in Paul.

49 See *Pastoralbriefe*, 169–70.

50 *Pastoralbriefe*, 173. See also Holtzmann's discussion of Tit. 3.7 on 498–9.

51 Holtzmann, *Pastoralbriefe*, 499. See also U. Luz, "Rechtfertigung bei den Paulusschülern," in J. Friedrich et al. (eds.), *Rechtfertigung* (Festschrift E. Käsemann; Tübingen/Göttingen: Vandenhoeck & Ruprecht, 1976), 365–83. Until Marcion, Paul's doctrine, Luz argues, plays a peripheral role in the second century (366). What knowledge of justification by faith there is appears in baptismal liturgies (see Eph. 2.1–10; Tit. 3.3–7) (370). The receding of apocalyptic expectation had the effect of marginalizing "Rechtfertigungslehre" (372–3). Luz notes its absence from the *paratheke* in the PE, drawing the conclusion that, in the place of the Pauline doctrine of justification by faith with its eschatological dimensions, there has been substituted a doctrine linked to baptism, namely,

justification by "Taufgnade" (379). Cf. Dibelius-Conzelmann, *Pastoral Epistles*, 150. But see also Hanson, *Pastoral Epistles*, 192–3 and Quinn, *Titus*, 228–9, both of whom are prepared to see far greater evidence of Pauline influence.

52 *Pastoralbriefe*, 179–80. Cf. von Lips, *Glaube*, 31.

53 *Pastoralbriefe*, 187: "Aehnlich wie im Epheserbriefe findet nämlich auch hier der bekannte Fortschritt statt von der Einzelgemeinde, an welche Paulus, wo er ἐκκλησία sagt, gewöhnlich denkt, zu dem nicht mehr socialen, sondern dogmatischen Begriff der *ecclesia universalis*."

54 R. Sohm makes the same point with respect to the ecclesiology of the PE. Sohm argued that that order seen already in the PE was a betrayal of the original charismatic endowment of the local congregations. See both his *Das Kirchenrecht* (Leipzig: Duncker & Humboldt, 1892) and *Wesen und Ursprung des Katholizismus* (Leipzig: Teubner, 1909). By restricting the work of the Spirit to the ordained clergy, and by seeking to establish the church by recourse to legal formulation—tendencies he noted at work in the later writings of the NT (including the PE)—he saw the first century church proceeding inevitably on its way to the Roman Catholic order that was to dominate western Christendom. In his essay "Paul and Early Catholicism," (see discussion at n. 41 above) Ernst Käsemann identifies the disappearance of the imminent expectation of the parousia as "marking the transition from earliest Christianity to the so-called ancient Church" (237), i.e., the church which developed into the *Una Sancta Apostolica*, the great Church, namely, the Church of Rome. As the imminent expectation of the parousia waned, the church found itself driven to institutionalize order by which the church might live out its life in the generations ahead.

55 *Pastoralbriefe*, 188: "Die Unbestimmtheit und Vagheit der Wiederkunftserwartung macht sich besonders bemerklich in der Art wie 1 Tim. 6,15 es Gott . . . überlassen wird, die ἐπιφάνεια 'zu seiner Zeit' . . . während der Verfasser sich mit seinen Anordnungen bezüglich der Lehrüberlieferung und Kirchenverfassung einstweilen nicht mehr blos für ein Provisorium, sondern für eine, immerhin belangreiche, irdische Gegenwart und Zukunft einrichtet."

56 *Pastoralbriefe*, 189.

57 Holtzmann, *Pastoralbriefe*, 189–190.

58 Heb. 3.1 and Eph. 1.3, Holtzmann argues, show that ἐπουράνιος means "in heaven" not "coming from heaven" (*Pastoralbriefe*, 189). See also J. Christiaan Beker, *Paul the Apostle* (Philadelphia: Fortress, 1980), 345–7. Beker stresses the material and earthly nature of Paul's hope over against the tendency to spiritualize it in the deutero-Pauline corpus.

59 *Pastoralbriefe*, 190.

60 *Theology of the New Testament* (2 Vols.; New York: Scribners, 1951 and 1955), 2.186. Cf. Schulz, *Die Mitte der Schrift*, 100–09.

61 *Theology of the New Testament,* 2.133. Cf. J. Christiaan Beker, *Heirs of Paul* (Philadelphia: Fortress, 1991), 38, 39, 46–47. Beker writes that the Pastor's "desire to contemporize Paul's authority for his churches directly contradicts Paul's own method of dealing with heretical movements . . . " (46).

62 *Theology of the New Testament,* 2.180. See also Bultmann's article "Pastoralbriefe," in H. Gunkel and L. Zscharnak (eds.), *Die Religion in Geschichte und Gegenwart* (Tübingen: Mohr, 1927–31), 4.995. The historical Paul, on the other hand, understands the divorce of the believer from the world much more radically (*Theology of the New Testament,* 2.186). See also Dibelius and Conzelmann, *The Pastoral Epistles*, 8. Dibelius and Conzelmann speak of "good Christian citizenship" ("christliche Bürgerlichkeit") as the ethical ideal of the PE, elements of which can be found in Paul. However, in Paul the ideal is eschatologically conditioned, i.e., "it results from the paradox of change in the world," and is concretized in the demand to serve others. In the PE, on the other hand, ethics are derived from "the order of creation," and from philosophical commonplaces. Cf. von Lips, *Glaube*, 76 and 87. Von Lips makes the point that the ethics of the Christian life are identical with those most valued in Greco-Roman culture, namely, σωφροσύνη, δικαιοσύνη, and εὐσέβεια. In fact εὐσέβεια replaces πίστις as the ground of the believers' existence with respect to God (80).

63 *Theology of the New Testament,* 2.185.

64 *Theology of the New Testament,* 2.184. Cf. 1.324–5. Bultmann adds that the term "sincere" (ἀνυπόκριτος) qualifies "faith" in 1 Tim. 1.5 and 2 Tim. 1.5, a term which Paul uses to qualify "love" (see Rom. 12.9; 2 Cor. 6.6). See also G. Friedrich, "Glaube und Verkündigung bei Paulus," in F. Hahn and H. Klein (eds.), *Glaube im Neuen Testament* (Festschrift H. Binder; Biblisch-theologische Studien 7; Neukirchen-Vluyn: Neukirchener Verlag, 1982), 93–113 and G. Kretschmar, "Der paulinische Glaube in den Pastoralbriefen," in *Glaube im Neuen Testament*, 115–40.

65 See, e.g., A. Jülicher's treatment of the PE in *An Introduction to the New Testament* (New York: G. P. Putnam's Sons, 1904), 174–200. Jülicher mounts the following major arguments against the authenticity of the PE: (i) their language and style, (ii) the writer discards the most distinctive elements of Paul's thought, especially the surrender of the imminence of the parousia, (iii) the excessive formality of the address to trusted fellow-workers (contrast Philemon), and (iv) the PE cannot be placed in the life of Paul as we know it from his letters and Acts. See also W. G. Kümmel, *Introduction to the New Testament* (17th rev. ed.; London: SCM, 1975), 370–84 and Brevard S. Childs, *The New Testament as Canon*, 378–9 for similar assessments.

66 *Pastoralbriefe*, 159.

67 *Pastoralbriefe*, 125. Cf. Young, *The Theology of the Pastoral Epistles*, 142.

68 *Pastoralbriefe*, 59.

69 *Les Épîtres Pastorales* (2 Vols.; Paris: Gabalda, 1969).

70 *Les Épîtres Pastorales*, 1.31.

71 *Les Épîtres Pastorales*, 1.37, 43.

72 See George W. Knight III, *The Pastoral Epistles* (Grand Rapids: Eerdmans, 1992), 10. The PE, he argues, have two common aims: (i) to warn against false teachers, and (ii) to instruct Christians in Ephesus and Crete through Timothy and Titus.

73 See Spicq, *Les Épîtres Pastorales*, 1.38–46. Cf. Quinn, *Titus*, 6–9; Johnson, *The Writings of the New Testament*, 391–2. For examples of paraenetic letters and further discussion see *inter alia* Abraham J. Malherbe, *Moral Exhortation: A Greco-Roman Sourcebook* (Philadelphia: Westminster, 1986), 122–4.

74 *Les Épîtres Pastorales*, 1.38–39. This is a mistaken identification of modes of moral exhortation in my view. See the discussion of the differentiation between protrepsis and paraenesis in ch. 2 section C.

75 *Les Épîtres Pastorales*, 1.38. Cf. Towner, *The Goal of our Instruction*, chs. 8, 9, and 10. Towner thoroughly examines the content of the paraenesis to the respective constituents of the church household.

76 See the use of verbs such as παραγγέλλω (1 Tim. 1.3; 4.11; 5.7; 6.13, 17), παρακαλέω (1 Tim. 1.3; 2.1; 5.1; 6.2; 2 Tim. 4.2; Tit. 1.9; 2.6, 15) and φεύγω (1 Tim. 6.11; 2 Tim. 2.22); the language of summons to responsibility in 1 Tim. 4.14; and the duties assigned various members of the "household" through the apostolic emissaries.

77 *Les Épîtres Pastorales*, 1.41–42. Cf. Kelly, *Pastoral Epistles*, 23.

78 *Les Épîtres Pastorales*, 1.41–42. Spicq operates with a conception of diatribe that is too loose to be of much help in the analysis of the PE. For a definition of the diatribe emphasizing its dialogical and didactic nature derived from the philosopher's classroom, and its presence in the letter to the Romans, see Stanley K. Stowers, *The Diatribe and Paul's Letter to the Romans* (SBLDS 57; Chico: Scholars Press, 1981).

79 *Les Épîtres Pastorales*, 1.86–87; see Gal. 5.12; 1 Cor. 4.8; 2 Cor. 10–12. He might also have added Rom. 16.20.

80 *Les Épîtres Pastorales*, 1.101–03. Spicq argues that the false teachers used the genealogical material as an aid to esoteric and speculative exegesis and

interpretation of scripture (103–10). See also Kelly, *Pastoral Epistles*, 44–45 and the attractive proposal of F. H. Colson, "'Myths and Genealogies'—A Note on the Polemic of the Pastoral Epistles," *JThS* o.s. 19 (1918), 265–71. Colson argues plausibly that the reference to "myths and genealogies" is an allusion to an esoteric and over intellectualizing approach to the Hebrew scriptures in which the personal details of the characters were reduced to lists and complex pedigrees after the manner of the treatment of the characters in the Homeric epics.

81 *Les Épîtres Pastorales*, 1.110. Cf. Knight, *Pastoral Epistles*, 11–12.

82 *Les Épîtres Pastorales*, 1.113 n. 1.

83 *Les Épîtres Pastorales*, 1.114.

84 *Les Épîtres Pastorales*, 1.65–83, 157. Cf. Kelly, *Pastoral Epistles*, 13–16.

85 *Les Épîtres Pastorales*, 1.67–70.

86 *Les Épîtres Pastorales*, 1.170–6. Cf. 121–46. Kelly, *Pastoral Epistles*, 6–8 admits the impossibility of harmonizing the PE and the missionary activity of Paul as we know it from Acts. However, see the summary of recent scholarship on the question of harmonization of the record in Acts with the PE in Towner, *1–2 Timothy & Titus*, 15–20. Towner is far more positive, though unpersuasive, in his assessment of the possibilities that the PE can indeed be harmonized with Acts. He supports the view that the activity of Paul presupposed in 1 Timothy and Titus could have occurred between Acts 19.20, 21.

87 It is by no means certain that Clement means that Paul reached Spain. Moreover, Clement seems unaware of Paul's release from prison. When Paul had "reached the limits of the west" (ἐπὶ τὸ τέρμα τῆς δύσεως ἐλθών, 5.7), Clement writes, he "bore testimony" (καὶ μαρτυρήσας) before rulers and received his heavenly reward. See the discussion in Dibelius and Conzelmann, *Pastoral Epistles*, 3; Hanson, *The Pastoral Epistles*, 19–20. Clement could have had Rome in mind rather than Spain when he writes of the "limits of the west." Harrison, *Problem*, 107–08 contends that the τέρμα of which Clement speaks is the "goal" of the apostle's life. Had Clement meant to denote "Spain" by his reference to "limit of the west" he would have written τέρματα. Incidentally, A. T. Hanson doubts that *1 Clement* was written as early as ca. 95–96 (where it is often dated), preferring instead to disassociate Clement from the "T. Flavius Clemens' affair", and, on the grounds of the reference to "Clement" (not T. Flavius Clemens) in *Herm. Vis.* 2.4.3, to date the letter to ca. 120. The late second century *Acts Pet.* 1 does actually speak of Paul's release and voyage to Spain (for text, see Schneemelcher [ed.], *New Testament Apocrypha: Volume Two*, 287). The Muratorian Canon also speaks of Paul departing Rome and journeying to Spain, thus implying that Paul was released from the first imprisonment. Note also Eusebius, *Ecclesiastical History*, 2.22 (in which the historian cites 2 Tim. 4.16–18 as evidence of Paul's release from that confinement recounted at the end of Acts). Eusebius, unlike *1 Clement*, *Acts of*

Peter, and the Muratorian Canon, explicitly speaks of a second imprisonment followed by the apostle's martyrdom.

88 So also Kelly, *Pastoral Epistles*, 9–10; Lock, *Pastoral Epistles*, 119. It is extremely likely, Kelly argues, that Paul was released from his first imprisonment. He expects to see his friends soon (Phil. 1.25; 2.24; Phlm. 22). Moreover, he surmises, Festus' report to Nero of the judicial proceedings would have disposed Nero to a favorable decision in Paul's case. It is by no means certain, however, that Clement means what Spicq, Kelly, and the other defenders of Pauline authorship of the PE argue. Dismissing *1 Clement* as a witness to Paul's supposed renewed missionary enterprise (see previous note), Harrison, *Problem*, 108–09 argues that the later witnesses to renewed missionary activity on Paul's part are derived only from the PE and intentions expressed in Rom. 15.24, 28 as well as from material, such as the *Acts of Peter*, which may be dependent on the biblical records. M. Prior, *Paul the Letter-Writer* (JSNTSS 23; Sheffield: JSOT Press, 1989), 91–112, is not persuaded that 2 Timothy should be regarded as Paul's "Farewell Address" before his execution. Having surveyed the vocabulary of 2 Timothy in passages normally taken to be referring to Paul's impending death, he concludes that the tradition of Paul's martyrdom has been read back into the text by commentators. Where Paul speaks about his "release" (ἀνάλυσις) in 2 Tim. 4.6 he refers not to his impending death but his release from imprisonment for renewed devotion to the task of missionary activity (111), this time in Spain.

89 See J. Jeremias, *Die Pastoralbriefe* (8th ed.; Göttingen: Vandenhoeck and Ruprecht, 1963), 2–3: "Der wichtigste Zeuge dafür, dass Paulus noch einmal freigekommen ist und auf einer vierten Missionsreise sein Werk abgeschlossen hat, sind die Pastoralbriefe selbst, auch für den Fall ihrer Unechtheit."

90 *Les Épîtres Pastorales*, 1.171. Cf. Childs, *The New Testament as Canon*, 380.

91 Cf. Kelly, *Pastoral Epistles*, 33. Even Dibelius and Conzelmann, *Pastoral Epistles*, 127, proponents of the pseudonymous authorship of the PE, note that the *personalia* are the strongest argument for the authenticity of the PE.

92 This is an important point in Kelly's argument for the authenticity of the PE (*Pastoral Epistles*, 33). However, see the contrasting point of view in, e.g., J. Zmijewski, "Die Pastoralbriefe als pseudepigraphische Schriften," *Studien zum Neuen Testament und seiner Umwelt* 4 (1979), 100–03, 113–7.

93 See Harrison, *Problem*, 115–30. He distinguishes the following genuine fragments: Tit. 12–15 (written soon after 2 Cor. 10–13 and before 2 Cor. 1–9); 2 Tim. 4.13–15, 20, 21a; 2 Tim. 4.16–18a; 2 Tim. 4.9–12, 22b. The sections now found in 2 Timothy once comprised Paul's no longer extant letter of farewell to Timothy. This letter is reconstructed in *Problem*, 126–7.

94 Knight, *Pastoral Epistles*, 46–47. Cf. E. Earle Ellis, "Pseudonymity and Canonicity of New Testament Documents," in Michael J. Wilkins and Terence Paige (eds.),

Worship, Theology and Ministry in the Early Church: Essays in Honour of Ralph P. Martin (JSNTSS 87; Sheffield: JSOT Press, 1992), 212–24.

95 David G. Meade, *Pseudonymity and Canon*, especially 118–39. See also James D. G. Dunn, "The Problem of Pseudonymity" in *The Living Word*, 65–85.

96 See Tertullian, *On Baptism*, 17. For discussion, see W. Speyer, *Die literarische Fälschung im Altertum* (München: C. H. Beck'sche Verlagsbuchhandlung, 1971), 210–2. While Paul appears in the third person in the *Acts of Paul*, *3 Corinthians* is written in Paul's name. The presbyter was removed from his office. For introduction and text see *NTA* 2.213–70.

97 *Les Épîtres Pastorales*, 1.176.

98 *Les Épîtres Pastorales*, 1.178.

99 *Les Épîtres Pastorales*, 1.179–80. See Knight, *Pastoral Epistles*, 22–23. Knight, citing Brox, contends that the argument which stresses the difference in the argumentative procedure between the authentic Paulines and the PE is ill-informed. Certainly the Paul of the undisputed letters often does argue his case against his opponents, answering their objections and setting forth his reasons for the positions he adopts. The author of the PE merely warns against the false teachers. But, adds Knight, there are many examples to the contrary. In the PE, Paul, it must be remembered, is writing in the first instance to individual associates, not to congregations. Nevertheless, even in the PE a theological case is reasoned by the author (e.g., 1 Tim. 4.1–5). Sometimes in the undisputed letters Paul does lay out precepts, appealing to what is already known and given (Phil. 3.17–18; Rom. 16.17) rather than arguing a coherent theological case. When addressing a third party, Knight argues, though not wholly persuasively, Paul's argumentative strategy in the undisputed letters corresponds to the PE.

100 *Les Épîtres Pastorales*, 1.193: "Mais l'explication la plus satisfaisante des particularités de style et de vocabulaire des Pastorales est celle du changement de *destinaire* et de *sujets* traités" (author's italics). Cf. Kelly, *Pastoral Epistles*, 19–20; Jeremias, *Pastoralbriefe*, 4.

101 *Les Épîtres Pastorales*, 1.199–200. One is reminded here of the similar "secretary hypothesis" by which differences between the PE and the Pauline corpus are sometimes explained. See Kelly, *Pastoral Epistles*, 25–27. Kelly points to evidence that other Pauline letters were written by secretaries (see Rom. 16.22 and, by implication, 1 Cor. 16.21 and Gal. 6.11). However, the PE give no explicit or implicit indication that a secretary was involved. Kelly also suggests that the presence of numerous hapaxes in the PE can be readily explained on the grounds that vocabulary increases with age (25). Furthermore, the "flatness" of style can be attributed to Paul's advancing years. Cf. Knight, *Pastoral Epistles*, 38–45. While the vocabulary of the PE demonstrate how versatile an author Paul was, Knight also entertains the possibility of Lukan influence, without positing Luke as the author

(see *Pastoral Epistles*, 48, cf. S. G. Wilson, *Luke and the Pastoral Epistles* [London: SPCK, 1979]). Taking much greater stock of the differences between the undisputed Paulines and the PE, Jeremias, *Pastoralbriefe*, 6, 8 is more convinced of the presence of the hand of a secretary (a Hellenistic Jew). However, he too sees evidence of Paul's usual style as well as signs of development. This is one of his arguments for the authenticity of the PE. Nevertheless, the defenders do not seem to realize that the vocabulary and style of the undisputed Pauline letters are homogeneous, whether Paul used secretaries or not. The PE, on the other hand, possess their own distinctive style. See Meade, *Pseudonymity and Canon*, 119–20.

102 *Les Épîtres Pastorales*, 1.243. Cf. Kelly, *Pastoral Epistles*, 16–17; Jeremias, *Pastoralbriefe*, 7; Knight, *Pastoral Epistles*, 32–35.

103 Cf. the analysis of the eschatology and theology of the PE in Towner, *The Goal of Our Instruction*, chs. 4 and 5. Towner assumes rightly that the theology of the PE should be interpreted in the light of the whole corpus, but seems to imply that this methodology is correct because Paul wrote all the letters of the ten-letter corpus, and may well have written the PE. For a more compelling analysis which takes into account real differences between the PE, the deutero-Paulines, and the undisputed letters without disputing the Pastor's claim to be actualizing Pauline tradition, see Trummer, *Die Paulustradition*, 161–240. Cf. Meade, *Pseudonymity and Canon*, 118–57; Zmijewski, "Die Pastoralbriefe als pseudepigraphische Schriften," 107–08.

104 *Les Épîtres Pastorales*, 1.249–52. Cf. Kelly, *Pastoral Epistles*, 19–20.

105 See, however, B. S. Easton, *The Pastoral Epistles* (New York: Scribners, 1947), 22, 234.

106 *Les Épîtres Pastorales*, 1.259.

107 *Les Épîtres Pastorales*, 1.261: "Les Pastorales envisagent le salut, moins comme un événement historique du passé ou un dogme à enseigner que comme un fait actuel qui s'accomplit incessamment dans l'Église . . . On ne peut dire que l'institution ecclésiastique a pris la place du Calvaire dans le salut des hommes, car le rôle personnel du Christ est toujours marqué . . . ." For discussion of the cross, and other Pauline distinctives, see Kelly, *Pastoral Epistles*, 18. That these are no longer central for the PE is to be explained on the ground that the occasion did not demand their explication.

108 *Les Épîtres Pastorales*, 1.262–4.

109 *Les Épîtres Pastorales*, 1.270–1.

110 *Les Épîtres Pastorales*, 1.274.

111 See Knight, *Pastoral Epistles*, 35–37 for his reply to the argument advanced by

Hanson, *The Pastoral Epistles*, 4–5 to the effect that the Pastor has a different attitude to doctrine than Paul. The use of παραθήκη does not imply a different attitude towards doctrine than that operating in the undisputed Paulines. Rather, Knight contends, he uses παραθήκη instead of the more usual word παράδοσις because of the negative connotations of the latter (see Gal. 1.14; Col. 2.8). There is every warrant in the undisputed Paulines, Knight argues, for the view that Paul was concerned to pass on the content of what he himself had received (see Rom. 16.17; 1 Cor. 11.2; 15.1–3). The issue of the shape of the "deposit" (παραθήκη) is an important issue in J. Christiaan Beker's analysis of the PE. See the discussion of Beker's *Heirs of Paul* in section D below.

112 *Les Épîtres Pastorales*, 1.278. The presence of the subjective sense of πίστις is also acknowledged by other defenders of the Pauline authorship of the PE. Kelly, *Pastoral Epistles*, 20 offers two instances of the use of πίστις in the Pauline corpus to denote the content of what is believed—Phil. 1.27; Col. 2.7. See also Jeremias, who instances Gal. 1.23 as an example in *Pastoralbriefe*, 4. Contenders for the pseudonymity of the PE also acknowledge the subjective use of πίστις in the genuine Paulines. See, e.g., J. Roloff, *Der erste Brief an Timotheus* (EKK 15; Zürich: Benziger Verlag, 1988), 31. He also instances Gal. 1.23 (νῦν εὐαγγελίζεται τὴν πίστιν ἥν ποτε ἐπόρθει) as well as 3.23 (πρὸ τοῦ δὲ ἐλθειν τὴν πίστιν); 3.25 (ἐλθούσης δὲ τῆς πίστεως); 6.10 (μάλιστα δὲ πρὸς τοὺς οἰκείους τῆς πίστεως); Phil. 2.17 (?) (σπένδομαι ἐπὶ τῇ θυσίᾳ καὶ λειτουργίᾳ τῆς πίστεως); Eph. 4.5 (εἶς Κύριος μία πίστις ἕν βάπτισμα); and Col. 2.7 (?) (βεβαιούμενοι τὴν πίστει καθὼς ἐδιδάχθητε). In the examples above from the undisputed Paulines, though Phil. 2.17 is not certain, πίστις signifies the content of what is believed. It might also be argued that in these passages the term is synonymous with the "gospel." See R. N. Longenecker, *Galatians* (Waco: Word Books, 1990), 42 for further discussion of Gal. 3.23, 25. However, it is undeniable that the preponderance of references to faith in the undisputed Paulines convey the objective meaning, while in the PE the preponderance of references convey the subjective meaning.

113 *Les Épîtres Pastorales*, 1.281. The PE, in common with the other Pauline letters, regard faith as a personal conviction characterized by sincerity. Essentially, faith for the PE means response to the apostolic message. Its exercise depends entirely on God, and it is inextricably linked to divine grace. Whereas Paul generally speaks of faith in Christ, the PE "envisagent surtout la foi en tant que professée et enseignée." It is nurtured by teaching (διδασκαλία, 1 Tim. 4.6).

114 *Les Épîtres Pastorales*, 1.296.

115 *Les Épîtres Pastorales*, 1.285.

116 *Les Épîtres Pastorales*, 1.293–7.

117 *Les Épîtres Pastorales*, 1.293–4.

118 *Les Épîtres Pastorales*, 1.294. Cf. C. F. D. Moule, *The Birth of the New Testament* (3rd edition; London: A. & C. Black, 1981), 68.

119 *Les Épîtres Pastorales*, 1.295. *Contra* Beker, *Paul the Apostle*, ch. 15.

120 For "evolution" in Paul's thinking, see C. H. Dodd, *New Testament Studies* (Manchester: Manchester University Press, 1953), 108–28. His argument is that Paul at the time of his conversion shared the "gloomy" apocalyptic outlook particularly exemplified in 4 Ezra with its depreciation of the natural world, its pessimistic expectation of the fate of the majority of people in the eschaton, and its unbending dualism. This framework is evident in 1 Thessalonians but is increasingly brought under the control of the gospel affirmation of natural human goodness, the relative value of human institutions, and the possibility of taking them up into the Christian life (118). The Epistle to the Ephesians, with its grand vision of the unity of Jew and Gentile in the Commonwealth of God, is the acme of Paul's later theological maturity (123–4). In sum, Paul "outgrew" the constraints of Jewish apocalyptic (126). He was baptized, as it were, into the world-view expressed in Ephesians, but as long as he still "made claims on life for power, satisfaction, and vindication (127)" that new understanding only came to the fore in the later epistles. Dodd argued that 2 Corinthians 10–13 testifies to a crisis in Paul's self-understanding as it was informed by Jewish apocalyptic. For another analysis, see C. Buck and G. Taylor, *Saint Paul: A Study of the Development of his Thought* (New York: Scribners, 1969). They argue that not only does the apostle's thinking undergo changes caused by suffering and further reflection, Paul revised the whole texture of his teaching in the light of the adjustments he made in the parts (see 16). See the response by Victor P. Furnish, "Development in Paul's Thought," *JAAR* 38 (1970), 289–303. Furnish contends that Paul's thought is not to be understood along the linear and developmental model argued by Buck and Greer, but rather along complex and dialectical lines (303). Note also Leander E. Keck, *Paul and his Letters* (Rev. ed.; Philadelphia: Fortress, 1988), 6–7.

121 On the assumption that 2 Timothy is Paul's testament, this particular genre gave the testator the opportunity to sum up the direction of his/her life and to express in terms of moral exhortation those matters which were held by the testator most dearly. See the discussion of the genre in ch. 2 section E.

122 See the discussion of the priority of Israel in Beker, *Paul the Apostle*, 335–7.

123 *Das Verständnis der Tradition bei Paulus und in den Deuteropaulinen* (Neukirchen: Neukirchener Verlag, 1962). The PE are discussed on 132–57 of the section on the deutero-Paulines. Treatments of Colossians (121–30) and Ephesians (130–2) account for the remainder of the chapter.

124 Particularly by Ranft, according to Wegenast. See Wegenast, *Das Verständnis*, 14–55. The chief elements of the early Jewish understanding of tradition, as outlined by Wegenast, are: (i) the exact words of the teacher must be transmitted, (ii) the present exponent must not only know word for word what is the tradition being

transmitted but also must know the name of the source, (iii) it must be possible to demonstrate, were such an investigation mounted, that the teaching goes back unerringly to a Mosaic source, and (iv) succession is conveyed by means of ordination (see 28–30).

125 See *Das Verständnis*, 11–23. These current theories are (i) the understanding of tradition in the NT, in Paul's letters especially, results from a break with the early Jewish concept of tradition, giving rise to the granting of equal authority to revelation and tradition, (ii) tradition for Paul and the early church is equivalent to the revelation to the apostle of Christ, and (iii) tradition amounts to the transmission of the content of the preaching of the Christian community in which Jesus is present by his spirit.

126 Wegenast, *Das Verständnis*, 44. Gal. 1.16 is, naturally, the fundamental passage in this discussion of the origin of Paul's gospel.

127 Wegenast, *Das Verständnis*, 40: "Mose und Christus sind für die Häretiker keine bloßen Urheber einer weiterzugebenden Tradition, sondern viel eher mythologische Figuren und Offenbarer einer Lehre." The opponents regard Paul's gospel as mere human teaching; the messenger (Paul) is neither called by a revelation nor is his message grounded in revelation (40).

128 Wegenast, *Das Verständnis*, 44: "Evangelium ist also nach der Meinung des Paulus aller Tradition voraus."

129 Wegenast, *Das Verständnis*, 51.

130 Wegenast, *Das Verständnis*, 65. See also 50: "Nach der Meinung des Paulus ist das Evangelium als offenbartes einer Tradition immer schon voraus und bleibt in jedem Fall Norm über aller Tradition."

131 Wegenast, *Das Verständnis*, 69: "Die Offenbarung ist dem Apostel unmittelbar von Gott als Offenbarung des Erhöhten als Herrn zugekommen." However, Gal. 2.2 shows that Paul knows that tradition can only confirm his "apocalypse." For this reason he values the confirmation of his message by the Jerusalem apostles, and esteems their fellowship, though he does not require their validation of his message. Without their confirmation, however, he would be "running to no effect (εἰς κενὸν τρέχω ἢ τρέχω)," the mission to preach the gospel to the Gentiles snared by disunity. On this verse, see also Longenecker, *Galatians*, 48–49.

132 *Das Verständnis*, 91.

133 *Das Verständnis*, 92.

134 *Das Verständnis*, 120.

135 *Das Verständnis*, 130.

136 According to Wegenast, *Das Verständnis*, 134.

137 The summary is drawn from Wegenast, *Das Verständnis*, 136–8.

138 Wegenast, *Das Verständnis*, 138. The basis of Wegenast's argument can be found in his excursus on 123–6. Here he shows that the παραδίδομαι terminology was current in the Gnostic writings emanating from the second/third centuries C.E. The Gnostics used the term παράδοσις to denote the teachings transmitted from the revelatory source (see 123–4; see also 124 n. 1 for citations from Gnostic literature). On 125 Wegenast argues that Gnosticism took its terminology in this respect from "late" Judaism.

139 *Das Verständnis*, 139.

140 Wegenast, *Das Verständnis*, 152. The extent and content of the παραθήκη is by no means agreed upon by scholars. See, e.g., J. Roloff, *Apostolat—Verkündigung—Kirche: Ursprung, Inhalt und Funktion des kirchlichen Apostelamtes nach Paulus, Lukas und den Pastoralbriefen* (Gütersloh: Gütersloher Verlagshaus G. Mohn, 1965), 249. As παραθήκη, the gospel is to be conceived as "unantastbares, unveränderliches Gut," the preacher having been given the task of guarding the gospel from violability after the manner of the original and first preacher, "Paul." Cf. N. Lohfink, "Paulinische Theologie in der Rezeption der Pastoralbriefe," in K. Kertelge (ed.), *Paulus in den neutestamentlichen Spätschriften: Zur Paulusrezeption im Neuen Testament* (Freiburg: Herder, 1981), 97. Brox, Jeremias, Wanke, Donelson, as well as Wegenast are proponents of the opposing view. Following Wegenast (*Das Verständnis*, 150–2), I would also prefer to enlarge the concept of the "deposit" to include more than "gospel," if by "gospel" one means only the proclamation of the saving events. The PE regard as "deposit" not just the message of saving acts (as understood above), but have extended the concept to cover both the ecclesiastical ordering and the content (i.e., the doctrines, paradigmatic portraits, the social teaching, the "sound words," and the virtue/vice lists) of the PE themselves. Cf. J. Wanke, "Der verkündigte Paulus der Pastoralbriefe," in W. Ernst *et al* (eds.), *Dienst der Vermittlung* (Leipzig: St. Benno-Verlag, 1977), 165–89 (171), and Donelson, *Pseudepigraphy*, 165, 167.

141 Wegenast, *Das Verständnis*, 157. Cf. von Lips, *Glaube*, 266–70.

142 Wegenast offers *1 Clem.* 42.7 and Pol. *Phil.* 6.3 as examples of this tendency.

143 For Hegesippus' statement of his drawing up a list of the succession of the bishops of Rome, see the fragments in *ANF* 8.764. For Eusebius' interest in the matter, see *Eccl. Hist.* 4.1; 5.6. In 5.6 he cites Irenaeus' list of the bishops of Rome to be found in *Against Heresies*, 3.3.3.

144 Wegenast, *Das Verständnis*, 162.

145 *Die Pastoralbriefe* (Regensburger Neues Testament, Vol. 7.2; Regensburg: Verlag F. Pustet, 1969, repr. 1989). His resume of the reasons against Pauline authorship are the familiar ones. None of the details of 2 Timothy can be fixed with certainty from what we know of Paul's life from the genuine letters and from Acts (16). Paul's work in the east already had concluded according to Rom. 15.19–20, 23. While the PE imply that Paul took this work up again, Brox considers *1 Clem.* 5.7 a witness to Paul's release and subsequent mission in *Spain*. Paul, like the churches of the PE, encountered teachers espousing gnosticizing ideas (32), though Marcion's work is probably not referred to in 1 Tim. 6.20. The Jewish-Gnostic character of the errorists (see 2 Tim. 2.18) suggests an early date from anywhere in Paul's own life-time to the end of the first century C.E. (38). Brox also notes differences between the polemic of the PE and the undisputed letters. The ecclesiastical officials of the PE are not to enter into dialogue with the errorists but to confront them with the speech of assertion (39, see 1 Tim. 6.20; 2 Tim. 2.24; Titus 3.9; 2 Tim. 2.14). How different this strategy is to that adopted by Paul as we know him in the genuine letters is noted by Brox (40; cf. Beker, *Paul the Apostle* and *Heirs of Paul*). On the question of the charismata, Brox argues that while Paul knew only charismatic order in the churches, the PE only know "das Anticharisma," which renders charismatically endowed prophets and teachers superfluous (44). Perhaps in the Gnostic conventicles under counter-attack by the PE the charismata yet lingered? Perhaps, too, the opponents of the PE claimed an authentic Pauline congregational order? Regardless of these speculations, the ecclesiastical organization of the PE with its hierarchical and juristic overtones speaks not only of a non-Pauline author but of a later generation than Paul (45). On the question of the vocabulary of the PE, Brox notes that there is considerable evidence of the use of words from the hellenistic religious culture, and a corresponding lack of whole series of Pauline terms. He aptly concludes: "In dieser Sprache schlägt sich eine andere theologische Denkart und eine veränderte kirchliche Situation nieder" (47). Note also Margaret Y. MacDonald's tracking of the growth of institutionalization in the Pauline churches of the second and third generation in her monograph *The Pauline Churches.*

146 *Pastoralbriefe*, 11.

147 *Pastoralbriefe*, 12.

148 See C. K. Barrett, *The Signs of an Apostle* (London: Epworth, 1970), 54–56. Note also the following articles: R. F. Collins, "The Image of Paul in the Pastorals," *LTP* 31 (1975), 147–73; H. -M. Schenke, "Das Weiterwirken des Paulus und die Pflege seines Erbes durch die Paulus-Schule," *NTS* 22 (1975), 505–18; S. G. Wilson, "The Portrait of Paul in Acts and the Pastorals," in G. MacRae (ed.), *SBL 1976 Seminar Papers* (Missoula, MT: Scholars, 1976), 397–411; M. C. de Boer, "Images of Paul in the Post-Apostolic Period," *CBQ* 42 (1980), 359–80; A. T. Hanson, "The Domestication of Paul: A Study in the Development of Early Christian Theology," *BJRL* 63 (1981), 402–18.

149 Brox, *Pastoralbriefe*, 12. Why, furthermore, does "Paul" venture to describe the "heretics" on Crete when Titus is on the spot (see 48)? The same could be said for the situation in Ephesus where Timothy is in charge.

150 Baur, *Pastoralbriefe*, 3 cites Schleiermacher's observation with approval.

151 Brox, *Pastoralbriefe*, 73. Cf. Barrett, *Signs*, 54.

152 Barrett, *Signs*, 54. *Contra* Brox, *Pastoralbriefe*, 74. Barrett (*Signs*, 55) also underscores the fact that the Paul of the PE is the guarantor of the tradition in a subsidiary sense only. God and the Holy Spirit are the ultimate defenders of the Pauline heritage (see 2 Tim. 1.12, 14).

153 Meade, *Pseudonymity and Canon*, 116. Paul uses τέκνον to refer to Onesimus (Phlm. 10) and Timothy (1 Cor. 4.17) and τέκνα for congregations (1 Cor. 4.14; 2 Cor. 6.13; Gal. 4.19). Cf. 1 Tim. 1.2, 18; 2 Tim. 1.2; 2.1; Tit. 1.4. Note also 2 John 1; 3 John 4; *Did.* 3.1, 3–6.

154 *Pastoralbriefe*, 49.

155 *Pastoralbriefe*, 50.

156 *Pastoralbriefe*, 51. Cf. Roloff, *Der erste Brief an Timotheus* (EKK 15; Zürich: Benziger Verlag, 1988), 384. Roloff contrasts the atmosphere of the PE with that of the Apocalypse. He suggests that the PE polemicize the kind of worldview espoused by the author of the Apocalypse. Tit. 2.11 speaks of the salvation of all. Cf. the phrase ὑπὲρ πόλλων in Mark 10.45 and 14.24 (cf. 2 Cor. 5.19). The church of the PE looks outward to the world. The author has much in common with Luke-Acts and 1 Peter. In these writings Roman institutions are valued. The church has nothing to fear from Roman officials. For its part, the church of the PE is the guardian of conventional cultural values. The author (though he is aware of the potential for persecution) seems to be confident that the state actually perceives the church as a vehicle committed to and modelling the preservation of the practical norms of everyday, household, and communal life long-sanctioned by practice and upheld by philosophical theory. Cf. MacDonald, *Pauline Churches*, 160–202.

157 Brox cites Schelkle on 53: "Der Verfasser verfügt nicht über den Geist des Paulus. Wer wird ihn deswegen rügen? Aber die Pastoralbriefe sind Schriften eines Mannes, der sich um das Verständnis des Paulus bemühte, der aus der Botschaft des Paulus Kraft für eines, späteres Geschlecht zu gewinnen suchte und gewann."

158 *Pastoralbriefe*, 63.

159 *Pastoralbriefe*, 68. Brox seems to agree with conclusions of Barnett, *Paul Becomes a Literary Influence*, 251–77 that the Pastor had access to ten letters of Paul (see Brox, *Pastoralbriefe*, 67 citing Schlatter, *inter alia*, in support).

160 *Pastoralbriefe*, 77.

161 *Pastoralbriefe*, 77.

162 *Der erste Brief an Timotheus*, 23–29.

163 See Roloff, *Der erste Brief an Timotheus*, 31–32. For the author, faith (πίστις) comes to denote *the* Christian faith, the content of what is believed, and also the quality of the believers' steadfastness, and not the means by which the believer appropriates the saving work of God in Christ. Important Pauline theological distinctives like "body" and "cross" do not appear in the PE. The letters are interested in the deposit: the faithful and sound formulations to be passed on from generation to generation of ordained ecclesiastical officials. Roloff also notes that the Pastor avoids the term παράδοσις, Paul's own term (see 1 Cor. 11.2; Gal. 1.14; cf. Col. 2.8). The παραθήκη of the PE is something that is already determined and laid down to be passed on unchangeably into the future. The Pastor scarcely mentions the Spirit, though at Titus 3.5 Pauline overtones are present. But this, argues Roloff, is a tradition-laden passage ("traditionsbestimmte Stelle") (32). The Spirit is not, as in Paul, an end-time gift given to all believers without discrimination. Rather, in the PE the Spirit operates as a gift of grace (*Gnadengabe*) which is received by the ecclesiastical officials at their ordination (32; 1 Tim. 4.14; 2 Tim. 1.6). The *personalia* (2 Tim. 4.9–21; Tit. 3.12–15) do not fit what we know of Paul's life, but they present Paul in a good light (32) and commend the image of Paul to the congregation. On the question of pseudonymity in general, Roloff (like Brox) stresses the fruitful parallels with the Pythagorean and Platonic pseudepigrapha, not just because they show that pseudepigraphy was a widespread phenomenon but because the personal notices of the PE bear some resemblance to the philosophical pseudepigrapha in function and content. By the writing of pseudepigrapha a philosophical school sought to confirm its origins and demonstrate continuity with the founding master. On this analogy, the author of the PE would belong to a Pauline school (cf. Holtzmann, *Pastoralbriefe*, 117). In terms of inspiration and sources the PE are heavily indebted to the Paul of the undisputed letters (39–40). Nevertheless, Roloff notes that the PE's dependence on liturgical traditions is also significant. It is these that bear the least specific marks of the Pauline tradition, testifying to their origin in the ecclesiastical theater (41). The date ascribed to the PE must take into account their hellenistic vocabulary—vocabulary which witnesses to their hellenistic ecclesiastical setting in the third Christian generation. Popular philosophy is the likely origin of the ethics of the PE, transmitted through the hellenistic synagogue and from thence into the PE (cf. 4 Maccabees).

164 *Der erste Brief an Timotheus*, 43–45. Roloff sees evidence of literary dependence on the Pauline corpus in the PE (39–40). See also n. 167 below.

165 Roloff, *Der erste Brief an Timotheus*, 42.

166 Roloff, *Apostolat*, 249. Cf. 252–3. See also 264 where Roloff states that his thesis is to show that the PE understands Paul and his "school" as "Typen und Urbilder rechter Episkopen."

167 Roloff, *Der erste Brief an Timotheus*, 377: "Die Briefe des Apostels gelten ihm als die geschichtliche Gestalt des Evangeliums, die bleibend verbindlich ist . . ."

168 Roloff, *Der erste Brief an Timotheus*, 377: "Er [the author] praktiziert keineswegs ein starres, mechanisch zu handhabendes Traditionsprinzip der bloßen Wiederholung vorgegebener Lehrsätze, sondern eine aneignende, auf neue Situationen hin anwendende Interpretation des Überkommenen."

169 Cf. Roloff, *Der erste Brief an Timotheus*, 378: "Das Wort des Apostels wird zum Gegenstand kirchlicher Verkündigung. Sein ursprünglich auf bestimmte geschichtliche Situationen hin ausgerichtetes Zeugnis wird so transformiert, daß es auch der in anderen Situationen lebenden Kirche der dritten Generation Orientierung und Weisung zu geben vermag."

170 Cf. Trummer, *Die Paulustradition der Pastoralbriefe*, 127. See also von Lips, *Glaube*, 141–4. Von Lips argues that in the PE authority in the church is analogous to the structures that exist within the household, whereas in Paul (Rom. 12.7ff.; 1 Cor. 12.8ff; 1 Cor. 14.26ff.) authority in the congregation depends on the use made of the charismata among the members.

171 Cf. Roloff, *Apostolat*, 241. See also Wanke, "Der verkündigte Paulus," 174ff.; Lohfink, "Paulinische Theologie," 79.

172 *Cf.* Roloff, *Der erste Brief an Timotheus*, 381: "Er [the author] will unter Rückgriff auf Paulus Direktiven für die Bewältigung einer kritischen Situation seiner Kirche, nämlich deren Bedrohung durch die gnostische Irrlehre, entwickeln."

173 *Der erste Brief an Timotheus*, 382.

174 Roloff, *Der erste Brief an Timotheus*, 382.

175 Roloff, *Der erste Brief an Timotheus*, 388. For "early catholicism" in general and in the PE, see H. Küng, "'Early Catholicism' in the New Testament as a Problem in Controversial Theology," in *The Living Church* (London: Sheed & Ward, 1963), 233–93; J. H. Elliott, "A Catholic Gospel: Reflections on 'Early Catholicism' in the New Testament," *CBQ* 31 (1969), 213–23; R. E. Brown, "The Unity and Diversity in New Testament Ecclesiology," *NovT* 6 (1963), 298–308; *The Churches the Apostles Left Behind* (New York/Ramsey: Paulist, 1984), ch. 2.

176 Cf. Beker, *Heirs of Paul*, 83–86. On 122 Beker has the following negative assessment of the success of what he terms the "pseudo-adaptations" of Paul's gospel in the deutero-Paulines: "All . . . have a common denominator, namely, their propensity to misrepresent or disregard the basic claims of Paul's original gospel."

They compel us, he continues, "to reflect on what constitutes an authentic adaptation of Paul's gospel."

177 *Die Paulustradition der Pastoralbriefe*, 17. They were, of course, not accepted precisely in this fashion in the early church, though Trummer notes that their first attestation is rather late in Athenagoras (32—alluding to 1 Tim. 2.2), and that heretical circles found some if not all three of the PE unacceptable.

178 See Tertullian, *On Baptism*, 17. Knight, *Pastoral Epistles*, 46–47 is particularly sensitive to the issue of the early church's suspicion of pseudonymous literature. However, the early church was not as dismissive as Knight and other scholars suppose. For discussion of the Muratorian Canon's acknowledgment of the pseudonymity of the *Wisdom of Solomon*, see Mark Kiley, *Colossians as Pseudepigraphy* (Sheffield: JSOT Press, 1986), 17–23. Kiley rightly observes that in the Greco-Roman era considerable respect was accorded the production of pseudepigrapha "when it was a type of exercise whose birthplace was in the schools" (18). Kiley contends that the Muratorian Canon implies that Wisdom was regarded as a "school" product. Wisdom was not universally received as scripture. See Origen, *On First Principles*, 4.1.33 (text in *ANF* 4.379); Eusebius, *Eccl. Hist.* 6.13.6.

179 *Paulustradition*, 68: "Dieselbe Funktion wie Jesus für die Evangelisten nimmt für P[aul] das Evangelium ein."

180 *Die Paulustradition*, 71–72. See further Trummer's "Corpus Paulinum—Corpus Pastorale: Zur Ortung der Paulustradition in den Pastoralbriefen," in Kertelge (ed.), *Paulus in den neutestamentlichen Spätschriften*, 122–45, in which he argues that the author wrote the PE as a corpus on the analogy of the *corpus Paulinum*.

181 *Die Paulustradition*, 88–89 (cf. 110). Trummer regards the theology of the PE as much indebted to that of (deutero-Pauline) Ephesians. See *Die Paulustradition*, 121. This observation is particularly apt with respect to the universalizing of the salvific purposes of God, the ecclesiastical focus, the use of *Haustafeln*, and the corresponding decline of the expectation of the imminence of the parousia common to both the PE and Ephesians. However, Ephesians' teaching about the "cosmic Christ," and preparedness to speak of the resurrection of believers as a present reality (see 2.6) are foreign to the PE. For this reason it is possible that the false teachers of the PE also espouse Pauline traditions. See also von Lips, *Glaube*, 155–6.

182 *Die Paulustradition*, 100: "an alle Kirchen auch für weitere Zeiträume gesagt." Thus the Pauline heritage is frozen for all time. Cf. Beker, *Heirs*, 41.

183 *Paulustradition*, 102.

184 *Paulustradition*, 86.

185 For further discussion, see Zmijewski, "Die Pastoralbriefe als pseudepigraphische Schriften," 111; Meade, *Pseudonymity and Canon*, 123–6.

186 Trummer highlights the following points of theological contrast. On the issue of justification by faith, he allows that the teaching of the PE (see 2 Tim. 1.9; Tit. 3.5ff.) is dependent on Paul (cf. Gal. 2.16; 3.11, 24). The fact that the PE are no longer wrestling with the issues of "faith" versus "works of the law"—issues so prominent in Romans and Galatians—means that the teaching of the PE reflects the changed historical and social situation of the churches (*Paulustradition*, 180–1). The Christology of the PE is contrasted with that of Paul and his strong focus on the cross. Trummer describes the PE as having a "title" Christology (note, e.g., the use of σωτήρ and μεσίτης [193ff.]). He considers that the Christology of the PE evidences a catholicizing tendency, its origins deriving from many sources in the early church such as the synoptics and the Fourth Gospel. The PE's stress on the epiphany of Christ, however, is a strong indication of the still prominent parousia expectation operating in post-Pauline circles, despite the un-Pauline terminology. Epiphany Christology must be understood over against the claims of the emperor cult, urges Trummer (200–01). The concept of suffering with Christ (see 2 Tim. 2.11–12) expresses the author's perception that the formulation encountered here not only serves as an authentic and proper summation of the Pauline gospel, but "auch dem nach pln Amtsträger den schweren Dienst für das Evangelium ermöglichen soll" (207).

187 *Paulustradition*, 172: " . . . die Antwort der Past auf das Phänomen der Häresie liegt in der Verlängerung der pln Funktion im Amt, das seinerseits der Irrlehre Widerstand entgegensetzen soll." Note also Margaret Y. MacDonald's thesis that the authors of the Pauline pseudepigrapha are engaged in maintaining the Pauline "symbolic universe" as they seek to stabilize (evidenced in Ephesians and Colossians) and protect (evidenced in the PE) the Pauline churches in the face of challenges to the Pauline heritage (see *Pauline Churches*, 127, 157–8, 204–05).

188 Assuming that ἐντολή in 1 Tim. 6.14 is synonymous with παραθήκη and the adjectives ἄσπιλος and ἀνεπίλημπτος qualify ἐντολή (see, e.g., Dibelius and Conzelmann, *Pastoral Epistles*, 89), then the statement also refers to the "spotless" and "undamaged" condition of the deposit in the hands of successive generations of trusted leaders. This view is shared by Kelly, *Pastoral Epistles*, 144–5. However, the meaning of 1 Tim. 6.14 is by no means settled. Roloff, e.g., argues that ἐντολή refers to ecclesiastical office bestowed by ordination; and the adjectives denote not the integrity of the deposit, but the personal integrity of the church leader (*Der erste Brief an Timotheus*, 352). That is why no criticism or modification of the deposit is envisaged. To my mind, no different social or ecclesiastical circumstances seem to be envisaged by the author of the PE which would warrant modification of the deposit. It is meant to function as a tradition frozen in time but passed on from generation to generation by trustworthy men (*sic*). Any modification of it is a betrayal of the Pauline heritage as it presently stands. Therefore, I find myself more in agreement with Wegenast who argues that it is the inviolability of the deposit which is at stake in 1 Tim. 6.14 (see *Das Verständnis*, 162). His interpretation

makes the better sense of the strong wording and considerable urgency to be encountered in the passage.

189 *Paulustradition*, 221–2. Trummer is critical of Wegenast's understanding of just what safeguarding the "deposit" entails. Wegenast contends (see previous note) that the task of "guarding" the παραθήκη permitted no modification of it. The Pastor regarded the tradition as "letzte und offenbarte Instanz" (*Das Verständnis*, 157). Any modification of it would amount to a betrayal of the Pauline heritage, and a transgression against the juridical nature of the παραθήκη.

190 *Paulustradition*, 129: "Die Paränese hat angesichts eines in den Tod gehenden P besonderes Gewicht und verpflichtenden Charakter und fordet dazu auf, diesen Amtsauftrag auch in der Situation nach dem Tod des P weiterzuführen." Cf. von Lips, *Glaube*, 144. The fulfilling of the roles society expects has salvific implications, as in 1 Tim. 2.15. The contrast with Paul is exceedingly marked at this point. Von Lips comments on Pauline ecclesiology: "Im Verband der Gemeinde gibt es . . . nicht mehr den Menschen, dessen Funktion von seiner natürlichen Stellung im sozialen Gefüge bestimmt ist . . . , sondern nur noch den Erlösten als Glied am Leib Christi. Jenseits von allen ethnischen und sozialen Strukturen ist eine neue Einheit geschaffen die ihre eigenen Lebensäusserungen und Wachstumsgesetze hat" (144). Moreover: "Die soziale Stellung des einzelnen ist durch das Heilsgeschehen neutralisiert, hat keine Heilsfunktion" (144).

191 *Paulustradition*, 150. Trummer is commenting here on 1 Tim. 2.15. Cf. 230 where εὐσέβεια is not merely a simple replacement of πίστις, but has to do with respecting "Ordnungen und Pflichten" (230). The ethics of the PE impresses Trummer as much more future-oriented than Ephesians or Colossians.

192 *Paulustradition*, 227–9.

193 *Die Pastoralbriefe als Paulustradition* (FRLANT 146; Göttingen: Vandenhoeck and Ruprecht, 1988), 11–25.

194 *Die Pastoralbriefe als Paulustradition*, 11.

195 *Die Pastoralbriefe als Paulustradition*, 13.

196 Wolter, 13 n. 13 cites as support for this view E. Dassmann, *Der Stachel im Fleisch: Paulus in der frühchristlichen Literatur bis Irenäus* (Münster: Aschendorff, 1979), 166, and Collins, "The Image of Paul," 147.

197 *Die Pastoralbriefe als Paulustradition*, 13.

198 *Die Pastoralbriefe als Paulustradition*, 15. Cf. MacDonald, *Pauline Churches*, Part 3 ("The Pastoral Epistles: Community-Protecting-Institutionalization" [160–234]).

199 *Die Pastoralbriefe als Paulustradition*, 22.

200 *Die Pastoralbriefe als Paulustradition*, 64. Wolter takes issue with Trummer, *Die Paulustradition*, 119, who argues that the account of Paul's conversion narrated in this passage (i.e., 1 Tim. 1.12–17) intersects with a paraenetic interest for the successors of Paul. They are to take heart that just as Paul was empowered by God in his fallen state, so God, and here Phil. 4.13 exercises a considerable literary influence, might empower the leaders in the church to fulfil their ministry. By contrast, Wolter is arguing that in 1 Tim. 1.12–17 the Pauline office is to be distinguished from all others in the church in terms of the apostle's determinative function in the saving purposes of God for his church.

201 *Die Pastoralbriefe als Paulustradition*, 81.

202 *Die Pastoralbriefe als Paulustradition*, 92.

203 *Die Pastoralbriefe als Paulustradition*, 99–102. He specifically appeals to Aristotle, *Rhetoric*, 1368a11, Isocrates, *Evagorus*, 78, and Quintilian, *Institutes*, 3.7.16.

204 *Die Pastoralbriefe als Paulustradition*, 113. See, e.g., Josephus on the antiquity of Moses as the lawgiver of the Jews in *Against Apion*, 2.154, and the stress on Jesus' pre-existence in Justin, *Dialogue with Trypho*, 48, 75 (for text see *ANF* 1.219, 236).

205 *Die Pastoralbriefe als Paulustradition*, 115: "Der Begriff παραθήκη verleiht der in den Pastoralbriefen auf Paulus zurückgeführten Tradition zunächst ganz allgemein die Konnotation der Normativität, insofern die Unversehrtheit des zu bewahrenden Depositums das konstitutive Element schlechthin des antiken Depositalrechts ist."

206 See the discussion of Roloff and Wegenast *inter alia* at n. 140 above.

207 *Die Pastoralbriefe als Paulustradition*, 241.

208 *Die Pastoralbriefe als Paulustradition*, 122. On 122–3 Wolter cites (*Pseudo-Clementine*) *Contestatio* 4 (*NTA* 2.494–6) as a parallel to 2 Tim. 1.12, 14. Continuity and identity with Petrine tradition is preserved by entrusting the deposit comprising the books of the preaching of Peter to his successors.

209 *Die Pastoralbriefe als Paulustradition*, 139. Wolter also cites 2 Peter as an example of a pseudonymous letter with paraenetic overtones.

210 *Die Pastoralbriefe als Paulustradition*, 157–61.

211 *Die Pastoralbriefe als Paulustradition*, 202–41.

212 *Die Pastoralbriefe als Paulustradition*, 261–2. Wolter cites renunciation of meat and wine (Rom. 14.2, 21), sexual abstinence and separation of marriage partners (1 Cor. 7). Sexual abstinence is also valued in Rev. 14.4. The reference to ascetic diet (cf. Col. 2.16, 21) is pejorative.

213 *Die Pastoralbriefe als Paulustradition*, 264. Cf. the thesis of Dennis R. MacDonald in his *The Legend and the Apostle* (see, especially, ch. 3) that the PE were written to counteract the socially subversive image of Paul disseminated by women "story-tellers."

214 *Die Pastoralbriefe als Paulustradition*, 269.

215 *Paul the Apostle*, 19.

216 Beker draws on the insights of P. Vielhauer and K. Koch (see *Paul the Apostle*, 135–6). Beker prefers Koch's understanding of the essence of apocalyptic thought, explaining cryptically that he does so "because it is more precise and more critical" (136). Beker rightly characterizes apocalyptic thought as the expression of a "deep existential concern," and that it is "in many respects a theology of martyrdom" (136). The apocalypticist, he continues, "has a profound awareness of the discrepancy between what is and what should be, and of the tragic tension between faithfulness to the Torah and its apparent futility" (136). Fundamental to Beker's understanding of Paul's interpretation of the Christ-event is the apocalyptic framework of early Judaism. In his *The Triumph of God: The Essence of Paul's Thought* (Minneapolis: Augsburg Fortress, 1990), xii, Beker also acknowledges his debt to Wrede in arriving at this conclusion that the Jewish apocalyptic framework provided the matrix in which Paul interpreted the Christ-event. Wrede insists that fundamental to apocalyptic is its future orientation which gives Paul's thinking its driving thrust. Present life is not the arena in which salvation becomes is realized. "All references to the redemption as a completed transaction," Wrede argued in *Paul* (London: Philip Green, 1907), 105–06, "swing around at once into utterances about the future." Note, however, the reverse in the interplay of Rom. 8.17, 30 (for discussion, see Kiley, *Colossians as Pseudepigraphy*, 68).

217 *Paul the Apostle*, 15.

218 Beker argues that there is a radical modification of apocalyptic in Paul. The Christ-event bears testimony to the incursion of the future into history and into the present. He contends for a point of view which stresses not the fulfillment of divine promises for the world and God's intention for his people—that would imply, of course, that all had been accomplished, and that palpably is not the case—but, rather, the gospel as the locus of the answer to the question of the God's faithfulness to his promises. These, Beker insists, are not fulfilled in Christ; rather, they are confirmed. The same issue occupies Beker in the excursus on Jewish-Christian dialogue in ch. 15 (337–42). There is still a triumph of God to be expected—and a future for Israel (presently partially hardened; see Rom. 11.25–27).

219 The problem of the definition of "coherence" is raised in Beker's article "Paul the Theologian: Major Motifs in Pauline Theology," *Int* 43 (1989), 352–65, reprinted in *The Triumph of God: The Essence of Paul's Thought* (Minneapolis: Augsburg Fortress, 1990), 117–35. He acknowledges the ambiguity of his use of the term.

See also the review of *Paul the Apostle* by J. Louis Martyn in *Word and World* 2 (1982), 194, 196–8.

220 *Paul the Apostle*, 16. On the same page, Beker observes that "the primordial experience of the Christ-event then nourishes, intensifies, and modifies Paul's traditional apocalyptic language."

221 *Paul the Apostle*, 16. Cf. 17 where Beker explains that the surface structure of Paul's theological language "operates as an interpretive field that mediates between the coherent center and its relevance to contingent situations." By this he means, he adds, "the authentic truth of the coherent center aims at relevance according to the demands of the dialogical situation."

222 *Paul the Apostle*, 27. See also N. A. Dahl's essay, "The Particularity of the Pauline Epistles as a Problem in the Ancient Church," in *Neotestamentica et Patristica* (Novum Testamentum Supplements; Leiden: Brill, 1962), 261–71. Dahl's point is that the early church could only justify the presence in the canon of the Pauline letters in all their evident particularity by treating them as if they were actually addressed to the wider general concerns of the Catholic church. Thus, from at least the time of the Muratorian Canon, it was stressed that Paul intentionally wrote to seven churches to indicate that he was in fact writing in general terms to the whole church.

223 This exercise is exemplified by Marcion's reading of Paul which focused on the distinctive "center and unity of Paul's thought" (30). Marcion, Beker argues, imposed a unity of thought—a body of selective concepts—on Paul, failing to note just how Paul brings the coherence of the gospel to bear in contingent circumstances (31). Rather, Beker proposes, the interpreter must, on the one hand, resist the temptation to see the letters as casual "fly-sheets" that have no normativity, and on the other to resist the attempt to "equate the coherent core of Paul's gospel with a systematic set of propositions or a doctrinal set of categories . . . " (31). In the place of Paul's own flexible and creative interpretation of the παράδοσις the danger is to establish a παραθήκη—a *depositum fidei*—as we see happening in the PE (32). In Paul the specific occasion or the contextual situation is not "suffocated by imposition from without" but becomes illuminated in the light of the gospel (32). Marcion's attempt to appreciate the distinctiveness of Pauline thought is to be lauded, but his attempt had the effect of imposing doctrinal unity on Paul based on an *a priori* assessment of what is essential and peripheral in Paul.

224 *Paul the Apostle*, 33.

225 *Paul the Apostle*, 35: [The] "manner in which the one gospel of 'Christ crucified and risen' achieves incarnational depth and relevance in every particularity and variety of human condition."

226 *Paul the Apostle*, 57. However, see the discussion of Paul's view of the law in

Galatians and Romans in Räisänen, *Paul and the Law*. Räisänen demonstrates that in general Paul's statements about the law are just as radicalized and inconsistent in both letters. Unlike Beker, Räisänen does not speculate about the contingencies that may have been operating in the respective communities Paul was addressing, which, as far as Beker is concerned, produced the differences in emphasis (highlighted above) between the two letters. Räisänen is aware of certain differences between the letters on the question of the role of the law, but these are of minor significance in the context of his overall thesis. See, e.g., *Paul and the Law*, 150–3. Thus in Rom. 7.10 the law could have had a positive intention, namely, to lead its "doers" to life, but it was just "too weak" to deliver this benefit. In Gal. 3.21–22 the possibility of the law providing this benefit is excluded by the syntax—"no life-giving law has in fact been given" (151). In 2 Cor. 3.6 the law "kills."

227 *Paul the Apostle*, 74.

228 *Paul the Apostle*, 177.

229 In *Paul the Apostle*, 157–8 Beker argues that this was the effect of the "intrusion of Hellenistic categories" into post-apostolic speculation. Beker (158) also alerts the reader to the use of παρουσία to refer to the nativity of Jesus in Ignatius and Justin. Cf. the teaching of Hymenaeus and Philetus alluded to in 2 Tim. 2.17–18 who insisted that the resurrection is already past.

230 This would appear to be the import of the message of Ephesians in which the believers' hope resides in the future life of the church, a life which has a robust content, and which arises out of a "growing up into Christ" (see, e.g., 4.13–16). This relocation of the hope is to be contrasted with the sparse and inconsequential references to the "coming age" in 1.21 and "the day of redemption" in 4.30.

231 *Paul the Apostle*, 171.

232 *Paul the Apostle*, 172. See also Beker's discussion of the centrality of ch. 15 in 1 Corinthians in *Paul the Apostle*, 173–6 and in his *The New Testament: A Thematic Introduction* (Minneapolis: Fortress, 1994), 11–19.

233 *Paul the Apostle*, 356.

234 Cf. the resurrection language denoting the present experience of believers in Col. 2.12; 3.1–4; Eph. 2.6. Note also the use of σεσωσμένοι of Eph. 2.8. See also C. Leslie Mitton, *Ephesians* (Grand Rapids: Eerdmans, 1973), 88–91 and MacDonald, *Pauline Churches*, 143. MacDonald insightfully observes: "Although one must remain cautious about building too strong a case on few verses, it remains notable that Col. 3.1–3; Eph. 2.6 come close to suggesting the kind of realized eschatology that Paul seems to struggle against in 1 Cor. 4.8 and throughout 1 Cor. 15." Moreover, I might add, with respect to other literature of the post-Pauline era, Luke-Acts transmutes the apocalyptic concept of the theocentric end-time triumph of God

into a non-apocalyptic and Christocentric salvation-historical schema, while the Fourth Gospel, in its insistence that the believer already possesses eternal life, gives expression to a realizing eschatology out of keeping with Paul's apocalyptic hope.

235 These are "Paul's Theology: Consistent of Inconsistent?," *NTS* 34 (1988), 364–77, and "Paul the Theologian: Major Motifs in Pauline Theology," *Int* 43 (1989), 352–65 (also printed as an Appendix in *The Triumph of God*, 117–35).

236 See, e.g., A. T. Hanson, "Review of *Paul the Apostle*," *JSOT* 14 (1982), 124; M. E. Thrall, *JThS* 33 (1982), 269. See also V. Branick, "Apocalyptic Paul?," *CBQ* 47 (1985), 664–75.

237 *Heirs of Paul*, 10–11.

238 *Heirs of Paul*, 15.

239 *Heirs of Paul*, 16.

240 *Heirs of Paul*, 20.

241 *Heirs of Paul*, 36.

242 *Heirs of Paul*, 73.

243 *Heirs of Paul*, 94–97.

244 *Heirs of Paul*, 95.

245 See the criticisms of Beker's defence of Paul's hermeneutical strategy in 1 Corinthians 15 in Robin Scroggs' review of *Paul the Apostle* ("'Apocalyptic' as the Center of Paul's Gospel") in *Int* 36 (1982), 76–77.

246 See, e.g., C. Roetzel's review of *Paul the Apostle* in *JAAR* 50 (1982), 117–9.

247 Käsemann, "Paul and Early Catholicism," 239–40, 241–2. Cf. Dahl, "Particularity," 261–71.

248 See Käsemann, "Paul and Early Catholicism," 249. Cf. Maurice F. Wiles, *The Divine Apostle: The Interpretation of St. Paul's Epistles in the Early Church* (Cambridge: University Press, 1967), 139.

249 See the Preface to the 1984 edition, xx.

250 See 2 Cor. 11.6 where Paul writes that he is ἰδιώτης τῷ λόγῳ—an amateur as far as speaking well is concerned. See further Wiles, *The Divine Apostle*, 16–17. Wiles argues that early commentators of Paul, such as Origen, Chrysostom, and Theodore

of Mopsuestia, take this protestation of Paul as helping to explain grammatical and syntactical inaccuracies, a sure sign of one's lack of rhetorical education.

CHAPTER TWO

The PE and the Rhetoric of Letters

This chapter builds on the conclusion that the majority of the approaches discussed in the previous chapter amount to an enterprise dominated by the need to address the theological issues arising from the perception that the PE are documents standing self-consciously in the Pauline tradition. As we have seen, much of the more recent study of the PE has demonstrated the Pastor's indebtedness to Pauline tradition, and has rightly cast him as a translator and communicator of the Pauline heritage to his audience. However, this enterprise has also propagated a limited appreciation of the Pastor's achievement as a theologian. While engaged in the task of actualizing and contemporizing the Pauline message he has, perhaps, failed to grasp the true essence of the apostle's ideas. The Pastor is rarely perceived as a persuasive communicator of the Pauline heritage with respect to his addressees.

This chapter will survey the different kinds of rhetorical strategies that were commended in letter writing theory and used by the letter writers of the classical and Greco-Roman eras. The focus here will be the epistolary tradition of moral exhortation derived in the most part from the conventions of classical oratory. More specifically, the PE will be examined with respect to their content and intent as letters of moral exhortation. As such they participate in a wide trajectory of hortatory literature embodied in other Greco-Roman letters, including the Pauline corpus.

Since the PE are self-evidently letters, and intentionally presented as letters written by the apostle, I will seek to underscore the extent to which the PE are redolent of the Pauline letter-writing tradition, and, further, to nominate what kind of letters in the Greco-Roman epistolary tradition of moral exhortation furnish the best analogies to the PE.

A. GRECO-ROMAN LETTERS

Letter Theory

As letters, the PE participate in a vast corpus of Greco-Roman letters. Kings, philosophers, clergy and cult functionaries, government officials, and common people wrote letters in varying degrees of literateness and facility.

What precisely is a letter? Artemon, the collector and publisher of Aristotle's letter deposit, is reported to have defined the letter as "half a conversation."[1] The question of definition is a significant one for the study of the PE, let alone the study of the Greco-Roman epistolary deposit of which the NT letters are a part. Adolf Deissmann's study of the papyrus letters that were being uncovered in his day in Egypt led him to posit what has been an influential and simple distinction between "real" letters and "non-real" epistles. The former, intended for immediate and private consumption, were exemplified by the often semi-literate papyri, as well as by the voluminous correspondence of Cicero and Seneca. A letter, Deissmann argued, echoing Artemon, is no different from a private conversation. A letter, writes Deissmann, is a

> confidential personal conversation between persons separated by distance.[2]

An epistle, on the other hand, is written conscious of literary style and public readership.[3] While letters are fully contingent, written for a specific occasion, epistles, Deissmann contended, are written for posterity.[4] The writer of epistles, therefore, looked beyond the implied epistolary context to the wider public. Deissmann classed the PE, as well as the Catholic Epistles of the NT, in the epistle category.[5]

Deissmann proceeded to class the genuine correspondence of Paul as "letters," as "real" as those of Aristotle and Cicero. Paul's letters are, in his estimation, informal and private. They are characterized by his intention to address the multi-faceted and immediate concerns of the churches in his care. Paul had no intention of contributing to the already rich "sacred literature of his nation."[6] He was not writing dogma. He was not self-consciously addressing the theological needs of future generations of believers. Rather, Paul was motivated by religious zeal to speak to the needs of the moment.[7]

Deissmann's arguments have recently been criticized by Stanley K. Stowers, William G. Doty, Klaus Thraede, and other scholars.[8] They have endeavored to show that Deissmann over-estimated the informal nature of Paul's correspondence, and drew unwarranted comparisons between the Pauline letters and the semi-literary, confidential papyrus letters.[9] Moreover, Stowers argues, Deissmann posed an unreal distinction between public and private correspondence, and was unduly influenced by his own "romantic" temperament which led him to differentiate supposedly spontaneous, artless private "letters" from formal and conventional "epistles."[10]

Furthermore, Doty proposes that Deissmann's distinction between letters and epistles is an unhelpful one because it was based on the grounds that Paul's intimate and informal letters were not susceptible to readings that imposed a dogmatic framework or theological system on them.[11] Instead, Doty argues, it would be preferable to adopt the broadest possible framework for interpreting letters. He defines the letter as

> a literary product, intended for a *private* or *public* reader(s), originally or only formally in letter form.[12]

This definition allows assessment by the interpreter concerning

> the degree to which their content is intended as public, or of the degree to which they are comprised of discursive or didactic materials.[13]

Much of the recent work on the NT letters is indebted to the earlier labor of Heikki Koskenniemi. In turn, his conclusions are very much in keeping with what can be gleaned from analysis of the Greco-Roman epistolary theorists. Koskenniemi's examination of the epistolary literature, chiefly that of the non-literary papyri, led him to conclude that the letters of the Greco-Roman era share the following three characteristics:

1. philophronesis—letters are the expression of a friendly relationship between the writer and the person addressed,
2. parousia—the letter-writer addresses the recipient as though physically present, and

3. homilia—the writer continues the dialogue begun when the two parties were present.[14]

Klaus Thraede's 1970 study investigates the literary letters of selected philosophers of the NT era, the second and third century literary papyri, and the letters of the later Church Fathers. He also discusses three passages in three Pauline letters to illustrate the concept of epistolary παρουσία.[15] Thraede is particularly concerned to apply Koskenniemi's isolation of the three main and defining literary characteristics of letters to his own selection of Greco-Roman and Christian letters.

In the Greco-Roman era, letter-writing remained a subject either not discussed in the rhetorical handbooks or relegated to the fringes of rhetorical theory. The reasons for this seem to have been that letters, as extensions of the medium of conversation, did not utilize the stylized and highly inventive techniques of oratory. However, as White argues, the techniques of oral discourse, such as the diatribe and the speech itself, were sufficiently akin to the literary medium of the letter that they attached themselves to it.[16]

The first rhetorician to incorporate epistolary theory into his handbook was the fourth century C.E. Julius Victor, who only does so by way of an appendix.[17] Nevertheless, it is evident that epistolographers were interested in the rhetorical effectiveness of letter-writing. Accordingly, some were concerned, as we shall see below, to set out the rules and construct examples of letter types by which letters might be more effective pieces of communication.[18]

The earliest extant theoretical discussion of letter-writing occurs in a digression in the treatise *On Style* (Περὶ Ἑρμηνείας). The work is attributed in the manuscript tradition to Demetrius of Phalerum (fl. 300 B.C.E.).[19] However, the treatise appears to date from the second century C.E. and could be as early as the first century B.C.E.[20]

The "plain" style (ἰσχνός) is one of the four styles of prose and poetry Demetrius discusses.[21] By "plain" style he means a prose style that is lucid and natural. Such a style is best able to persuade. By contrast, a style that is not clear does not persuade (§221). A persuasive style does not convince by means of the application to the written medium of conventional canons of rhetorical effectiveness which operated in the sphere of formal speeches. Rather, the plain style persuades precisely because it lacks the art of invention appropriate to oratory. It is from these observations on prose style that Demetrius proceeds to discuss the style of letters.

According to Demetrius, who cites Artemon as his authority, a letter should be written in the same manner as a dialogue or conversation, with the letter representing one of the sides in the conversation.[22] However, the letter should not be a mere reporting of conversation, as he understands Artemon to believe, but should be somewhat "studied." By this he means that a letter should be a little more attentive to rhetorical effect and style than would be the case if letters were merely couched in reported speech. In penning a letter, one is writing a gift (δῶρον), as it were, to someone else.[23] Nevertheless, Demetrius understands letters as familial communications, rather than opportunities for oratorical display, criticizing Aristotle's obscure and semi-metrical style on this point.[24]

Although Demetrius discusses letter-writing as a digression in his examination of the "plain" prose style, he does, nonetheless, admit that in expression letters should be a mix of the "graceful" and "plain" styles.[25] In other words, letters can bear ornamentation.[26] The "plain" style is shorn of the kind of oratorical inventiveness recommended for speeches. Clarity of expression and the concomitant avoidance of stilted expression is the goal.[27] The only ornamentation of a philosophical nature that Demetrius allows is that applicable to friendly pieces of advice (φιλοφρονήσεις). He who speaks in "sententious maxims and exhortations" is no longer speaking "familiarly" but "ex cathedra" (μηχανῆς).[28] Aristotle, he observes, used "proofs" (ἀποδείξεις) when writing letters, but did so in a way appropriate to the familial tone.[29] Even when writing to city-states (πολεῖς) and kings one should heighten one's tone and style, but without writing a treatise.[30]

Letters, Demetrius argues, should provide glimpses of character, adding that of all the forms of composition, it is the epistolary medium that reveals character most keenly.[31] This observation is thoroughly in keeping with the concept of a letter as a communication between friends. Moreover, letters should be brief and free of "periods," i.e., the writer should not write discursively in well-rounded and well-framed syntactical and thematic units.[32] The "plain" style of a letter is admirably appropriate to the object of speaking to a friend since rhetorical effect, especially of the exaggerated kind, is not of the essence.[33] Nevertheless, there are examples of letters which do employ rhetorical effect and studied persuasive technique.[34]

There is good reason to believe that letter-writing exercises under the tutelage of the "grammaticus" were part of the educational regimen at the secondary level in schools throughout the Empire. In these exercises, Malherbe surmises, letter form and grammar were the focus.[35] The handbooks Malherbe surveys in *Ancient Epistolary Theorists* may have been used in conjunction with this didactic purpose and helped maintain continuity of form. The rhetorical schools may also have encouraged letter writing as an exercise in imitating the style (rather than mere letter-writing form) of the masters.[36] Furthermore, one cannot rule out the value of such letters as propaganda or as actualizations of the master's tradition against competing teachers claiming to represent the master's legacy.[37]

It has also been argued that the collections of pseudonymous letters, often purporting to be written by philosopher-masters, may be important for understanding how the collection of the PE, as well as the other deutero-Pauline letters, originated.[38] In company with a number of scholars I would contend that there was a Pauline "school" in which former *disciples* (not just associates or converts) of the apostle continued to give literary expression to their master's ideas.[39] Whether that "school" was a formal one or not, and whether one should rather term it a "movement," we do have to reckon with a number of individual writers operating in Asia Minor who were committed to the same task—they were vitally interested in securing Paul's heritage in the present and for the future. The deutero-Pauline corpus and the Book of Acts represent the extent of their legacy received into the New Testament.

I have suggested in chapter 1 that the best explanation of the shape of the Pauline tradition that comes to expression in the PE is that it expresses the actualization of Paul's teaching as it had already been received by the Pastor through the ten-letter corpus, at least as far as the literary embodiment of that legacy was concerned. The pseudepigrapher responsible for the authorship of the PE may or may not have belonged to a formal "school," but he certainly did what many of the students of the philosophers were prepared to do, namely, to seek to perpetuate, perhaps in circumstances hostile to the maintaining of their master's legacy, the tradition in which they had been tutored and enlightened. For the Pastor the existence of Pauline letters represented the literary legacy of the apostle and embodied what he took to be the Paulinism he was committed to securing and perpetuating once and for all by his own letters, i.e., the PE. Schenke puts it well when he writes:

> Echten Paulinismus kann es nur da geben, wo man den Paulus der Briefe kennt und das briefliche Wort des Apostels als Richtschnur nimmt, und wo man, wenn man das Wort des Paulus in veränderter Situation neu zu Gehör bringen will, es eben in der Form von Paulus-Briefen tut.[40]

Before turning to the important question of the Pauline form of the PE, a discussion of the types of letters identified by the Greco-Roman epistolary theorists is in order.

Letter Types

Pseudo-Demetrius' *Epistolary Types* (Τύποι Ἐπιστολικοί) derives from anywhere between the second century B.C.E. and the third century C.E.[41] The work is a practical manual with descriptions of twenty-one categories of letters appropriate to a variety of occasions and needs. The author appends a brief epistolary example to each category. A number of these are significant for the discussion of the NT epistolary material, and the PE in particular.

Pseudo-Demetrius' "advisory" letter (συμβουλευτικός) is apposite to the task of identifying possible analogies to the PE. In this type of letter, the author observes, writers offer their own judgment on particular matters (τὴν ἰδίαν γνώμην προφερόμενοι). "We are seeking," the theorist contends,

> either to exhort (προτρέπωμεν) or to dissuade (ἀποτρέπωμεν) someone from a course of action.[42]

This kind of letter has obvious affinities with the species of deliberative oratory as defined by Aristotle and the rhetorical handbooks. The following passages from Aristotle's *Rhetoric*, the later *Rhetorica ad Alexandrum,* and Quintilian's *Institutes* bear this judgment out:

> *Rhetoric,* 1.3.3
> The deliberative kind [of speech] is either hortatory (προτροπή) or dissuasive

(ἀποτροπή); for both those who give advice in private and those who speak in the assembly invariably either exhort or dissuade. (trans. J. H. Freese [LCL])

ad Alex. 1 (1421b)
Speaking generally, exhortation (προτροπή) is an attempt to urge people to some line of speech or action, and dissuasion (ἀποτροπή) is an attempt to hinder people from some line of speech or action. (trans. H. Rackham [LCL])

Institutes, 3.8.6
The deliberative department of oratory (also called the advisory department), while it deliberates about the future, also enquires about the past, while its functions are twofold and consist in advising and dissuading (*suadendi ac dissuadendi*). (trans. H. E. Butler [LCL])

The letter example provided by Pseudo-Demetrius purports to be written by a ruler to a colleague seeking to persuade him to adopt the same course of action for winning the affection of his subjects as has been outlined in a "previous" letter. If the addressee emulates the example set by the writer he will, so the writer urges, enjoy a good reputation among the masses. The general tone of the PE accords with Pseudo-Demetrius' characterization of the advisory letter in so far as the author sets forth courses of action for the protection of the Pauline heritage within the churches for which the addressees have responsibility.

The first of the letter categories discussed by Pseudo-Demetrius is the "friendly" letter (φιλικός). The theorist's discussion of this type is the longest devoted to any of the categories. The friendly letter is written by a superior to an inferior. Such a letter, he counsels, "seems to be written by a friend" (ὁ δοκῶν ὑπὸ φίλου γράφεσθαι). Moreover, the friendly letter need not be written by a person who is in an already established relationship with the recipient. The writer might choose to write this type of letter because he or she wants something in return. He thinks, observes Pseudo-Demetrius, that no one can refuse him when he writes in this way. This is so in the following letter example which purports to be written by an absent householder to the manager, probably a slave, of the affairs he has left in his keeping. He begins by assuring the addressee that he, the writer, is absent in body only. He alludes to the childhood they shared together. He continues:

> Knowing that I myself am genuinely concerned about your affairs, and that I have worked unstintingly for what is most advantageous to you, I have assumed that you, too, have the same opinion of me, and will refuse me nothing. You will do well, therefore, to give close attention to the members of my household (καλῶς οὖν ποιήσεις πυκνότερον ἐπισκοπῶν τοὺς ἐν οἴκῳ) lest they need anything . . . [43]
> (trans. Malherbe)

While there are some noteworthy thematic and verbal similarities to the PE here,[44] this letter is formally analogous to the PE on the grounds that it is written by a superior to an inferior, namely, one who is reminded of the charge to which he has been committed by the master, and the relationship which exists between them. The persuasive strategies employed in the example are quite explicit. It is not difficult to note the rhetorical implications of some of the other types of letters in Pseudo-Demetrius either, especially the letters of "praise" (ἐπαινετικός and "blame" (ψεκτικός), the tenth and ninth of his twenty-one categories respectively.

The discussion of epistolary types in the handbook entitled *Epistolary Styles* (Ἐπιστολιμαῖοι Χαρακτῆρες), attributed to Libanius, has been dated from the fourth to the sixth centuries C.E.[45] Like Pseudo-Demetrius, Pseudo-Libanius lists a number of categories of letters, this time forty-one types, each supplied with its own example. Again, there is evidence of precise rhetorical interest, not only in defining the types but in adapting them to various situations.[46]

The chief interest here is the theorist's discussion of the paraenetic letter. Similarities between this type of letter and the rhetoricians' delineation of deliberative rhetoric cited above are immediately obvious:

> The paraenetic style is that in which we exhort someone by urging him to pursue something or to avoid something. Paraenesis is divided into two parts, encouragement and dissuasion.[47] (trans. Malherbe)

However, Pseudo-Libanius makes a point of distinguishing between paraenesis and advice (συμβουλῆς). In function his category of advisory letter looks very much like the definition of deliberative oratory offered above by Aristotle, the *Rhetorica ad Alexandrum,* and Quintilian. According to Pseudo-Libanius, advisory speech is speech "that does admit of a counter-statement."[48] On the other hand, paraenesis, according to Pseudo-Libanius, is hortatory speech aiming at inculcating what is commonly regarded as self-evidently true, as his brief letter example (no. 52) indicates. No counter-statement can be reasonably offered against paraenesis.

However, this does not mean that paraenesis might not offer concrete and specific exhortation.[49] It is not always concerned with the inculcation of generalities alone. As Stowers observes, there are examples among the letters of purely traditional exhortation, while there are other letters of particular and occasional paraenesis. Still others offer a mixture of the traditional and occasional.[50] Stowers also observes correctly that the advisory letter of Pseudo-Demetrius (discussed above) largely corresponds to Pseudo-Libanius' paraenetic letter.[51] By analogy, Pseudo-Libanius' paraenetic letter is related to epideictic rhetoric in which the orator commends and confirms the values held by his audience.

I have already remarked that although letter-writing is not incorporated into rhetorical theory (at least not in the extant handbooks), and is only discussed in an appendix to Julius Victor's fourth century C.E. *Rhetoric*, it is evident, nonetheless, that rhetorical theory and consideration of rhetorical effect did play a significant part in the letter writing tradition, as it did in all other written media.[52] This is particularly relevant in the case of letters of paraenesis and advice in which, as we saw above in the discussion of Pseudo-Demetrius' letter types, the similarities between deliberative rhetoric and paraenetic letters are pronounced and intentional. Both seek to persuade or dissuade. The best hearing is guaranteed when good rapport can be established, or indebtedness appealed to. The latter is especially noticeable in the example (cited above) of the friendly letter of Pseudo-Demetrius. In such letters, we can expect to see evidence of the contours of the epideictic species of rhetoric. The presence in letters of the rhetorical "proofs" is also to be expected. These are arguments grounded in appeals to reason, ethos, and pathos which play a significant role in oratory, as we shall see in chapter 3.

Nevertheless, we encounter a potent mix of *naïveté* with rhetorical and prescriptive force even where rhetorical invention and ornamentation are eschewed, the unadorned plain-speaking style is highly commended, and where a concern is shown that letters be persuasive communications of friendship and embodiments of the writer's personality (such as in the discussion of the kind of letter that looms so large in Demetrius' *On Style*). Thraede rightly observes:

> Zum Indikativ des im bloßen Vorkommen von Korrespondenz überhaupt liegenden 'naiven' Verhältnisses Person-Brief tritt jetzt der Imperativ, das Gebot an den Gebildeten, die Möglichkeit wirklich und angemessen auszuschöpfen. So fließen Persönlichkeiten und Stilisierung, Briefpraxis und Rhetorik zusammen.[53]

B. THE PE AS PAULINE LETTERS

This section addresses a matter which received considerable attention in the first chapter, namely, the contours of the Pastor's actualization of Pauline theology and ethics. However, my focus here is the shape of the actualization of that tradition in the form of the Pauline letter. The PE warrant investigation as persuasive Pauline epistolary formulations with respect to their letter framework. However, because the PE claim to be specifically Pauline letters, it will also be necessary to address briefly the theology of the letters, and the image of Paul the PE embody.

The Pauline Letter Framework

The author of the PE wrote three letters. Each is directed to an individual. The author's task, I repeat, was to re-present Pauline tradition for the needs of the Pauline church(es) of the third generation. As we have seen in the discussion above, letters were primarily regarded as substitutes for the presence of the conversation partners. Letters enabled correspondents already in relationship with one another to continue their conversation.[54]

Robert W. Funk has argued persuasively that Paul's writing of letters was one of three strategies he adopted in giving expression to his apostolic "presence" (parousia) with respect to the congregations in his care.[55] The other two strategies were his actual bodily presence and the use of emissaries. The presence of the apostle conveyed in his letters is of great significance for his pastoral oversight. His desire is to sustain his relationship with the churches. This is a particularly urgent need when he is absent from them, and they are at the mercy of false teachers and false models. Letters, therefore, were an indispensable means of keeping alive the "conversation" he had begun while present with the churches bodily. That Paul's letters are dialogical in nature is, therefore, no accident, but an essential aspect of his apostolic office with regard to the churches. The Pauline letter, therefore, embodies the apostle's claim to be patron, patriarch, and spiritual director (*Seelenführer*) of his churches. Paul's letters, like the friendship letters of the Greco-Roman era, functioned as substitutes for his presence.

Paul's letters represent a new phenomenon in the early Christian movement.[56] Paul writes to communities, just as a Greek philosopher might keep in touch with his scattered groups of disciples, or Palestinian Jews with their diaspora fellows. He wrote out of an acute sense of being a divinely appointed apostle with authority analogous to that of a Hebrew prophet, even writing to churches he had not founded, convinced of his appointment to the office of apostle by Christ himself.[57] He wrote not just to keep in touch, but to continue his guidance and nurture of the believers.

It was incumbent on the author of the PE to give voice to that tradition of pastoral care in the form of letters such as Paul had himself written to the churches. It was by this medium that the apostle had been able not only to communicate with those in his care but to actualize his own apostolic authority for their exhortation, admonition, and warning while he was absent from them. It was an elemental but integral part of the Pastor's persuasive strategy to write a recognizably Pauline letter. Allowing for different circumstances and content, the letters the Pastor wrote had to follow a recognizable Pauline format, since that was the form in which the apostle sustained the thrust and dynamic of his bodily presence with his congregations.[58] Apart from any consideration of the theological content of Pauline tradition, the Pauline letter, with its reflection of the authority of the apostle, was part of the received tradition the author of the PE sought to actualize.

William Doty observes that Paul's letters are his own developments of the basic letter pattern of an introduction, body, and conclusion. His personal mode of writing produced a format, which, in its broadest outline, can be broken down into the following sections:

1. *opening*—including sender (prescript), addressee (adscript) and greeting,
2. *thanksgiving* or *blessing*—often with an eschatological climax,
3. *body*—commencing with a disclosure or request formula,
4. *paraenesis*—arising out of the apostle's perception of ethical life in the congregations addressed, and
5. *conclusion (postscript)*—with formulaic blessings and greetings.[59]

John L. White correctly observes that the Pauline letters are redolent of early Christian worship.[60] He notes the evidence of prayers, hymns, appeals to scripture, paraenesis, doxologies and blessings in the letters. These are all suggestive of a homiletic and liturgical context. Indeed, the remainder of the NT epistolary deposit not only preserves something like the Pauline formulae to be observed in prescript and postscript but the same reflection of the liturgical life of the congregations to which the letters were addressed. White argues that the contours of the post-Pauline letter-writing deposit were dependent on the earlier Pauline letters.[61] Not only are Pauline formulae imitated by later letter writers but one encounters prayers, hymns, doxologies and blessings. The PE are particularly laden with prayers and hymns.[62]

The investigation below of the PE as Pauline letters firstly focuses extensively on the more formulaic details of the prescript and postscript of the Pauline letters, and then on the introductory thanksgivings and *personalia* of the corpus. However, with respect to the body and the paraenesis of the Pauline letter, comments will be briefer since these sections were not as stereotyped as the openings and closings.[63]

Superscript. Each letter begins as follows:

1 Tim. 1.1
Παῦλος ἀπόστολος Χριστοῦ 'Ιησοῦ κατ' ἐπιταγὴν θεοῦ σωτῆρος ἡμῶν καὶ Χριστοῦ 'Ιησοῦ τῆς ἐλπίδος ἡμῶν

2 Tim. 1.1
Παῦλος ἀπόστολος Χριστοῦ 'Ιησοῦ διὰ θελήματος θεοῦ κατ' ἐπαγγελίαν ζωῆς τῆς ἐν Χριστῷ 'Ιησοῦ

Tit. 1.1–3
Παῦλος δοῦλος θεοῦ, ἀπόστολος δὲ 'Ιησοῦ Χριστοῦ κατὰ πίστιν ἐκλεκτῶν θεοῦ καὶ ἐπίγνωσιν ἀληθείας τῆς κατ' εὐσέβειαν ἐπ' ἐλπίδι ζωῆς αἰωνίου,

ἣν ἐπηγγείλατο ὁ ἀψευδὴς θεὸς πρὸ χρόνων αἰωνίων, ἐφανέρωσεν δὲ καιροῖς ἰδίοις τὸν λόγον αὐτοῦ ἐν κηρύγματι ὃ ἐπιστεύθην ἐγὼ κατ' ἐπιταγὴν τοῦ σωτῆρος ἡμῶν θεοῦ

In their apostolic claim and their ascription to the will of God as the source of the apostolic office, the superscripts of the PE conform most closely to Romans, 1 and 2 Corinthians, Galatians, Ephesians, and Colossians.[64] Quinn argues that the elaborate and theologically discursive superscription of Titus suggests that it originally headed the three-letter corpus.[65]

The superscript of Titus invites comparison with Rom. 1.1–6. Like the theologically laden superscript of Romans, that of Titus heralds distinctive theological themes to be encountered elsewhere in the PE as a corpus, such as the entrusting by God to Paul of the message of eternal life (1.3; cf. 1 Tim. 1.11), and the virtue of religious duty (1.1, εὐσέβεια). The author's self-designation as δοῦλος in Tit. 1.1 is also used by Paul, though always "of Christ," never "of God" as here.[66]

Adscript. Each letter addresses the recipient as follows:

1 Tim. 1.2
Τιμοθέῳ γνησίῳ τέκνῳ ἐν πίστει

2 Tim. 1.2
Τιμοθέῳ ἀγαπητῷ τέκνῳ

Tit. 1.4
Τίτῳ γνησίῳ τέκνῳ κατὰ κοινὴν πίστιν

The adscripts of the PE are, as we would expect, much more personally suited to the individual nature of the correspondence, and are best paralleled within the Pauline corpus by Phlm 1b.[67] However, there are many parallels to this intimate form of address within the Greco-Roman letter writing tradition.[68]

Opening greetings. The PE contain the following greetings:

1 Tim. 1.2

χάρις, ἔλεος, εἰρήνη ἀπὸ θεοῦ πατρὸς καὶ Χριστοῦ Ἰησοῦ τοῦ κυρίου ἡμῶν

2 Tim. 1.2
χάρις, ἔλεος, εἰρήνη ἀπὸ θεοῦ πατρὸς καὶ Χριστοῦ Ἰησοῦ τοῦ κυρίου ἡμῶν

Tit. 1.4
χάρις καὶ εἰρήνη ἀπὸ θεοῦ πατρὸς καὶ Χριστοῦ Ἰησοῦ τοῦ σωτῆρος ἡμῶν

The "grace and peace" terminology of the PE is closely paralleled in the Pauline corpus. However, the tri-partite greetings of 1 and 2 Timothy are unusual in that context.[69] Nevertheless, Gal. 6.16 does use the same tri-partite formula in the recapitulation section of the postscript.[70] By contrast the "grace and peace" of Tit. 1.4 reverts to the Pauline pattern found in the opening greetings encountered in Rom. 1.7, 1 Cor. 1.3, 2 Cor. 1.2 and elsewhere.[71]

The postscripts of the Pauline corpus are rather fluid in their construction. *Personalia*, doxologies, benedictions, greetings, and exhortations all figure in no apparently prescribed order.

Final exhortations. The Pastor writes these concluding exhortations to his addressees:

1 Tim. 6.20–21
ὦ Τιμόθεε, τὴν παραθήκην φύλαξον, ἐκτρεπόμενος τὰς βεβήλους κενοφωνίας καὶ ἀντιθέσεις τῆς ψευδωνύμου γνώσεως, ἥν τινες ἐπαγγελλόμενοι περὶ τὴν πίστιν ἠστόχησαν.

2 Tim. 4.21
σπούδασον πρὸ χειμῶνος ἐλθεῖν.

Tit. 3.12–14
ὅταν πέμψω Ἀρτεμᾶν πρὸς σὲ ἢ Τυχικόν, σπούδασον ἐλθεῖν πρός με εἰς Νικόπολιν, ἐκεῖ γὰρ κέκρικα παραχειμάσαι. Ζηνᾶν τὸν νομικὸν καὶ Ἀπολλῶν σπουδαίως πρόπεμψον, ἵνα μηδὲν αὐτοῖς λείπῃ. μανθανέτωσαν δὲ καὶ οἱ ἡμέτεροι καλῶν ἔργων προΐστασθαι εἰς τὰς ἀναγκαίας χρείας, ἵνα μὴ ὦσιν ἄκαρποι.

Exhortatory parallels occurring in the postscripts of other Pauline letters can be found in 2 Cor. 13.11 (λοιπόν, ἀδελφοί, χαίρετε, καταρτίζεσθε, παρακαλεῖσθε, τὸ αὐτὸ φρονεῖτε, εἰρηνεύετε) and in the lengthy 1 Thess. 5.12–22. Eph. 6.21–22 and Col. 4.7–9 associate the visit of Tychicus (cf. 2 Tim. 4.12) with the postscript. These two passages can be compared with the travel plans outlined in the postscripts of 2 Tim. 4.9–21 and Tit. 3.12–13.

Final greetings

1 Tim. ————————

2 Tim. 4.21
ἀσπάζεταί σε Εὔβουλος καὶ Πούδης καὶ Λίνος καὶ Κλαυδία καὶ οἱ ἀδελφοὶ πάντες.

Tit. 3.15
ἀσπάζονταί σε οἱ μετ᾽ ἐμοῦ πάντες. Ἄσπασαι τοὺς φιλοῦντας ἡμᾶς ἐν πίστει.

Closing greetings, sometimes from Paul alone (2 Thess. 3.17) or more usually from associates of Paul and the addressees, are common to all Pauline letters, except 1 Timothy, 1 Thessalonians (where Paul asks that the addressees greet all the brethren), and Ephesians.[72] Their often intimate nature, as in 1 Cor. 16.20, 2 Cor. 13.12, and 1 Thess. 5.26, is somewhat muted in the PE where the closing greetings are less personal and more formal. Indeed, some scholars note that the *lack* of closing greetings in 1 Timothy is evidence of non-Pauline authorship.[73]

Final benedictions

1 Tim. 6.21
ἡ χάρις μεθ᾽ ὑμῶν.

2 Tim. 4.22
ὁ κύριος μετὰ τοῦ πνεύματός σου. ἡ χάρις μεθ᾽ ὑμῶν.

Tit. 3.15
ἡ χάρις μετὰ πάντων ὑμῶν.

Mark Kiley perceptively observes that the PE, in common with other letters in the post-Pauline corpus (2 Thess. 3.18 is the exception), do not tie χάρις with the Lord Jesus Christ as is Paul's usage in the undisputed letters.[74] It is also noteworthy that in common with all the Pauline letters, even that to Philemon (v. 25), the final benediction is couched in the plural. Although the PE are addressed to individuals, the communities of Ephesus and Crete are addressed indirectly through their respective apostolic delegates.[75]

Introductory Thanksgiving. Paul Schubert observed that there are no fully-fledged introductory thanksgivings in the PE.[76] He was prepared to concede, however, that there is a "trace" of such a thanksgiving in 2 Tim. 1.3–5 (χάριν ἔχω τῷ θεῷ . . .), and that 1 Tim. 1.12–16 (χάριν ἔχω . . .) functioned as one.[77] These thanksgivings are part of the structure of the Pauline letter. Among the NT letters, only the Pauline corpus, with the exception of Galatians and 2 Corinthians, features thanksgivings after the prescript. Schubert proceeds to observe that Christian epistolary literature of the second century, in common with the PE, shows only

> sporadic and fragmentary imitation of the Pauline thanksgivings, while the non-epistolary Christian literature of that period shows none whatsoever.[78]

Schubert observes that the introductory thanksgivings included an eschatological climax. This is observable in 1 Cor. 1.8, Phil. 1.10, and 1 Thess. 1.10. In the PE, 1 Tim. 1.12–16 does indeed close on an eschatological note:

> ἵνα ἐν ἐμοὶ πρώτῳ ἐνδείξηται Χριστὸς Ἰησοῦς τὴν ἅπασαν μακροθυμίαν, πρὸς ὑποτύπωσιν τῶν μελλόντων πιστεύειν ἐπ' αὐτῷ εἰς ζωὴν αἰώνιον.

However, 2 Tim. 1.3–5 lacks this feature.

In the wake of Schubert's study, Jack T. Sanders' investigation of the transition from introductory thanksgiving to the body of the Pauline letter further establishes the indebtedness of 1 and 2 Timothy to the Pauline model.[79] Sanders observes that after the thanksgiving the addressees are either exhorted or commanded or informed of some matter. In the case of exhortation or command, the issue being raised is expressed in the accusative or by a prepositional phrase (introduced by περί, ὑπέρ, or ἐπί), or sometimes the subject is omitted altogether. The command or exhortation is expressed by a ἵνα clause preceded by παρακαλέω.[80] In the latter, the disclosure takes the form of a ὅτι clause introducing what the apostle wishes his addressees to know.[81]

In 1 Tim. 1.12–16, the thanksgiving period, delayed by the imparting of urgent commands in vv. 3–11, is concluded by a doxology (v. 17), followed by a variation of the characteristic Pauline exhortation formula—ταύτην τὴν παραγγελίαν παρατίθεμαί σοι, τέκνον Τιμόθεε . . . ἵνα . . .—in v. 18. The situation of the thanksgiving in 2 Tim. 1.3–5 is not as easily fitted into the Pauline schema. There is no eschatological climax. Although v. 6 does contain exhortation, it is not introduced in the characteristic way noted above.[82] Titus, like 2 Timothy, is also difficult to fit into the schema, though it should be noted that after the lengthy superscript (1.2–3) the writer turns to exhortation in 1.5 at the commencement of the body of the letter by way of reminder to Titus of the apostle's charge.[83]

Finally, Sanders shows how the formulae marking the transition from the thanksgiving period to the body of the letter are by no means restricted to the introductory thanksgivings, but occur throughout the letters, and also in the PE.[84]

The Body and Paraenesis. In the body of the letter the reader encounters the occasion of the writing of the letter. This is the least stereotypical aspect of the letter format. The issues taken up in the body of the Pauline letter are anticipated in the introductory thanksgiving.[85] The issues Paul addresses in the body of his letters are often related to the status of the Jewish law in the life of the believer and the role of the Jewish people in the purposes of God. In Galatians and Romans we find these concerns discussed not only at the theological but also at the paraenetic level, and not necessarily near the conclusion of the letters as is sometimes supposed. In 1 Corinthians Paul addresses a number of issues relating to the intrusion of unacceptable moral behavior into the church well before the conclusion. 1 Thessalonians is almost all paraenesis.

It is not the rule, therefore, that Paul discussed theological matters first and then, near the conclusion, offered some traditional, non-specific and generalized exhortation. This view was stated with vigor by Dibelius in his *From Tradition to Gospel*.[86] Drawing from the Greco-

Roman paraenetic tradition exemplified in Isocrates' *To Nicocles*, Pseudo-Isocrates' *To Demonicus*, and their early Jewish and early Christian counterparts in *Pseudo-Phocylides*, Tobit 4, 12, *Ahikar*, James, and *Did.* 1–6, he argued that Pauline paraenesis "contains no far-reaching discussion based on religion or theology," but is presented as loosely connected maxims or proverbs. Moreover, Pauline paraenesis lacks "an immediate relation with the circumstances of the letter."[87]

Rather, it is much more the case that Pauline paraenesis embodies the moral implications of his teaching.[88] Beker demonstrates with respect to Romans, for instance, that the paraenesis of chapters 12–15 is vitally linked with the teaching that precedes them.[89] While Keck may be correct in arguing that the paraenesis of the Pauline letter can on occasion be unrelated to the theological issues Paul discusses,[90] a good case can be made for the integration of theology and paraenesis in Paul and, for that matter, in the PE.

What is different about the PE when contrasted with the majority of the letters of the Pauline corpus is the almost exclusive concentration in the PE on moral exhortation. Even the *Kirchenordnungen* of 1 Timothy and Titus are subsumed under exhortation to the addressees. The actual addressees (the leadership of the Pauline churches in Ephesus and on Crete) are exhorted through the assumed addressees (Timothy and Titus) to maintain their faithfulness to Paul and his heritage and to see to it that the congregations in their care continue to be organized in the prescribed manner in order that the Pauline legacy might be sustained. Extended discussion of the paraenetic aspects of the PE will be reserved until section D.

Personalia. The *personalia* of the PE will be also treated below (see section D). In many of Paul's letters personal notes are present, often concerning his travel plans or those of his emissaries. Their presence in the PE in 1 Tim. 3.14–15, 2 Tim. 1.15–18, 4.6–8, 9–18, and Tit. 3.12–14 find counterparts in, e.g., Rom. 15.22–29, 1 Cor. 16.5–12, 2 Cor. 13.1–2, 10, Eph. 6.19–20, 21–22, Col. 4.7–9, and Phlm. 22. Moreover, the PE have several references to the "charge" which "Paul" gave Timothy and Titus in person (see 1 Tim. 1.3 [cf. 6.13 and 2 Tim. 4.1]; Tit. 1.5). I have already drawn attention above to the theme of the apostolic parousia in these letters, and will also return to the subject below.

It might be noted here that, in the Pauline corpus I judge the Pastor to have received, Paul combines what White terms "private" sentiment with "apostolic" authority.[91] The PE, especially 2 Timothy, are persuasively Pauline at this juncture because of the evocation of Paul's apostolic authority. This authority is heightened because as far as the Pastor is concerned Paul is the only apostle.

In keeping with the Pastor's purpose of actualizing Pauline tradition, we can note the debt to Pauline literary form and usages in the prescript-postscript framework of the PE. The PE evoke the Pauline correspondence, their different ecclesiological situation and theological emphases notwithstanding. In the use of *personalia* and the recurrent theme of the apostolic parousia, the Pastor can also be observed at work actualizing the Pauline epistolary tradition through his own literary formulations. The Pastor's use of the characteristic Pauline thanksgiving period in 1 Tim. 1.12–16, as well as his use of a variation of the disclosure formula in 1 Tim. 1.18 and elsewhere in the body of the PE (see 2 Tim. 3.1), also commend the letters as vehicles of the actualization of Pauline tradition.

The PE as Embodiments of Pauline Theology

This issue has received considerable treatment in chapter 1. I have already registered my agreement with those scholars who have argued for the pseudonymous authorship of the PE on the grounds that many of the Pastor's theological emphases can be contrasted with those of the undisputed Pauline letters.

The theological issues Paul was wont to address in his genuine letters either do not surface in the PE or they do so in a modified manner. The theology of the false teachers is not directly engaged. To that extent, Paul's argumentative strategy is not emulated, since Paul, unlike the Pastor, is prepared to carry the argument to his opponents. In the PE, on the other hand, the teachers are targets of unrelenting polemic or invective, or are indirectly addressed in this fashion through the advice and warnings given to the audience. F. C. Baur demonstrated this long ago in his interpretation of the PE. Thus the duties of ecclesiastical officials, the paraenesis to various groups in the congregations, even the advice given Timothy in 1 Tim. 5.23, have as their aim the countering of the positions taken up by the false teachers. With the possible exception of 1 Tim. 2.11–15 and 4.1–5 we do not encounter sustained theological arguments which persuade by appeal to reason in the PE. However, it would be unjust to charge that the Pastor is no theologian or that his moral exhortation does not derive its motivational dynamic from his theological presuppositions, i.e., from his perception of the significance of the Christ-event.

Much of the debate concerning the authenticity of the PE has focused on the issue of the relationship of the theology of the PE to that of Paul. Investigation of this issue in the nineteenth century by Baur, Holtzmann, and other scholars has demonstrated the incompatibility of the theology of Paul with that of the PE at a number of inescapable points, as much by what the Pastor in the name of Paul omits as by what he commits to writing. In the scholarly debate of this century, there has been little reason to change or modify their overall conclusions. While the author of the PE has some grounding in the distinctives of Pauline theology, there is sufficient evidence, on balance, to doubt that the apostle is directly responsible for the PE.

It is demonstrable that the PE owe their outlook as much to the situation of the third generation of believers as to the Pastor's actualization of the Pauline tradition. This tradition was encapsulated in literary form not only in what we might term the seven undisputed Pauline letters, but may well have extended to the post-Pauline letters of the second generation (Ephesians, Colossians, 2 Thessalonians). Presumably the latter were actualizations of the Pauline tradition their respective authors had received. If the Pastor did know the ten-letter corpus, it is likely that he regarded all ten as authentically Pauline. It is also possible that the Pastor knew Acts.

Thus, one might regret the changed focus in the PE of such distinctly Pauline concepts as faith (πίστις). One might note the blurring of the apocalyptic coordinates of Paul's interpretation of the significance of the Christ-event. We might also lament the adoption of strategies which would seem to indicate accommodation of the church to many of the structures of conventional wisdom and ethical expectation in the post-Pauline era. However, in the passage of time Pauline distinctives no longer "connected" with the situation of the Pauline churches. As a general rule, Paul's theology was hammered out in the crucible of intense dialogue over questions that pertained uniquely to the naissance of the early Christian movement—questions like those which concerned the function of the Jewish law, the status of the Jewish people in God's saving purposes, and the application of distinctly Jewish apocalyptic categories in Hellenistic church contexts. These issues, I adjudge, are no longer live ones for the churches of the PE. In the PE the struggle is much more focused on the maintaining and securing of the Pauline heritage in the churches for future generations as the means of protecting those communities.

It is my conviction that the theology of the PE contains echoes of the theological tradition contained in the undisputed Paulines. But, generally, the theology, ethics, and ecclesiology we see developing in the deutero-Pauline deposit has been encapsulated in the PE at an even later stage of the development of the Pauline corpus. The PE could be described as embodiments of "Paul for a new day." The Paul of the PE, like the Paul of the undisputed Pauline corpus, is committed to addressing the contingencies operating within the Pauline churches beset by false teachers who, perhaps, also appealed to their own fund of Pauline tradition for their authority. But for the author of the PE there was much of what he inherited which was part of an unusable and non-repeatable past. By the time he wrote, the church had been situated within Greco-Roman culture for at least two generations. It was perceived that the second epiphany of Christ may take place many generations hence. It made sense, therefore, to marry the Pauline tradition with those strategies for virtuous and commendable living which seemed to accord with the life-orientation based on the Christ-event originally imparted by the apostle himself, or his historic delegate(s).

The gospel of the PE might not be couched in the same language as Paul's, and does not share all the coordinates of his apocalyptic framework. But gospel it is, grounded on the author's keen sense of the salvific intervention of God for all in the person of Jesus Christ.

The Image of Paul in the PE

This matter has also been discussed at some length in chapter 1. Beker, e.g., is particularly harsh in his assessment of the image of Paul in the PE. The Paul of the undisputed Pauline letters has been transmuted into the sole apostle of Christendom. Though we must take into account the perceived threat the Pastor felt to the Pauline legacy, the Paul of the PE has become a dogmatic teaching authority who issues decretals and "freezes" the deposit (παραθήκη) of his message for generations to follow (see 2 Tim. 2.2). He refuses to engage in theological argument with the false teachers and dismisses them as heretics and enemies of the truth.[92]

There is truth in Beker's observations. Paul is the only apostle as far as the PE are concerned. The Paul of the PE certainly does indulge in vituperation against the false teachers. He does mandate his legacy for future generations. Beker is right to draw our attention to the threat to the survival of the apostle's legacy as an explanation for the image of Paul the Pastor has constructed. However, I hope to show in this chapter that these negative judgments are somewhat precipitate. We cannot hope to understand the Pastor solely on these terms. Rather, I am contending, the Pastor sought to actualize the image of Paul as it is had already been transmitted to him in order to address what he perceived to be the urgent needs of the Pauline churches to be protected from the inroads of false teachers. Furthermore, he exhorted communities, whose identity in the Pauline tradition was threatened, by affirming conventional ethical and social wisdom. He communicated persuasively and literately. As such, his achievement deserves more than to be contrasted with the letters of the historical Paul.

As pseudonymous writings, the PE effectively locate the authority of Paul in the church leaders who share the author's understanding of Paul. I adjudge the author of the PE to have mounted a highly practical image of the revered apostle Paul in the face of crises in which the Pauline heritage was under grave threat. The Pastor also created a remarkably durable and effective ecclesiastical anchoring of the Pauline legacy in the interests of securing his interpretation of the apostle's teaching and vision of life for successive generations of believers.

As letters standing self-consciously in the Pauline tradition of letter-writing, the PE are, in my estimation, persuasive embodiments of that tradition. With some exceptions, the PE incorporate not only the broad format and formulae of the Pauline letter, but also, under the circumstances operating in the Pastor's ecclesiastical context, give expression to an interpretation of Pauline theology and promote a recognizably authoritative image of the apostle.

C. Moral Exhortation in the Greco-Roman World

My concern in this section of the chapter is to investigate the Greco-Roman tradition of hortatory discourse and the practice of writing letters of moral exhortation in order to understand better both the epistolary function of the PE as letters in their own right and the extent to which they share with other NT material, particularly the letters of Paul, the same tradition. First, however, a clearer definition of what I mean by the term "moral exhortation" will be attempted.

Paraenesis and Protrepsis

In the Greco-Roman world there existed an hortatory tradition in which a writer appealed to an addressee to continue in a certain way of life by commending conventional morality and traditional wisdom. This appeal was reinforced by positive and negative examples, as well as by reminder to the recipient of what he/she already knew of a commendable ethical life-style. While the principles appealed to might be traditional, this did not mean that such discourse did not accommodate itself to the specific situation of the recipient. A mixing of general and occasional exhortation is frequently encountered.

Another mode of hortatory literature, less broad than that identified above, called for an addressee to change a present life-orientation and to devote him/herself to philosophy or to virtue. Both of these modes of address, however, were termed "paraenesis" in the Greco-Roman era.[93]

Rudolf Vetschera, noting the consequent confusion that exists in the attempt to define paraenesis, adopted the following differentiation. He reserved the term "paraenesis" for that mode of address in which the whole conduct of the addressee's moral life and duties was the subject of the address. The addressee is exhorted to *maintain* adherence to traditional or accepted modes of behavior. The opposite modes of behavior were the subject of dissuasion. Vetschera termed "protrepsis" that mode of address which takes the form of an appeal to *change* one's life-orientation, an appeal which often had devotion to the study of philosophy as its aim as the most sure path to virtue.[94] He observed that both modes of address aimed at inculcating virtue.[95] It can be observed that there is a good deal of blurring of these modes of address.[96] This is true of the PE, especially in the Pastor's address to the actual addressees—the churches of Ephesus and Crete—whose goodwill must be secured and might not be assumed, as well as other hortatory material in the NT.

Occasionally, the term "advice" will be used in the discussion of ancient letters and of the PE. This term will be restricted to matters which concern persuasion or dissuasion where the writer offers his/her own opinion of a course of action to be taken without explicitly appealing to traditional ethical wisdom.[97]

Vetschera locates the origin of literary paraenesis in the *Works and Days* of Hesiod (ca. 700 B.C.E.), the elegies of Theognis (mid sixth century B.C.E.), and the work of other early Greek poets, Chiron and Phocylides.[98] Their concern was to give expression to strategies for successful living by means of precepts and maxims, in much the same manner as the wisdom literature of the Hebrew Bible, but derived from the perspective of the Greek mythical and wisdom tradition.[99] The *Sentences of Pseudo-Phocylides*, written probably in Alexandria about the turn of the era, is a paraenetic work that seeks to give voice to the Greek paraenetical tradition, but is also influenced by Jewish religious traditions and Stoic ethics.[100] The work of the original sixth century B.C.E. Phocylides exists only in fragments.[101] This kind of literature either explicitly addresses another person, or implies such an address.

The most extensively discussed category of ancient letters surveyed by Stowers in his *Letter Writing in Greco-Roman Antiquity* is that devoted to letters of moral exhortation and advice. The search for clear definitions, which has been the subject of this section so far, is further hampered by the confusion that exists on the matter of paraenesis and advice in the tradition of epistolary theory. Pseudo-Libanius (see discussion in section A of this chapter) defines paraenesis and advice along lines analogous to epideictic and deliberative rhetoric respectively. He defined paraenesis as the commending of traditional and self-evident moral truths which admit of no counter-argument. Advice, he argued, was that mode of address in which the author offers his/her persuasion or dissuasion concerning a course of action under consideration by the recipient.

However, the distinction offered by Pseudo-Libanius breaks down when we compare the definition of advice and the example of an advising letter in the earlier epistolary theorist Pseudo-Demetrius. He offers an example of the advising letter which effectively mixes both paraenesis and advice as would be later understood by Pseudo-Libanius. Unfortunately, Pseudo-Demetrius does not provide an example of a paraenetic letter. The lesson to be learnt here is that definitions of these terms are elusive, not least, I suspect, because there was an overlapping of persuasive strategies and modes of address.

This study of the tradition of exhortatory epistolography is important not only for understanding the tone of the PE but also the self-understanding of the author. Stowers observes that much of the extant literature was written by or attributed to philosophers, both Greek and Latin, keeping in touch with their students, clients or family members. Malherbe terms this a tradition of psychagogy, i.e., pastoral care or guidance.[102] The same trajectory is manifest in the PE and in the Pauline corpus as a whole, not to mention early Jewish and early Christian literature in general. In this literature, as well as in the Greco-Roman materials, there is exhibited the concern of writers to further the moral and spiritual well-being of those in their charge.

Stowers, like Vetschera, uses the term "protrepsis" to denote the kind of exhortation in which a writer exhorts the one addressed to a new and radical way of life. He reserves the term "paraenesis" for exhortation to continue in a way of life already assented to.[103] There are affinities, he observes, between the two modes of exhortation and the deliberative and epideictic species of rhetoric respectively. In protrepsis the speaker or writer underscores the advantages or disadvantages of following a life-orientation should that option be taken by the addressee.[104] This corresponds somewhat to deliberative rhetoric.[105] In paraenesis, on the other hand, continued adherence to a set of moral values is encouraged and assent to them is sought, rather in the manner of epideictic rhetoric's focus on praise and blame.

However, as Stowers points out correctly, exhortation transcends rhetorical conventions.[106] A protreptic appeal can be deliberative or epideictic depending on one's point of view. For the author of the appeal, the life-orientation being envisaging is already one to which assent has been has given. The author writes epideictically. For the addressee, however, the appeal becomes a matter for deliberation. Furthermore, one could say that there were occasions when paraenetic address is directed to those who were once the subject of protreptic appeal and had heeded it.[107] Moreover, it is often the case that the distinctions between the two modes are blurred in the material to be examined.[108]

Stowers also notes, as I have already indicated above, that many hortatory letters bear witness to a mixing of modes of exhortation, combining positive appeals, such as praise and encouragement, and negative ones like censure, blame, and warning, with perhaps one mode predominating in the letter. However, he concludes:

> What all complex letters of moral exhortation have in common is an explicit or implicit model of what it means to be a good person in general or a good person in a certain role.

He adds:

> The rhetoric of exhortation, then, attempts to persuade and move the audience to conform to that model and to elicit corresponding habits of behavior.[109]

The models for later hortatory prose in discourses, treatises and letters were provided by the discourses of Isocrates and Aristotle.[110] The latter's *Protrepticus*, now extant in fragments only, addressed Themison, King of Cyprus, exhorting him to adopt, as king, the life of philosophical enterprise. Themison is urged, in effect, to convert to a new and radical life-style, lived in opposition to prevailing societal conventions and expectations, making the study of philosophy his priority.[111] Thus, fragments 50 and 51 urge the addressee to make philosophy pre-eminent in his life. The philosopher "moors his life to that which is eternal and unchanging" (ἐξ αἰδίων καὶ μονίμων ἀναψάμενος), and lives as his own master (ζῇ καθ' ἑαυτόν).[112] Though philosophy is theoretical, "it enables us," Aristotle writes, "to frame all our practice in accordance with it."[113] If the pursuit of wisdom is fraught with many risks, "we should not shrink from labor or expense."[114]

Protreptic address was often used by philosophers in exhorting those they addressed to adopt the life of philosophical detachment from the world and its pleasures. That such a mode of address was adapted to the letter form can be seen in Pseudo-Anacharsis' letter to Croesus. The writer exhorts the fabulously wealthy king to give up his great wealth and possessions, the fruit of the "disease" (νόσημα) of the desire to possess many things which has made him a slave, and, instead, to seek wisdom and pursue virtue.[115]

The philosopher Epicurus (341–271 B.C.E.) also addressed a number of his contemporaries, including his mother and his students, in letters written in the protreptic mode. Diogenes Laertius preserves several of these. To Pythocles, a favorite of the philosopher, Epicurus writes:

> Hoist all sail, my dear boy, and steer clear of culture.[116]

The lengthy letter to Menoeceus is an appeal to him to devote his life to acquiring wisdom and to follow Epicurus' ethical and religious teaching.[117] The chief aim of such a life is pleasure, defined as the absence of both pain in the body and trouble in the soul.[118] The constant discipline of the exercise of one's own mind, in company with one's fellows, in Epicurean precepts is a sure way to the goal of the undisturbed life of wisdom and virtue.[119]

In early Christian literature, the anonymous *Epistle to Diognetus* (perhaps second century C.E.) is to be classed as a protreptic letter. It is written to an enquirer who is zealous to learn the "religion of the Christians" (ἡ θεοσέβεια τῶν Χριστιανῶν μαθεῖν, 1.1). As in other protreptic addresses, the views of other religious "philosophies," namely, Greek idolatry and Judaism are countered in the interests of showing the superior rationality of Christian insight and the surpassing advantages of becoming a believer.[120] The writer argues that God's sending of his Son demonstrates that he is seeking to persuade, not compel, people to believe (ὡς πείθων, οὐ βιαζόμενος, 7.4). Furthermore, the evident pretentiousness of humankind's quest for access to knowledge of God is put to rest by God's imparting of the truth to his Child alone (8.9). In turn, God gives believers both a share in the benefits of salvation and the ability to see and understand the truth hitherto hid from them (8.11). Not unimportant is the stress the writer places on loving one's neighbor as an imitation of God's goodness. In taking up the burden of one's neighbor and helping the weak, such a person becomes an imitator of God to those he helps (οὗτος μιμητής ἐστι θεοῦ, 10.6).[121] Finally, the writer urges Diognetus to consider the benefits God bestows on those who love him, none other than access to the tree of knowledge and the tree of life, which God alone can give (12.1–3).

Klaus Berger defines protrepsis in terms too broad to be of much help. For him protrepsis is any address which makes the past as well as the future choice of the Christian life-orientation its theme.[122] Accordingly he argues that all of Paul's letter to the Romans belongs to this genre.[123] According to this definition, protreptic address is found elsewhere in the NT, especially in Matt. 7.13–27, 11.25–30, John 3.1–21, 1 Cor. 13 (with its focus on the "höchster Weg"), 1 Tim. 4.7b–10, as well as the so-called Sermons on the Mount and Plain.[124] Although Berger rightly classes appeals to repentance and separation from influences damaging to one's Christian commitment as protreptic in character, he also places in the protreptic category general exhortations to holy living and to persevere in what the addressee(s) have learnt from the beginning, as well as exhortations to demonstrate Christian maturity and to accept suffering.[125] His reasoning is that all the categories of protreptic he isolates have to do not only with the decision to adopt but also to maintain the Christian life-commitment.[126] One would have thought, however, that protrepsis denotes more specifically the appeal to become a Christian, rather than such wide-ranging appeals to faithful expression of one's commitment or duty, such as contained in 1 Tim. 4.7b–10 and the two Sermons.

I contend that protreptic address seems best designed as a mode of exhortation for "insiders" to appeal to "outsiders" to make the same commitment they have made, be it to virtue, philosophy or the Christian faith. Nevertheless, there is a potential for considerable blurring of hard and fast distinctions between protrepsis and paraenesis, especially when goodwill is sought between the writer and addressee.

Isocrates

In contrast to writers utilizing the protreptic mode of appeal, Isocrates wrote in the paraenetic mode of address. A number of his discourses to kings and young officials are extant. As noted above, his works provide the literary models for a paraenetic tradition which is encountered throughout the Greco-Roman era in the work both of moralists and epistolarists.

In his works of this temper, Isocrates appeals to ethical standards with which he is sure the recipient is familiar and, indeed, is already following. He wrote two hortatory works in this vein, namely, *To Nicocles* and *Nicocles*, written in King Nicocles' name to his subjects. *To Demonicus*, addressed to a prospective official, is a work attributed to Isocrates. With good reason, Benjamin Fiore argues that these three addresses are letter-like—all three are dialogical in nature, they are written by a friend of the addressee, and profess to be written in a spirit of exhortation and helpful advice.[127]

To Nicocles, with its string of apparently detached maxims, is a loosely constructed discourse of personal exhortation which has the recipient's progress in virtue in his station in life as its aim. The author exhorts and advises the young ruler of Cyprus, Nicocles, whose father Evagorus was the subject of an encomium by Isocrates, to devote his life to the art of being a good king in all its multi-faceted nature. The teaching, as the reader soon discovers, is, in the main, traditional and conventional.

As Nicocles' adviser (§6), Isocrates sets out to lay down precepts most appropriate for one who governs a multitude (§8), and who is seeking to live a life of virtue. Isocrates offers this definition of the function of kings: maintaining and relieving the state in times of prosperity and distress, and making the state "great" when it is "small" (§9).[128] Therefore, it is necessary, writes Isocrates, for kings

> and for you, Nicocles, who surpass all others in rank to surpass them also in the exercise and possession of virtue (ταῖς ἀρεταῖς αὐτῶν διοίσεις, §11).[129]

Association with the wisest and most virtuous of his subjects and of foreign nations is essential (§12).[130] In worship of the gods, following ancestral custom with respect to rites is enjoined. Nevertheless, Isocrates continues:

> [T]he noblest sacrifice and the highest devotion (θεραπεία) is to show yourself in the highest degree a good and just man (§20).

The use of harshness or undue severity is to be avoided when demonstrating one's authority (§24).[131] Avoidance of slavery to pleasure and the need to rule over one's passions more firmly than over one's subjects are urged (§29).[132] One's self-control (σωφροσύνη) stands as an example to one's subjects (§31).[133] Combining courtesy (ἀστειότης) and dignity (σεμνότης) is the kind of outward behavior one should make one's aim (§§34–35).[134]

Isocrates acknowledges the conventional nature of the precepts (see §§40–41). "Do not be surprised (μὴ θαυμάσῃς)," he writes,

> that in what I have said there are many things which you know as well as I (§40).

Novelty is not the purpose of such discourses. It is not possible

> to say what is paradoxical or incredible or outside the circle of accepted belief (ἔξω τῶν νομιζομένων, §41).[135]

"I have offered you all the good counsel I know" (ἐγὼ μὲν οὖν ἅ τε γινώσκω παρῄνεκα, §54), Isocrates concludes. This penchant for reminding recipients of moral exhortation of what they already know is characteristic of the mode. It is a strategy designed to commend the good-will of the author since it implies that the addressee already is fully apprised of his/her moral duty. In other words, the addressee is exhorted as an "insider."

Seneca deals with the question of why one would encourage someone to do those things with which he is already familiar. These are his justifications:

1. whereas we may have been taught what we ought to do, we might not see with sufficient clarity what those things are,
2. emotions hinder us, as does
3. lack of experience in knowing what things we ought to do in particular situations, and
4. our minds may be inactive and untrained in finding the path of duty.[136]

Thus, such advice (*admonitio*), Seneca contends, makes clear what we should do. Moreover, though we may infer from "proofs" what our duties are, precepts also have their place since they clearly define the nature of the duties to which one is called. This characteristic of addressees being reminded of what they already ostensibly know occurs in moral exhortation in the NT and early non-canonical Christian literature with frequency.[137]

The discourse entitled *Nicocles*, written by Isocrates in Nicocles' name, refers to Isocrates' hortatory discourse to the assumed author (*To Nicocles*). *Nicocles* concludes with exhortations on various topics concerning the appropriate behavior of Nicocles' subjects (§§48–64). However, the paraenesis follows a lengthy encomium on the superiority of monarchy as a form of government (§§14–28) and the virtues of Nicocles, who reigns, by virtue of the sanction of gods and men, as the exemplar of a monarch (§§29–47). This is part of the strategy of the assumed author to secure the obedience and cooperation of his subjects for the enjoyment of all manner of blessings in the state (see §§63–64).

The exhortation, *To Demonicus*, attributed to Isocrates, is addressed to another Cypriot. As scholars have noted, the form the paraenesis takes in the discourse belongs, in many instances, to standard ethical τόποι.[138] Moreover, the loose construction of this work, as well as its ethical injunctions and their form, can be effectively compared with *To Nicocles*. The author commences by noting that he has written a παραίνεσις (§5), not mere "protreptic words" (προτρεπτικοὶ λόγοι) designed, as such addresses could be, to encourage the addressed to devote his attention to gaining oratorical proficiency. Rather, the author is interested in the ethical life of the addressed. Virtue (ἀρετή) is long lasting: it is better than riches (§7). Demonicus should recall the example set by his father, who "trained his body by toil, and by his spirit withstood dangers" (§9). It is right to pay devotion to the gods, Isocrates continues, not merely by the performing of sacrifice, but by assiduously keeping one's vows (§13). Adornment that is truly becoming consists in modesty, justice, and self-control.[139] Moreover, what is shameful (αἰσχρός) should not be the subject of conversation (§15).[140] With respect to pleasure, gain, and bursts of temper, Demonicus is to practise self-control (§21).[141] He is not to be quarrelsome (§31). He is to avoid drinking parties (§32).[142] He should obey the laws established by kings (§36). "Do not be surprised," (μὴ θαυμάσῃς) the author adds, if some of these precepts are not applicable just now in his youthful station in life (§44). Underscoring the paraenetical mode he has adopted, the author is confident that the treatise will have its effect, especially in the light of what he has heard about Demonicus' commitment to his general education (§45).[143] However, if the good neglect virtue, he concludes, they can expect to be rebuked (§48). It is worth noting here that the appeal to exemplars, as in the address above (§9), is a commonplace in hortatory literature. These can be both positive and negative.[144]

Nevertheless, the discourse does not play out entirely in the sphere of the conventional and general. Isocrates does appeal to the concrete example of the recipient's father, Hipponicus (see §§9–12). Isocrates himself implies that he, as Hipponicus' friend, is an example of a faithful friend and educator (see §§2–3) in writing to Demonicus, since he "guides students of philosophy" (τοὺς φιλοσοφοῦντας ἐπανορθῶ).

Discourses addressed to kings and officials of the types surveyed above occur frequently, as noted already, in the Greco-Roman hortatory tradition. Dio Chrysostom's first four discourses are on the subject of the exercise of kingship. Plutarch wrote several treatises devoted to the subject of political responsibilities, including the fragmentary *To an Uneducated Ruler*.[145] P. Tebt. 703 (third century B.C.E.) is a memorandum of duties incumbent on an official prescribed by the *dioecetes*.[146] Although the instructions have already been delivered in verbal form before the official embarked on his duties, the writer thought it best to write them down.[147] Of particular interest to me, however, is the fact that the list of responsibilities concludes with moral exhortation, and with the prospect of further advancement should the addressee be faithful in the discharge of his duties:

> I considered that your prime duty is to behave well and be upright in your district, to keep clear of bad company, to avoid (φεύγειν) all base collusion, to believe that, if you are without reproach in this, you will be deserving of higher functions . . . [148]

Letters of Exhortation

Letters of exhortation—both in the paraenetic and protreptic modes, as well as in a mixture of these and other modes—occur mainly in Greco-Roman philosophical literature, much of it extant in pseudonymous collections.

Pseudonymous collections. The collection of thirty-six letters attributed to the Cynic philosopher Crates, e.g., exhibits a wide range of hortatory types, including invective (see *Letters*, 7, 24, 25), reproof (10), and advice (33). A large number are addressed to his students. They fall into the category of ethical and philosophical exhortation. This is expressed in maxims and precepts sanctioned by the sage, whose example is beyond reproach.[149] "Take care of the soul (μελέτω ὑμῖν τῆς ψυχῆς)," Crates urges his students in letter 3, because happiness and indulgence in pleasure are not synonymous.[150] "Flee (φεύγετε) injustice and self-indulgence, and also their causes, pleasures," he writes to them in letter 15, adding:

> [P]ursue (διώκετε) not only the best of goods, self-control (ἐγρατεία) and perseverance (καρτερία), but also their causes, toils (πόνοι), and do not shun them on account of their harshness.[151]

Often Diogenes, Crates' teacher and model, is upheld as the example *par excellence* to follow, as in letters 6, 13, 16, and 17.

The letters of Pythagoras and the Pythagoreans are also pseudonymous. A number of these are written in the paraenetic mode by and to women. The letter *Melissa to Kleareta* concerns the subject of modesty and the dress and adornment proper for women. Beginning with commendation for the noble qualities Kleareta has already acquired, Pseudo-Melissa proceeds to set out requirements for modesty in dress and appearance. The teaching here corresponds for the most part with the precepts of 1 Tim. 2.9–11 and 1 Pet. 3.3–4.[152]

Pliny. The Latin hortatory epistolary literature of the first and early second century C.E. displays traits similar to that noted in the Greek tradition of exhortation. A few examples drawn from the correspondence of Seneca and Pliny will suffice to demonstrate the affinity.

Pliny's letter to Valerius Maximus (ca. 100 C.E.) is an excellent example of the paraenetic letter with roots in the tradition of Isocrates' exhortation on statecraft *To Nicocles* and Pseudo-Isocrates' *To Nicocles*. Valerius is about to commence duties as special commissioner for Achaea, a post to which he was appointed by the emperor.[153] Pliny, as his patron, takes the opportunity to address the exhortation to him. He commences with the conventional:

> I know you need no telling, but my love for you prompts me to remind you to keep in mind and put into practice what you already know, or else it would be better for you to remain ignorant.[154]

The sentiment invites comparison with Rom. 15.14–15. Paul is persuaded that what he has been imparting is indeed known by the addressees, but he writes boldly by way of reminder (ὡς ἐπαναμιμνήσκων) as a "minister" (λειτουργός) of Jesus Christ.[155]

The succeeding string of precepts covers matters such as remembering the reason for which he is being sent and to respect the rights of the Greeks. The Greeks are a free people, Pliny observes, who have maintained that freedom by

> their courage, merits and friendly relationships, and finally by treaty and sanction of religion (§2).

Valerius should, moreover, respect

> the gods their founders, pay regard to their antiquity, their heroic deeds, and their glorious past (§3) . . . ,

remembering what each city once was (§5). As one with authority, he is to remember that he will not be despised unless he wields that authority with meanness and ignobility. Pliny adds that it is a poor thing

> if authority can only test its powers by insults to others, and if homage is to be won by terror (§6).[156]

Finally, Pliny underscores the concrete purpose for which Valerius has been commissioned, namely, to order the constitutions of free cities (§7), and repeats the sentiment that his exhortations are simply a reminder of what he, Valerius, already knows (§10).

Seneca. The letters of Seneca to Lucilius represent the only extant extended ancient correspondence of the tutelage of a *protégé*.[157] The letters derive much of their persuasion from the already existing friendship of the correspondents. I have noted above in the discussion of the nature of letters that the epistolary genre was widely perceived as an extension of the relationship of friendship.[158] In letter 6, e.g., Seneca feels free to be able to share within the bounds of the letter-form something of his own experience of inner transformation for the better through the practice of philosophy. He wishes to foster his relationship with Lucilius in this particular instance so that their already firm friendship may be placed on an even more sure footing (see 6.2).[159]

Also with respect to letter 6 of this corpus, Stowers observes how approximate it is to the Pauline and post-Pauline correspondence in which precepts are not simply set forth but are supported by examples for increased persuasive effect. These examples are derived in many instances from the author's own behavior, as we shall see below.[160] On the value of examples, Seneca ventures the opinion that the way to virtuous living

> is long if one follows precepts (*per praecepta*), but short and helpful, if one follows patterns (*breve et efficax per exempla*, 6.5).

Moreover, he adduces the example of Cleanthes, Plato, Aristotle, and the "whole throng of sages" (6.6) who did not merely hear their masters deliver their lectures but lived the common life with them and learned from observing their character. The correspondence of Seneca (the master) and Lucilius (the student) is analogous to this hallowed and venerable enterprise.

Letter 52 is devoted to the subject of finding models for one's own advancement in virtue. These may be living or past. Seneca urges Lucilius not to seek out men who merely talk about virtue but

> men who teach by their lives, men who tell us what we ought to do and then prove it by practice, who show us what we should avoid, and then are never caught doing what they have ordered us to avoid.[161]

In letter 26 Seneca himself is an example. He mentions his own physical infirmities as a means of exhorting Lucilius to persevere in the way of philosophy. He explains:

> Only my vices, and the outward aids to these vices, have reached senility; my mind is strong and rejoices that it has but slight connection with the body (§2).

In letter 78 Seneca's youthful bouts with sickness, which were so severe as to make him think about suicide, prompt him to inform the addressee, who appears to be suffering the same symptoms, that at such times he was consoled by philosophy. "I owe my life to philosophy," he confesses in §4. His friends also helped him through these difficult times. Their conversation and affection refreshed him. "All these things," he adds,

> gave me the inclination to succor myself and to endure any torture (§4).

It is not hard to perceive the thrust of Seneca's appeal to Lucilius, who would do well to follow Seneca's example.[162]

This letter (78) has much to say about the wise man's endurance through suffering. For this reason the letter is an extremely valuable witness to the value placed on suffering and endurance in the PE.[163] The philosopher does not seek to avoid suffering, but rather welcomes it as inevitable in this world, and as an opportunity for one's virtue and moral worth to be tested. Thus, his intention is to endure in the midst of torment. If he gives way

> he will be vanquished; but if he strives against his sufferings, he will conquer (§15).[164]

Appealing to the example of athletes who endure all kinds of physical sufferings in the interests of being prepared, equipped, and conditioned for their particular sporting endeavor, how much more, writes Seneca, should the philosopher "train" himself for the reward of virtue as he struggles against that which Fortune decrees for him (§16). The mind, he writes elsewhere, should be disciplined "to understand and to endure its own lot."[165] Whatever calamities may be visited upon the sage, we must not cry out against any of them, because "into such a world have we been born."[166]

Seneca also regards poverty as an honorable estate, if those who endure it are content. He asks: What is the proper limit of wealth? His answer, also reminiscent of the PE, is the observation:

It is first, to have what is necessary, and, second, to have what is enough.[167]

The friendship of Seneca and Lucilius does not rule out the master's writing reproachfully.[168] Letter 48 is such a letter. Seneca accuses Lucilius of indulging in logical hair-splitting. The letter commences, however, with a reminder of the nature of friendship as a true partnership effecting the interests of both parties. Seneca offers his reproach in the spirit of friendship, and concludes on the note of protreptic appeal to Lucilius to re-commit himself to the task of pursuing philosophy in fellowship with his master.

Ignatius. The letter of Ignatius to Polycarp has been rightly heralded as providing the closest analogy to the PE.[169] Ignatius wrote this personal paraenetic letter to Polycarp, Bishop of Smyrna, on his way to Rome and eventual martyrdom. Wolter draws attention to the fact that the letter, like the PE, addresses an individual with respect not only to his own personal piety but to his oversight of the various constituencies of his charge. Unlike the PE, however, the letter also explicitly exhorts the congregation (see ch. 6). The brief letter begins, as do many other paraenetic letters, with affirmation of the addressee.[170] At the conclusion of the letter, Ignatius, in keeping with paraenetic convention, also underscores the esteem in which he holds the addressee:

I exhort you by no more than these few lines, for I recognize your fervor for the truth.[171]

In the body of the letter, athletic imagery abounds in exhortation directed to Polycarp and the congregation. Polycarp is exhorted to "press forward on your course" (προσθεῖναι τῷ δρόμῳ σου, 1.2), to bear the "sicknesses" of all as the "perfect athlete" (ὡς τέλειος ἀθλητής, 1.3), to be sober as God's athlete (νῆφε, ὡς θεοῦ ἀθλητής, 2.3[172]) and to suffer punishment, as is the task of great athletes, and yet conquer (3.1). The congregation is exhorted to labor together (συγκοπιᾶτε), struggle together (συναθλεῖτε), run together (συντρέχετε), to suffer together (συνπάσχετε, 6.1), and, to change the imagery, to be pleasing to him "in whose ranks you serve" (ἀρέσκετε ᾧ στρατεύεσθε, 6.2).[173] The athletic imagery is precisely the imagery one encounters in the paraenetic letter tradition as exemplified in Seneca.[174] Moreover, Polycarp is exhorted to be gentle with the more troublesome of his congregation as a means to win them over (see 2.1).[175] There is much in this letter which is obviously reminiscent of the PE.

Turning to the NT materials, Klaus Berger defines paraenesis as exhortation, which, as far as content is concerned, concerns itself with traditional and conventional norms of living.[176] The themes of such discourse, he writes, are loosely connected syntactically. The function of such material is to elicit remembrance of these general behavioral norms. NT paraenesis deals with responsibilities towards society at large and towards members of the Christian community, sexual ethics, the renunciation of retaliation, power, and luxury, the acceptance of difficulties such as oppression, poverty, and suffering, instruction for the newly converted, leadership duties, warnings, and virtue and vice lists.[177]

While Berger's examination of the kinds of NT materials is exhaustive, his understanding, however, does not allow sufficiently for the concretization of paraenesis. This is apparent even in the discourses of Isocrates which are often held up wrongly as examples *par excellence* of exhortation in the general and non-specific mode.

Defining Characteristics. This section has concentrated on the Greco-Roman tradition of moral exhortation, especially in the form of its embodiment in letters. I have spent considerable time investigating letters and discourses exhorting kings, officials, and subjects in their duties because the PE are ostensibly written by a superior to inferiors concerning the duties the assumed author has bestowed upon them.

Based on the work of scholars such as Stanley Stowers, Abraham Malherbe, and other scholars whose work has been reviewed so far, the following conclusions regarding the characteristics of hortatory and advising letters can now be offered as way of preparing the way for an examination of the PE as letters standing within this tradition:

1. Letters of moral exhortation are written by a superior to one who is an inferior in terms of social rank or moral attainment;

2. There is an already existing relationship of friendship between writer and recipient. Such letters, therefore, evidence φιλοφρόνησις, ὁμιλία, and παρουσία;

3. The writer often exhorts by way of reminder. The content of the exhortation, whether the duties of statecraft, or officialdom, or moral duties in general are in view, is often conventional and traditional, but can also be concrete, specific, and occasional;

4. The use of examples, both positive and negative, enhance the persuasive dynamic of the exhortation. The writer him/herself often poses as an example to the recipient.

A fifth element can also be isolated, though it should not be regarded as definitive for the genre of the letter of exhortation. Letters of moral exhortation sometimes use other modes of exhortation in a subsidiary manner. These modes include protrepsis, admonition, rebuke, and consolation. These are employed to further enhance the writer's purpose of moral guidance or psychagogy.

D. THE PE AS LETTERS OF MORAL EXHORTATION

The analysis which follows investigates the shape of the hortatory texture the author created in the PE with respect to the first four of the characteristics nominated above. I shall also address the relationship of the fifth to the PE.

Superior to Inferior

In the tradition of letters of moral exhortation, a superior writes to an inferior. In the case of the PE, the assumed author is the apostle Paul while the assumed recipients are his emissaries Timothy and Titus. We have already had cause to note the fact that the PE, as letters standing self-consciously in the Pauline letter-writing tradition, present Paul as an apostle, the self-identification he adopted in the rest of the Pauline corpus (see, e.g., Rom. 1.1; 1 Cor. 1.1; Eph. 1.1). As an apostle, Paul was acutely aware of his role in the effecting of the purposes of God. He had been called and set aside by divine command (κατ' ἐπιταγὴν θεοῦ, 1 Tim. 1.1; Tit. 1.3; cf. 2 Tim. 1.1). And, yet, he is also a "slave" of God (δοῦλος θεοῦ, Tit. 1.1; cf. Rom. 1.1; Gal. 1.10; Phil. 1.1), one who cannot please himself, but is found doing the will of his master. His authority derives from both his apostleship and his servanthood. As apostle, Paul knows himself to be set apart for the establishing of the purposes of God wherever the gospel is preached and people respond positively. As "slave of God/Christ" he is conscious both of his relationship of exclusive service and loyalty to God/Christ and the suffering and humiliation with which his life for the churches in his apostolic care has often been characterized.

The PE, as I have already argued in section B of this chapter, sharpen the authority of Paul for the churches to whom the Pastor is writing. Not only is Paul presented as the only apostle, his sufferings as δοῦλος θεοῦ have increased to the point where he is on the point of being executed, ready to be "sacrificed" in the service of his Master. Consequently, Paul, as the superior writing to his emissaries, can plead not only his apostleship but also his sufferings for the sake of the gospel with which he has been entrusted. At the end of his life, the Paul of the PE is able to address the churches in his care through their apostolic delegates. He is one who has spent his life, and been spent, in the service of the gospel. Moreover, he can summon Timothy and Titus as trusted associates to take up the task of maintaining and securing the legacy of Paul. This legacy comprises the message of God mediated directly to the apostle (see 1 Tim. 1.12; 2 Tim. 1.11–14) as well as the compendium of teachings and directives associated with Paul in the tradition.

If this is the picture of the assumed writer, the "superior," of the PE, who are Timothy and Titus? What is the form of the relationship each has with Paul? What were their roles in the Pauline corpus and in the tradition received by the Pauline churches addressed by the Pastor?[178]

Timothy is associated with Paul in the superscripts of 2 Cor. 1.1, Phil. 1.1, Col. 1.1, and Phlm. 1, and with Paul and Silvanus in 1 Thess. 1.1 and 2 Thess. 1.1. Victor P. Furnish argues persuasively that the association of Timothy does not indicate that he was Paul's secretary or that he was the co-author of these letters. Rather, such an association, as Phil. 2.2 eloquently testifies, suggests that Timothy was highly regarded by Paul as one who had shown great loyalty and service to him. Indeed, in 2 Cor. 1.19 Timothy, together with Paul and Silvanus, is mentioned as a preacher of the gospel to the Corinthians (cf. Acts 18.5). The device is also a means by which the recipients are assured that Timothy, an associate of Paul they know well, continues to care for them.[179]

Paul's association with Timothy may be traced in the NT to Acts 16.1–3. Now, it is a moot point whether the Pastor knows Acts or not.[180] The references to Timothy's upbringing and family life in 2 Tim. 1.5–7 are certainly not out of keeping with the account recorded in Acts 16. Moreover, Paul's farewell address (*Abschiedsrede*) in Acts 20.18–35 is reminiscent of several passages in the PE, especially 1 Tim. 4.1–3, 2 Tim. 3.1–9 and 4.3–4.[181] Intriguingly, however, when Paul refers in 2 Tim. 3.10–11 to the sufferings he endured in his missionary journeys, and which Timothy "had followed closely" (παρηκολούθησας, v. 10), he alludes to experiences which might conceivably have been known to the PE from Acts 13 and 14. But Acts places these *before* Paul's association with Timothy, i.e., before he had the advantage of being not only a "follower" of such matters but an eye-witness.[182] One would have expected Paul to have alluded to deprivations both he and Timothy might have experienced *together*, of which Acts furnishes many examples.[183] Moreover, and this is a substantial difference, Acts does not number Paul among the apostles, whereas Paul is the sole apostle for the PE.[184] In the light of the lack of clear and unambiguous evidence, it is best, therefore, that we assume that the author does not know Acts, and confine our attention to the Pauline corpus.

On a number of occasions in the Pauline corpus Timothy is designated an emissary of the apostle.[185] Tychicus (Eph. 6.21; Col. 4.7), Onesimus (Col. 4.9), and Titus are also entrusted with this responsibility. A brief discussion of a number of relevant passages follows:

> 1 Cor. 4.16–17
> παρακαλῶ οὖν ὑμᾶς, μιμηταί μου γίνεσθε. διὰ τοῦτο ἔπεμψα ὑμῖν Τιμόθεον, ὅς ἐστίν μου τέκνον ἀγαπητὸν καὶ πιστὸν ἐν κυρίῳ, ὃς ὑμᾶς ἀναμνήσει τὰς ὁδούς μου τὰς ἐν Χριστῷ ['Ιησοῦ], καθὼς πανταχοῦ ἐν πάσῃ ἐκκλησίᾳ διδάσκω.

This is a particularly significant passage for understanding the assumed relationship between Paul and Timothy. One notes the designation of Timothy as "beloved child" (τέκνον ἀγαπητόν) with its implication (note 1 Cor. 4.15) of Paul as "father" (πατήρ).[186] In the PE, this nurturing relationship is clearly mirrored. In the Corinthian situation, Timothy's task is to bring about remembrance of Paul's way of life in order that the Corinthians "might continue" in the task of emulating their "father." Here, of course, Paul is using a common convention of the paraenetic letter-writing tradition, reminding his charges of what they already know. The imagery of father/son and father/children is also common to the tradition of moral exhortation. It is also found in other passages of the Pauline corpus, such as 1 Thess. 2.11.[187] One even encounters maternal imagery in Gal. 4.19.[188] However, the father/son imagery is not confined to the Greco-Roman context. It is used in the literature of the sapiential tradition of the master/disciple relationship of the Hebrew Bible and early Judaism, including the Qumran writings, especially where the transmission of wisdom from the sage is concerned.[189]

In the greetings of the PE both recipients are termed "child."[190] The attributive "true" (γνήσιος) refers to legitimacy.[191] Indeed, Quinn and other scholars rightly contend that the term, especially when "in the faith" (ἐν πίστει) is added (see 1 Tim. 1.2; cf. Tit. 1.4), has a polemical edge. None other than the apostle Paul is their "father." There is nothing spurious about their grasp of the faith. They bear the image and likeness of their spiritual father.[192] The implication of the term for the testamentary overtones of the PE will be discussed in section E of this chapter.

1 Cor. 16.10–11
ἐὰν δὲ ἔλθῃ Τιμόθεος, βλέπετε ἵνα ἀφόβως γένηται πρὸς ὑμᾶς, τὸ γὰρ ἔργον κυρίου ἐργάζεται ὡς κἀγώ· μή τις οὖν αὐτὸν ἐξουθενήσῃ. προπέμψατε δὲ αὐτὸν ἐν εἰρήνῃ, ἵνα ἔλθῃ πρός με, ἐκδέχομαι γὰρ αὐτὸν μετὰ τῶν ἀδελφῶν.

In this passage, Timothy is on the point of being sent by Paul to the Corinthians. Nothing is to cause Timothy discomfort, Paul directs, in his stay among them. For, Paul writes, he, "like me," is doing the "work of the Lord" (ἔργον κυρίου). In fact, the Corinthians are to treat him as they would treat Paul himself. They are directed to send him back to Paul "in peace." The intrusion of the idea of apostolic parousia here is most interesting. Timothy, sent by Paul, who expects him back with a report, is the manifestation of the apostle's presence (parousia) (cf. 1 Thess. 3.2 below).

The use of ἐξουθενέω in this passage suggests the similar use of καταφρονέω in 1 Tim. 4.12.[193] The PE portray Timothy as a young man, whose "youth" provides the pretext for detractors to disdain him.[194]

1 Thess. 3.2
καὶ ἐπέμψαμεν Τιμόθεον, τὸν ἀδελφὸν ἡμῶν καὶ συνεργὸν τοῦ θεοῦ ἐν τῷ εὐαγγελίῳ τοῦ Χριστοῦ, εἰς τὸ στηρίξαι ὑμᾶς καὶ παρακαλέσαι ὑπὲρ τῆς πίστεως ὑμῶν

Here Paul is sending his delegate, Timothy, back to the Thessalonians to strengthen and encourage them in their faith. He is termed familiarly as "our brother" (ὁ ἀδελφὸς ἡμῶν), common in the plural in Paul as a designation of believers, but used in the singular of those especially esteemed by the apostle.[195] As one who is closely associated with Paul in the work of the gospel he also calls him "God's fellow worker" (συνεργὸς τοῦ θεοῦ).[196] The term συνεργός is also encountered in 1 Cor. 3.9 in which Paul designates himself as well as Apollos συνεργοὶ τοῦ θεοῦ.

Phil. 2.19–22
ἐλπίζω δὲ ἐν κυρίῳ 'Ιησοῦ Τιμόθεον ταχέως πέμψαι ὑμῖν, ἵνα κἀγὼ εὐψυχῶ γνοὺς τὰ περὶ ὑμῶν. οὐδένα γὰρ ἔχω ἰσόψυχον ὅστις γνησίως τὰ περὶ ὑμῶν μεριμνήσει, οἱ πάντες γὰρ τὰ ἑαυτῶν ζητοῦσιν, οὐ τὰ 'Ιησοῦ Χριστοῦ. τὴν δὲ δοκιμὴν αὐτοῦ γινώσκετε, ὅτι ὡς πατρὶ τέκνον σὺν ἐμοὶ ἐδούλευσεν εἰς τὸ εὐαγγέλιον.

This passage again demonstrates the esteem in which Timothy is held by Paul. Paul knows that he will sustain Paul's own pastoral care for them even though he cannot be there in person. Indeed, the apostle has no one like Timothy in this regard. In this respect, even if in no other, Timothy is the very image of the apostle himself and represents Paul's presence with the Philippians. Moreover, Timothy is single-mindedly fixed on "the interests of Jesus Christ" (τὰ 'Ιησοῦ Χριστοῦ).

One recalls the nurturing imagery of 1 Thess. 2.1–12 in which Paul rehearses the guileless and non-demanding mode in which the apostolic band (including Timothy) first came among the Thessalonians. By contrast with the "superior apostles" of 2 Corinthians, Paul abased himself, refusing to be a burden to any of the believers there (2 Cor. 11.7–11; 12.13). Moreover, neither he nor his associates, including

Titus, took advantage of them (see 12.14–18).

As we have seen in Phil. 2.22, Paul regards Timothy as a son; Paul is his father. Not only are we dealing here with an intimate personal relationship but one in which Timothy is closely related to Paul's apostolic authority. This is a vital issue in the PE. Paul reminds Timothy and Titus of their charge to guard the apostle's deposit and sustain the "work of God" (ἔργον τοῦ θεοῦ) Paul has begun and is now, especially in 2 Timothy, bequeathing to faithful fellow-workers.

In contrast to the wealth of material on Timothy to be gleaned from the Pauline corpus, Titus, on the other hand, is only mentioned in 2 Corinthians and Galatians. In the latter, he appears as a Gentile believer whom Paul took to Jerusalem. He is, therefore, an important witness for Paul's establishing the credentials of his law-free gospel (see Gal. 2.1, 3).[197] However, in 2 Corinthians we glimpse something of the esteem in which Paul held this otherwise rather shadowy figure. In Troas, a town in which an opening for the gospel had been opened up, Paul had expected to find Titus, "my brother" (ὁ ἀδελφός μου). Not finding him—indeed Paul's mind cannot rest because he did not find him—he moved on to Macedonia. Thus Paul surrendered an opportunity to preach the gospel at Troas because Titus was not there. His reasons for hastening on are probably meant to indicate to the Corinthians his desire to hear Titus' report of the situation in Corinth.[198] His arrival, recorded in 2 Cor. 7.6, does in fact give relief to Paul, not only because he is re-united with his associate but because of his news about the Corinthian church. Titus' news is good (7.7). Paul notes with evident joy how the Corinthians, who had fallen out with their apostle, were now repenting. Paul uses terminology in 7.7 and v. 11 which one might interpret as the Corinthians' "longing" (ἐπιπόθησις) for the parousia of the apostle in their midst.[199]

Titus is to return to Corinth to complete the work of the collection (see 8.6, 17)—no easy task. As Rom. 15.25–27 as well as 2 Corinthians 8–9 make clear, Paul regards the collection not only as an opportunity for more wealthy believers to aid the poor saints of Jerusalem but as an essential and defining factor in the exercise of his apostleship to the Gentiles.[200]

In 2 Cor. 8.23 Paul calls Titus his "fellow worker" (συνεργός) and "partner" (κοινωνός). The latter term is echoed in the greeting of Tit.

1.4 (Τίτῳ . . . κατὰ κοινὴν πίστιν). The term συνεργός is accorded Timothy in Rom. 16.21 and 1 Thess. 3.2. Indeed, Titus is encountered, once more in the office of delegate, in the closing verses of 2 Timothy (ἐπορεύθη . . . Τίτος εἰς Δαλματίαν, 4.10).[201]

Timothy and Titus, therefore, emerge from the Pauline corpus as trusted fellow-workers of the apostle.[202] They are clearly in a subordinate relationship to Paul, for it is he who charges them with the office of delegate. Nevertheless, apostolic delegates are vital for the maintenance of Paul's apostolic claim over the churches as Pastor and "founding-father." That these two associates should be addressees of the PE does not surprise given their already faithful service recorded, with the apostle's grateful imprimatur, in the Pauline corpus. It was service which the apostle, the historical Paul, had acknowledged and to which he had declared his indebtedness. This, then, is the relationship presupposed in the PE between assumed author and assumed recipients, between superior and inferior.

Friendship between Writer and Recipient

In examining the superior/inferior relationship between writer and addressee in the PE as letters of moral exhortation, I also discussed at some length the contours of the existing relationship presupposed between Paul and his associates in the PE. However, as friendship letters more can be said about the PE than already broached.

Philophronesis. The intimacy of each of the greetings is supplemented by other material similar in tone. This is especially noticeable in 2 Timothy. In 1.3 Paul assures Timothy that he is constantly in his prayers. If they are separated from each other, Timothy is present (πάρων) in the prayers of the apostle. Paul remembers Timothy's tears at their leave-taking (v. 4; cf. 1 Tim. 1.3), the evidence of the parting of intimates. He longs "night and day" to see Timothy that he might be filled with joy.[203] This brings Paul to recall the faith of Timothy, and the faith of the women of the family circle from which Timothy has come. This reminiscence is a particularly poignant one, and it gives Paul an effective opening for reminding Timothy of his sober responsibilities as his delegate (see 1.6). At the conclusion of the letter Paul urges him to come soon (4.9), and to come before winter (4.21).

Parousia. The theme of the apostolic parousia, noted above with respect to Paul's desire for Timothy to come to him (2 Tim. 4.9), is also to be encountered elsewhere in the PE. In 1 Tim. 3.14, it is Paul who hopes to come to Timothy soon. If delayed, he writes in 3.15, Timothy will know how people ought to behave in the household of God by the instructions he is conveying.[204] In 2 Tim. 4.9 Tychicus has already been sent to Ephesus, thus allowing Timothy to come to Paul. In Tit. 3.12 Paul intends to send Artemas or Tychicus, requesting Titus' presence with him in Nicopolis for the winter. Zenas and Apollos, presumably delegates sent by Paul at some earlier date, are to be sent speedily on their way.[205] By contrast, the assumed author of 2 Tim. 4.9 requires the presence of Timothy since all others, except Luke (v. 11), have either deserted him or are currently employed elsewhere as his emissaries (v. 10).

Homilia. 2 Timothy is especially conversational and intimate in its address to Timothy. We have already noted Paul's desire to see Timothy again (2 Tim. 1.4; 4.9). There are many reminders in the PE of the charge Paul delivered to Timothy in person (1 Tim. 1.3; 2 Tim. 1.13; 2.2; cf. Tit. 1.5). The letters function as extensions or supplements, as well as re-applications, of the initial verbal instructions.[206]

The series of "faithful words" (πιστοὶ λόγοι) found in 1 Tim. 1.15, 3.1, 4.9, 2 Tim. 2.11 and Tit. 3.8 should also be assessed as initially verbal traditions. They stem from the assumed author, the fellowship of like-minded men, or are transmitted by them from earlier sources. The authority of these sayings is unquestioned. They have to do not only with Christological and soteriological truth (1 Tim. 1.15) but with the exercise of godliness (1 Tim. 4.9; 2 Tim. 2.11; Tit. 3.8) and church order (1 Tim. 3.1–13). Perhaps, as apparently fixed statements, they were used liturgically in the Pauline congregations of the PE.[207]

It is true to say that the PE, as letters, represent the extension of the conversation of the apostle with his trusted "friends" and delegates, and, through them, to the congregations in their care.

Exhortation by Reminder

Letters of moral exhortation deliver their paraenesis often by way of reminder. The convention can be observed in the PE. The body of both

1 Timothy and Titus begins with reminders of the charge bestowed on them by the apostle (1 Tim. 1.3–4; Tit. 1.5). This reminder is particularly urgent in the former letter, coming as it does before the thanksgiving of 1.12–16. This feature of reminding the addressee of the task to which he/she has been committed or assigned as has already been noted in the Greco-Roman letters already surveyed. Indeed, 1 Tim. 1.18 repeats the initial apostolic charge. Here Paul reminds Timothy of the prophetic oracles that singled him out.

The reminder in 2 Tim. 1.6 is a clear evocation of 1 Tim. 1.18 with its note of the gift of God already bestowed on Timothy and now to be fanned into flame by him for application to the task ahead. The calling to mind of his "sincere faith," together with that of his grandmother and mother, is a particularly powerful exhortation to Timothy because it implies not only that he has been set aside for the task by God himself (through the gift of his Spirit) but that he possesses inherited aptitude, as it were, from two generations of women in his family for the faithful discharge of his duties in maintaining the legacy of the apostle. Paul, who knows these women, is also a witness of Timothy's aptitude and spiritual gifts through the laying on of his hands. Moreover, he encourages Timothy in v. 7 (using the inclusive first person plural):

> οὐ γὰρ ἔδωκεν ἡμῖν ὁ θεὸς πνεῦμα δειλίας, ἀλλὰ δυνάμεως καὶ ἀγάπης καὶ σωφρονισμοῦ.

In turn, Timothy is to remind his hearers of what they know. Speaking of the example of Jesus Christ (2.8) as the exemplar of the kind of perseverance and commitment commended in 2.1–7 (cf. 1 Tim. 6.11–13), Paul exhorts Timothy to remind his people to aspire to the same whole-hearted life-commitment (2 Tim. 2.14). For, as Paul says in 2.11–13, the issue of faithfulness and endurance has decided implications for eschatological reward, a reward that is guaranteed by Christ himself.

In 2 Tim. 3.10–11 Paul reminds Timothy:

> σὺ δὲ παρηκολούθησάς μου τῇ διδασκαλίᾳ, τῇ ἀγωγῇ, τῇ προθέσει, τῇ πίστει, τῇ μακροθυμίᾳ, τῇ ἀγάπῃ, τῇ ὑπομονῇ, τοῖς διωγμοῖς, τοῖς παθήμασιν, οἷά μοι ἐγένετο ἐν Ἀντιοχείᾳ, ἐν Ἰκονίῳ, ἐν Λύστροις, οἵους διωγμοὺς ὑπήνεγκα· καὶ ἐκ πάντων με ἐρρύσατο ὁ κύριος.

While we shall have cause to return to this passage below, it should be pointed out that Timothy, as an eyewitness and as one who had "followed closely" (παρακολουθέω),[208] was singularly blessed in having access as an associate and eye-witness to the type of guardian of the deposit the Pastor regarded as absolutely necessary for the protection of the Pauline communities.[209] Paul is the embodiment of such a guardian. He had received the gospel from Christ himself and kept it secure. After holding up a negative example of the certain regress in virtue of "evil men and imposters," the Pastor continues in the following vein in 2 Tim. 3.14–15:

> σὺ δὲ μένε ἐν οἷς ἔμαθες καὶ ἐπιστώθης, εἰδὼς παρὰ τίνων ἔμαθες, καὶ ὅτι ἀπὸ βρέφους [τὰ] ἱερὰ γράμματα οἶδας, τὰ δυνάμενά σε σοφίσαι εἰς σωτηρίαν διὰ πίστεως τῆς ἐν Χριστῷ Ἰησοῦ.

Here, once again, we meet the phenomenon, frequently encountered in the Greco-Roman letters, of the exhortation to continue in what the addressee already knows. Its occurrence here picks up the theme of Timothy's childhood and the marvellous opportunities he has had to be acquainted with all that is necessary for salvation and for faithful service of the gospel. The links with 2 Tim. 1.5–6 are manifestly clear.

The body of the letter to Titus commences with a reminder of the initial directive Paul had given the addressee (see 1.5). A further reminder, this time concerning the appropriate social behavior incumbent upon believers, is issued to the people through Titus in 3.1–2 (cf. 2 Tim. 2.14).

This is not to say that there is no new instruction in the PE. The *Kirchenordnung* of 1 Tim. 2.1–3.13 should be regarded as a substantial supplementing of the assumed author's initial charge, especially in the light of 1 Tim. 3.14–15:

> ταῦτά σοι γράφω, ἐλπίζων ἐλθεῖν πρὸς σὲ ἐν τάχει· ἐὰν δὲ βραδύνω, ἵνα εἰδῇς πῶς δεῖ ἐν οἴκῳ θεοῦ ἀναστρέφεσθαι, ἥτις ἐστὶν ἐκκλησία θεοῦ ζῶντος, στῦλος καὶ ἑδραίωμα τῆς ἀληθείας.

However, the similar material in Tit. 1.6–9 is presented as a rehearsal of the original commission (see v. 5).

As we have seen, the content of the exhortations in the Greco-Roman letters can follow a traditional and conventional format. Although moral exhortation may be general or concrete, when one compares the exhortations emanating from the earlier classical and Greco-Roman eras there is nothing new in the virtues commended as appropriate to the situation of life of the recipient.

What makes the PE such a contentious corpus in NT studies is that since the early nineteenth century scholars have detected a radical shift from the ethical insights of the undisputed Pauline letters to the moral exhortation urged on the addressees in the PE. In the undisputed letters, Paul, it is rightly claimed, was motivated by a lively sense of the imminence of the parousia. He placed a high priority on justification by faith as setting the tone of ecclesial fellowship, especially where Jews and Gentiles found themselves together in the same "body." He perceived that the break with the Jewish law had radical implications for relationships between once-divided people (see Gal. 3.28). The effect of these insights amounted to the engendering of largely non-conventional and non-traditional expressions of social interaction in the Pauline communities. From both the Jewish and Greco-Roman points of view, these expressions cut across racial, gender, and social mores. All this Paul celebrated, though not without reservation lest social conventions be undermined.[210] The PE, on the other hand, inculcate traditional values not just within the family but in the exercise of ministries in the church.

What is perceived to be the case with the PE and more traditional morality has long been observed in Ephesians and Colossians also. Indeed, one of the reasons why these two letters have been regarded as deutero-Pauline is their use of so-called "household codes" (*Haustafeln*) in Col. 3.18–4.1 and Eph. 5.22–6.9 with their schema of reciprocal duties for the various constituents according to the Hellenistic and Greco-Roman household structure. Here is evidence, it is fairly argued, that, for all their preparedness to adapt the codes along Christian lines, the Pauline churches of the immediate post-Pauline era are coming to terms with the structures and conventions of society. This strategy is intentionally promoted by the authors of the post-Pauline letters. Paul has departed the scene; the expectation of an *imminent* parousia is waning; the churches are coming to terms with the need to co-exist with the wider society.[211]

In the PE this same process is going on, though at a more advanced stage. Margaret MacDonald insightfully terms the PE as monuments to the process of "community-protection institutionalization."[212] This can be seen in the explicit silencing of women teachers in the congregations of the PE and the address to embryonic orders of ministers in the household of God. Martin Dibelius has been credited with the idea that the Pastor is inculcating the ideals of a "bourgeois" Christianity (*bürgerliches Christentum*). The hope of an imminent parousia and the inbreaking of the Kingdom of God has been replaced by the stance of accommodation with and conformity to prevailing conventional mores. The Pauline communities standing self-consciously in this heritage are being exhorted to live out their life in society.

Responses to this reading of the PE have picked up pace in the last decade. Roland Schwarz, Philip H. Towner, and Reggie M. Kidd all address the issues raised by Dibelius concerning the ethical stance of the PE. All three have made the challenge of responding to him a major concern of their respective monographs. Nevertheless, although Dibelius' views warrant modification in the light of the research of recent scholarship, he did demonstrate that, at a number of points, the Pastor and Paul have different ethical agendas for their communities. The hellenistic ethical terminology—the language of the virtues—encountered in the post-Pauline corpus is not Paul's. The ecclesiological structure of the churches of the PE has evolved beyond the charismatic and occasional leadership exercised in the Pauline communities as he knew them. The church of the PE understands itself as having a future in society. The PE are coming to terms with a second epiphany of Christ which may yet be many generations distant in time. The contingency plan calls for securing the Pauline legacy for future generations, not just because the future may be long but because of serious challenges from false teachers whose work is already bearing fruit in the congregations.[213]

Roland Schwarz argues that the PE do not adopt the stance Dibelius characterized as "bourgeois" Christianity in their commendation of virtue and quiet living.[214] Neither is it the case that the church is trying to come to terms with the allegedly delayed parousia. Rather, the threat posed by the false teachers has necessitated the formulation of ethical ideals by the author in the language of Greco-Roman ethical convention.[215] The injunction of 1 Tim. 2.2 concerning quiet living is amply paralleled in the wisdom literature of the Hebrew Bible and early Judaism in which this mode of existence is regarded as an ethical ideal.[216] Moreover, the church finds itself unable to accept the ascetic, world-denying practices of the false teachers. Significant for Schwarz is the fact that the Christian life is presented in the PE as the expression of gospel reception, i.e., the ethics of the PE are anchored in the gospel of the death and resurrection of Christ.[217]

Philip Towner's reading of the ethical stance of the PE in his *The Goal of Our Instruction* amounts to a particularly sustained attack on Dibelius' views. Without actually contending for Pauline authorship, Towner finds nothing of consequence that commends the PE as post-Pauline. Moreover, the ethics and theology of the PE are compared with the remainder of the Pauline corpus, all the letters of which are regarded as genuine by Towner. Throughout his monograph, he argues that what Dibelius and Conzelmann considered accommodationist and "bourgeois" in the PE is to be interpreted as the author's concern lest the congregations of the letters fail in their missionary endeavor by causing undue offence to their neighbors. Towner sees the PE as committed to a missionary enterprise which will otherwise fail. Dibelius and Conzelmann would prefer, I suspect, to call the PE's injunctions to good Christian citizenship a strategy for survival in the light of the unexpected continuation of history in which the communities of the PE find themselves.

Reggie Kidd's monograph, *Wealth and Beneficence in the Pastoral Epistles*, is more germane to my task. Whereas Towner reads the paraenesis of the PE in a straight-forward manner preferring to accept the authorship/addressee situation generated in the letters as an actual one between Paul and his delegates, Kidd accepts the double pseudonymity of the PE. Moreover, he perceptively analyzes the social setting of the PE. He seeks to elucidate how the wealthy members of the congregations would have heard the PE. I shall return to Kidd's analysis of this issue below.

David Verner's *Household of God* underscores the fact that the paraenesis of 1 Timothy and, to a lesser extent, Titus is directed along the lines of the duties commended in the *Haustafeln*. According to 1 Tim. 3.15, the church is actually conceived in household terms. Here the Pastor writes:

> ἐὰν δὲ βραδύνω, ἵνα εἰδῇς πῶς δεῖ ἐν οἴκῳ θεοῦ ἀναστρέφεσθαι, ἥτις ἐστὶν ἐκκλησία θεοῦ ζῶντος, στῦλος καὶ ἑδραίωμα τῆς ἀληθείας.

Under the image of the οἶκος θεοῦ Paul addresses its various constituents—men, women, leaders, widows, the wealthy, slaves—through his delegate into whose charge the οἶκος has been delivered. Thus 1 Timothy and Titus resemble the paraenetic discourses and letters surveyed earlier in which the author exhorts the addressee—perhaps a monarch, statesman, or family member—with respect to their duties and responsibilities in their official capacity. Not without significance here is the summons to official duty in 1 Tim. 4.13–15 (my italics):

> *πρόσεχε* τῇ ἀναγνώσει, τῇ παρακλήσει, τῇ διδασκαλίᾳ. *μὴ ἀμέλει* τοῦ ἐν σοὶ χαρίσματος, ὃ ἐδόθη σοι διὰ προφητείας μετὰ ἐπιθέσεως τῶν χειρῶν τοῦ πρεσβυτερίου. ταῦτα *μελέτα*, ἐν τούτοις *ἴσθι* . . .[218]

The personal paraenesis of these two letters is also paralleled in the relevant Greco-Roman materials since the writer knows that personal exercise of and progress towards virtue is the foundation of successfully fulfilling one's responsibilities. On the other hand, 2 Timothy, resembles the letters of Seneca to Lucilius in which personal exhortation predominates. Official duties are not far removed in 2 Timothy, however. Timothy is directed and exhorted to maintain and secure the Pauline heritage. This is a matter of great moment because it requires as leader and teacher a truly Pauline persona (see, e.g., 1 Tim. 4.11) to effect such a guarding of the deposit.

What might one say about the content of the paraenesis directed to the various orders in the οἶκος θεοῦ? Much of it follows the τόπος pattern suggested by Terence Y. Mullins, namely, injunction, reason, and discussion with respect to some independent moral issue or subject.[219] Indeed, as already noted, the exhortation of 1 Timothy and Titus is indebted to the τόπος on household management which grew out of Aristotle's discussion of the household in his *Politics*, and is particularly evident in neo-Pythagorean sources, as David Balch has argued.[220] What follows below is a brief analysis of three paraenetic *topoi* in 1 Timothy, namely, 1 Tim. 2.1–7 (directed to all members of the household), 2.8–15 (directed to men and women), and 6.17–19 (directed to the wealthy).

In 1 Timothy the household paraenesis begins with a *topos* directed to all members of the household on the subject of proper respect for authorities. The injunction, given in the indicative mood in vv. 1–2a, requests prayer for all in authority, including kings and all in high positions, followed in v. 2b by the reason:

> ἵνα ἤρεμον καὶ ἡσύχιον βίον διάγωμεν ἐν πάσῃ εὐσεβείᾳ καὶ σεμνότητι.

The hellenistic tone of this injunction can be observed in the reference to the virtues of godliness (εὐσέβεια) and gravity (σεμνότης). Living a "quiet life" in "godliness" and "gravity" sums up for Dibelius all that is "bourgeois" about the Christianity of the PE. The Pastor is seeking to inculcate the ideals so highly esteemed in his culture.[221]

Moreover, the parallels with Rom. 13.1–5 and 1 Pet. 2.13–17, also in *topos* form, are striking. In the latter passage, the reason given in v. 15 is similar to that given by the Pastor, since such behavior is motivated by what others in society might think:

> ὅτι οὕτως ἐστὶν τὸ θέλημα τοῦ θεοῦ, ἀγαθοποιοῦντας φιμοῦν τὴν τῶν ἀφρόνων ἀνθρώπων ἀγνωσίαν.

However, the reason for being subject to governing authorities in Rom. 13.1b–2 is decidedly eschatological in its outlook and provides motivation at the level of appealing to the wrath of God against all, including believers, who resist the order he has established in this age:

> οὐ γὰρ ἔστιν ἐξουσία εἰ μὴ ὑπὸ θεοῦ, αἱ δὲ οὖσαι ὑπὸ θεοῦ τεταγμέναι εἰσίν· ὥστε ὁ ἀντιτασσόμενος τῇ ἐξουσίᾳ τῇ τοῦ θεοῦ διαταγῇ ἀνθέστηκεν, οἱ δὲ ἀνθεστηκότες ἑαυτοῖς κρίμα λήμψονται.

Indeed a further reason for conducting oneself "becomingly" (εὐσχημόνως, Rom. 13.13), whether with respect to governing authorities or to one another, is precisely because the time has grown short (v. 12). The contrast between this sentiment and the PE is marked.

Dibelius' excursus ("The Ideal of Good Christian Citizenship"), which follows his discussion of 1 Tim. 2.1–2, does acknowledge the fact that for the PE, and 2 Timothy in particular, "good citizenship" has its limits.[222] This is an important point since the PE underscore the reality of the potential for suffering and persecution for all who would live a godly life. The Pastor draws on Pauline tradition for confirmation of this expectation.[223]

The paraenesis which follows in 1 Tim. 2.8–15 is devoted to men and women. The injunction concerning men (ἄνδρες, v. 8), however, is cut short before reason and discussion are given. This leaves a comparatively lengthy treatment of the proper behavior for women in the church. Adornment and aptitude for learning with a submissive disposition are the subjects of injunctions in vv. 9 and 11. Strictly speaking the *topos* comprises the further injunction of v. 12, followed by the reason in v. 13 and its supplement (v. 14), with concluding discussion in v. 15.

The aim of the paraenesis is not hard to detect. The assumed author appeals to convention as a means of imposing traditional mores on women both in their dress and adornment and in the area of exercising teaching authority over men.[224] He does this not only by appealing to social convention[225] but to arguments based on the Hebrew Bible and early Jewish tradition.[226] A number of commentators have noted the potential in these injunctions for confrontation between the Pastor and the women of the congregations of the PE, especially those who were wealthy (if one is to judge by 2.9b).[227]

The third *topos* concerns instructions to the wealthy in 1 Tim. 6.17–19. In this passage the injunction is located in v. 17:

> τοῖς πλουσίοις ἐν τῷ νῦν αἰῶνι παράγγελλε μὴ ὑψηλοφρονεῖν μηδὲ ἠλπικέναι ἐπὶ πλούτου ἀδηλότητι, ἀλλ' ἐπὶ θεῷ . . .

The reason is implied in the ascription of God in v. 17b as

> . . . ὁ παρέχων ἡμῖν πάντα πλουσίως εἰς ἀπόλαυσιν.

The discussion is found in vv. 18–19. In this passage an eschatological motivation is added to the theological one provided in v. 17b. Liberality and generosity are the hallmarks of the wealthy who aim for godliness.[228] Indeed, scholars note the parallels between the attitude towards the wealthy who show no compassion (see v. 19) with that encountered in Matt. 6.19–20, Luke 12.21 and 16.1–9. This tradition rests in turn on the prophetic and wisdom traditions of the Hebrew Bible which castigate the wealthy who do not pay due regard for the poor and widows.[229] These traditions were mediated to the writers of the NT through early Jewish literature in passages like Sir. 29.10–13. The passage (i.e., 1 Tim. 6.17–19) is well-balanced by the earlier *topos* in 6.6–10 on the mortal dangers of seeking to be rich.

The implication of 1 Tim. 3.4, 12 is that candidates for the positions of bishop and deacon will come from the householder group in the congregation, i.e., from the more wealthy members.[230] However, possession of wealth is not made a prerequisite for exercise of leadership, rather a number of other qualities are required. For the bishop these include hospitality (1 Tim. 3.2), aptitude for teaching others (3.2), and a peaceable, gentle attitude (3.3). Deacons require qualities of seriousness (1 Tim. 3.8), absence of greed (3.8), and prior testing (3.10). The qualifications listed in Tit. 1.6–9 are in basic agreement with these. Although being a manager of one's own household is not listed here, the household metaphor is evoked in the ascription in 1.7 of the bishop as the οἰκονόμος θεοῦ, the "manager" for God.[231]

Kidd argues that the wealthy would have expected to function as leaders by virtue of their wealth and status, and, moreover, because the historical Pauline mission seems to have placed great store by wealthy patrons and patronesses.[232] However, the Pastor insists that the leadership of a Pauline church will be open only to those who show the requisite *spiritual* dispositions and aptitudes. These are actually reflected in the apostolic delegates—the PE's assumed recipients. Their task is to order the church and its leadership in the name of the apostle for the generations ahead. While their tenure might not be life-long, as is possibly implied of these leaders of the congregations on the evidence of 2 Tim. 2.2,[233] they are, nevertheless, plenipotential. Timothy and Titus are exhorted not merely to represent the absent Paul but, in effect, to model the kind of leadership the assumed author regards as indispensable for the securing of his apostolic legacy into the next generation and beyond.[234]

I conclude that the paraenesis examined in this sub-section of this chapter demonstrates affinities with the prevailing conventions of Greco-Roman culture with respect to traditional household duties. The church is clearly perceived as a household. Its constituents have an obligation to reflect prevailing societal norms. However, the PE also expect that believers will suffer. By holding up to the congregations the mirror of the suffering apostle, the Pastor heralds no easy and acculturated rite of passage for the church. This is made particularly evident in the exhortation directed to the wealthy. They are expected to provide the leadership of the congregation but only in so far as they fashion their lives after the image of the self-giving example of "Paul" and his legates in the service of the gospel. The paraenesis directed to (wealthy) women disenfranchises them as teachers of men. The paraenesis directed to the rich seems to approve of their wealth rightly used, and affirms the significance of their rank as heads of households for congregational leadership. Just as the wealthy could expect to serve with honor in society and in clubs,[235] so a certain continuity of expectation of service and honor lies before them within the congregation as leaders. However, the PE set before the wealthy exacting moral and personal prerequisites for exercising congregational leadership. Moreover, the Pastor confronts them with sobering realities concerning suffering and persecution, which, despite the considerable affirmation of conventional household mores, only underscore the perceived discontinuity between church and society.

Use of Examples

The use of examples by the Pastor is a marked aspect of his style of address. These are both positive and negative. Jesus himself is a prominent example in the PE. He too suffered and bore a faithful testimony, fighting the fight of faith as should Timothy (1 Tim. 6.12).[236] By contrast, there are several negative examples of individuals, no doubt known to the audience of the PE. Among these are Hymenaeus and Alexander (1 Tim. 1.20) as well as Jannes and Jambres (2 Tim. 3.8). Most sobering of all are the faithless associates of the apostle, namely, Phygelus and Hermogenes (2 Tim. 1.15), and Demas (2 Tim. 4.10), who all deserted him when they were most needed.[237] However, I want to concentrate here on the Pastor as example.

The assumed author of the PE frequently poses as an example to be followed by his delegates. This is particularly apparent in those passages in which he speaks of his suffering for the believers in the discharge of his ministry. He is the paradigm—the ideal, the prototype (ὑποτύπωσις)—for the church leaders. As such he furnishes a most powerful motivating example of the true teacher and psychagogue.

Just how persuasive this aspect of the image of Paul is for the PE can be gauged in John T. Fitzgerald's study of the Greco-Roman background of the suffering catalogues of the Corinthian correspondence in which Paul speaks of his apostolic labor.[238] Fitzgerald's results can be selectively applied to the PE, as he himself foreshadows in a number of footnotes in his monograph.[239] In his sufferings and, importantly, in his endurance in the face of affliction, the Pastor presents an image of the apostle to the audience of the PE after the model of the sage whose afflictions and endurance constitute the proofs of his worth as an exemplar. This is a concept with wide currency in the Greco-Roman world, as we saw with respect to the moral exhortation of the letters of Seneca. Adversity, writes Fitzgerald, is the litmus test of character, and the mark of the true worth of the philosopher/sage.[240] Not only does the wise man speak of his own sufferings as divine education and training towards virtue and the overcoming of passion and evil, he exhorts his students/friends to devote themselves to the same training (ἄσκησις). He offers himself as their model in the struggles he knows all who strive for virtue must face and, hopefully, overcome without being overcome by them.

In the PE the sufferings of the apostle/teacher, as well as the exhortations to suffering and training, must loom large in the estimation of the persuasive strategies employed by the author. Timothy is exhorted: "Train yourself for godliness" (γύμναζε δὲ σεαυτὸν πρὸς εὐσέβειαν, 1 Tim. 4.7) and "Take heed to yourself and to your teaching" (ἔπεχε σεαυτῷ καὶ τῇ διδασκαλίᾳ, 1 Tim. 4.16). Such heeding benefits not only Timothy but those for whom he is responsible.[241] The exhortations in 1 Tim. 6.12 strike a similar chord:

> ἀγωνίζου τὸν καλὸν ἀγῶνα τῆς πίστεως, ἐπιλαβοῦ τῆς αἰωνίου ζωῆς, εἰς

ἣν ἐκλήθης καὶ ὡμολόγησας τὴν καλὴν ὁμολογίαν ἐνώπιον πολλῶν μαρτύρων.

In 2 Tim. 1.8 Paul exhorts Timothy to "share [with him] in suffering for the gospel" (συγκακοπάθησον τῷ εὐαγγελίῳ), the gospel for which Paul was appointed preacher, apostle, and teacher (v. 11).[242] The same thought is expressed in 2 Tim. 2.3:

συγκακοπάθησον ὡς καλὸς στρατιώτης Χριστοῦ Ἰησοῦ.

The inclusive first person plural verb forms in 2 Tim. 2.11–13 convey the certain hope of eschatological reward for those who endure and suffer in the present. The Pastor is under no illusions as to the realities of the hardships the faithful ministers of the Pauline gospel will have to face, as 1 Tim. 4.7, 6.3–5, 2 Tim. 2.16–18, 22–23, 3.1–9 and 4.3–5 make clear. Timothy will have to face opponents (2 Tim. 3.1–9). He will have to be on guard against youthful passions (2 Tim. 2.22). He will have to contend with temptations to get involved in pointless controversies (2 Tim. 2.23). All this Timothy knows. He has already been well-informed and has personally encountered the shape of things to come in his own ministry in Ephesus. The urgent exhortation in 1 Tim. 1.3–7 had already asserted that the agenda of the false teachers did not promote "the stewardship of God which is in the faith" (οἰκονομία θεοῦ τὴν ἐν πίστει, v. 4).

Titus is also exhorted to submit to training and to practise godliness. In Tit. 2.11–12 the appearance of the salvation of God "trains us" (παιδεύουσα ἡμᾶς), the Pastor writes inclusively, to disavow ἀσέβεια and κοσμικαὶ ἐπιθυμίαι. This salvation, which is the manifestation of God in the world, "trains us" to live virtuously (σωφρόνως καὶ δικαίως καὶ εὐσεβῶς) with respect to ourselves, other people, and God.

Turning to Paul's experience of suffering in the PE, the following passages should be noted. In 2 Tim. 1.12 Paul suffers because of his appointment as an apostle. He is neither ashamed nor downcast, but fully confident in God's commitment to the work God has been doing through him (v. 12). "Imitate my pattern of sound words," urges Paul in v. 13. The prospect of suffering might have turned others aside from identifying with Paul (v. 15) but not Onesiphorus, who was not ashamed of Paul's chains (vv. 16–17). He receives a blessing from Paul. In 2.9 Paul is depicted wearing the fetters of a criminal because of the gospel.

The brief catalogue of labors in 2 Tim. 3.10–11 warrants comparison with similar materials in 1 Cor. 4.9–13, 2 Cor. 4.8–9 and 11.23–33. In the Corinthian passages Paul underscores his degradations and those of his associates as an apostle in Christ's service. The Corinthian catalogues amount to a declaration of his apostolic demeanor in which the sufferings of Christ himself are reflected for the sake of the well-being of the churches. However, unlike the function of the Corinthian suffering catalogues, Timothy is implicitly urged to follow Paul's suffering example in 2 Tim. 3.12, 14–17 (cf. 2 Tim. 1.8; 2.1–7). Suffering, the true mark of the genuine believer as it was of the genuine philosopher/sage, is an integral part of the Christian life (v. 12). When faced by adversity, it is then that Timothy is to recall Paul's example and the training he has had. He is to continue in what he has learned from childhood, especially in the scriptures (v. 16).[243] The reward amounts to being complete and equipped for every good work, i.e., for every deed of virtue and leadership (v. 17).

Finally, Paul surveys the prospect of his impending death, calmly expectant but fully prepared for what he knows must come. He is ready to die. He has "fought the good fight" he had earlier urged Timothy to wage. He has finished the race for which he has been trained by God and for which Jesus is the example *par excellence*. Not only is he not cast down, he is sure that he will receive the crown of eschatological life already set aside for him.[244] But it is not only he who can have this assurance, all who have "loved the Lord's appearing," and been trained by it for a life of virtue and suffering (cf. Tit. 2.11–13), can likewise live and work in hope.

Use of Other Modes of Exhortation

Letters classed in the category of moral exhortation sometimes use other modes of exhortation in a subsidiary manner. Letter 48 of Seneca's correspondence to Lucilius provides an example of this.

However, there is no doubt that paraenesis is the major hortatory mode in the PE. In the main, the addressees are exhorted to carry out their appointed official tasks, the contours of which they have already been apprised, with appropriate and sometimes urgent calls to attend to their individual spiritual health.[245] The motivations for faithfulness are located in eschatological rewards and in the benefit their faithfulness will accrue to the general good of the household of faith and society as a whole—God, it must be remembered, desires that all people might be saved (1 Tim. 2.4). Faithfulness is reinforced by exemplars, both negative and positive. I have addressed this characteristic above.

Not only do Timothy and Titus guard the deposit of the apostle, in doing so faithfully there is held out to them the prospect of eternal reward, both for them and for the people they serve. In 1 Tim. 4.8 the godliness (εὐσέβεια) to which Paul summons Timothy is of value "in every way" (πρὸς πάντα ὠφέλιμος), including holding out to him the promise of eternal life.[246] In 4.10 faithful discharge of his duty is motivated by

> our hope in God who is savior of all men, especially those who believe.

The capstone of this argument comes in 4.16. Just as the conversion of Paul himself is fundamental to the saving purposes of God, so Timothy, if he is faithful, will save both himself and his hearers.

Furthermore, in 1 Tim. 6.12 Timothy is urged:

> ἀγωνίζου τὸν καλὸν ἀγῶνα τῆς πίστεως, ἐπιλαβοῦ τῆς αἰωνίου ζωῆς, εἰς ἣν ἐκλήθης καὶ ὡμολόγησας τὴν καλὴν ὁμολογίαν ἐνώπιον πολλῶν μαρτύρων.

Reminding him of his baptismal oath (or ordination vow),[247] the Pastor once again focuses the addressees' attention on his calling and its eschatological scope. This focus is not far from the author's mind in v. 14 in which Timothy is urged to "keep the commandment" until the ἐπιφάνεια of "*our* Lord Jesus Christ." The note of eschatological accountability is struck implicitly in 2 Tim. 1.12. Here Paul is supremely confident that God/Christ is capable of guarding what has been entrusted to him, and which he now bequeaths to Timothy. Ultimately, his guardianship, like Paul's exercise of his own apostolic ministry, is not one which Timothy fulfils by virtue of his own training or his own natural ability. The Holy Spirit, "who dwells within us," guards the apostolic delegate and watches over his work.[248] Significantly, then, echoing the confidence of 2 Tim. 1.7 and the several references to the giving of the Spirit, the final blessing to Timothy is "the Lord be with your spirit" (ὁ κύριος μετὰ τοῦ πνεύματός σου).[249]

In 2 Tim. 2.10–13, Paul gives his reason for enduring the suffering which has marked his life. He has endured, he says, because of the elect (διὰ τοὺς ἐκλεκτούς, v. 10):

> ἵνα καὶ αὐτοὶ σωτηρίας τύχωσιν τῆς ἐν Χριστῷ Ἰησοῦ μετὰ δόξης αἰωνίου.

But Paul associates Timothy and others with that reward. Endurance cannot fail to receive its due. By contrast, Hymenaeus, Alexander, and other people have come to grief by falling away from the faith (1 Tim. 1.19–20).

Reward is a prominent theme in 2 Tim. 2.1–6. In a series of metaphors Timothy is exhorted, as a good soldier, not to get entangled in matters extraneous to his charge. Just as the soldier does not get distracted by civilian affairs but aims to please the one who enlisted him, so Timothy should be prepared to endure suffering so as to please his Master. Moreover, he should run the race to claim the prize, and work hard as the farmer does in order to enjoy the fruit of his labor. At the end of his life, Paul can declare utter confidence in having run the race set before him; he has kept the faith (2 Tim. 4.7). Consequently, he is sure of ultimate rescue from every evil and of being saved for God's heavenly kingdom (4.18).

In Titus 2.11–14, the Pastor reveals his perception that the grace of God has appeared for the salvation of all. This grace, he writes in vv. 12–13,

> παιδεύουσα ἡμᾶς ἵνα ἀρνησάμενοι τὴν ἀσέβειαν καὶ τὰς κοσμικὰς ἐπιθυμίας σωφρόνως καὶ δικαίως καὶ εὐσεβῶς ζήσωμεν ἐν τῷ νῦν αἰῶνι, προσδεχόμενοι τὴν μακαρίαν ἐλπίδα καὶ ἐπιφάνειαν τῆς δόξης τοῦ μεγάλου θεοῦ καὶ σωτῆρος ἡμῶν Ἰησοῦ Χριστοῦ . . .

Such a life-orientation leads surely to life in the eschatological era. The evidence that that salvation has already appeared is the fact that "regeneration and renewal" (παλιγγενεσία καὶ ἀνακαίνωσις) are present experiences of believers, manifest in lives of godliness (3.3–5).

Advice, fitting for letters of exhortation, is given on two occasions, once each in 1 Timothy and 2 Timothy. In 1 Tim. 5.23 the author writes:

> χεῖρας ταχέως μηδενὶ ἐπιτίθει, μηδὲ κοινώνει ἁμαρτίαις ἀλλοτρίαις· σεαυτὸν ἁγνὸν τήρει. Μηκέτι ὑδροπότει, ἀλλὰ οἴνῳ ὀλίγῳ χρῶ διὰ τὸν στόμαχον καὶ τὰς πυκνάς σου ἀσθενείας.

This seemingly naïve advice expresses concern for Timothy's health. It is precisely the kind of matter one meets in the letters briefly surveyed in section C, as well as in the familial papyrus letters.[250] However, it appears to be a qualification of the injunction "keep yourself pure" (σεαυτὸν ἁγνὸν τήρει), a maxim that might have been interpreted to affirm Timothy's apparent abstinence in the interests of ascetic purity. As such, this piece of anti-ascetic advice has polemical, perhaps anti-Gnostic, overtones.[251]

In 2 Tim. 4.14–15, the Pastor writes:

> Ἀλέξανδρος ὁ χαλκεὺς πολλά μοι κακὰ ἐνεδείξατο· ἀποδώσει αὐτῷ ὁ κύριος κατὰ τὰ ἔργα αὐτοῦ· ὃν καὶ σὺ φυλάσσου, λίαν γὰρ ἀντέστη τοῖς ἡμετέροις λόγοις.

This advice seems to be a friendly urging on Paul's part to avoid a troublesome and habitually intransigent local craftsman. Defenders of Pauline authorship treat this advice at face value.[252] The trouble-maker may well be the "Alexander" (of 1 Tim. 1.20) whom, with Hymenaeus, Paul had "delivered to Satan." Yet, on the other hand, the attribution—"coppersmith"—may also be intended to differentiate him from the Alexander of 1 Tim. 1.20.[253] It seems likely, in my view, though unprovable, that the author of the PE is injecting into his actualization of the Pauline tradition a veiled reference to a heretic who was active in the midst of the Pauline congregations, one who had "strongly opposed our message."[254]

E. The PE and the Testament Genre

The testament, writes John J. Collins, is a "discourse delivered in anticipation of imminent death."[255] Although there are testaments (διαθῆκαι) extant in Greek philosophical literature,[256] Collins argues that the genre attested in the Hebrew Bible—specifically in Genesis 49, Deuteronomy 33, Joshua 23–24, 1 Samuel 12, 1 Kings 2.1–9, and 1 Chronicles 28–29, and in the literature of early Judaism—is to be differentiated from its putative Greek counterparts, which deal with the disposal of property and the like, and are not hortatory. However, Benjamin Fiore has demonstrated that moral exhortation is present in the testamentary letters 6 and 27 of the pseudepigraphic Socratic collection imparted, as in the PE and the Jewish testamentary literature, by example and ethical argument.[257]

Eckhardt von Nordheim defines the genre as a category of wisdom literature the aim of which is moral exhortation. This exhortation is oriented toward faithfulness to the Jewish law, and is often centered on the dangers of idolatry and sexual sins.[258] The other elements commonly associated with testaments—historical review and prediction of the future—serve as vehicles for the exhortation, and are secondary to the main purpose of the writing.[259] He writes:

> Ohne eine Anweisung zu einem bestimmten Verhalten ist also ein Testament kein Testament, nicht jedoch ohne die beiden anderen Elemente. Das Herz der Testamentsform schlägt also in der Verhaltensanweisung.[260]

Collins, however, suggests the following three distinctive characteristics with respect to the early Jewish work *Testaments of the Twelve Patriarchs* (*T. 12 Patr.*) which he takes as the normative document for distinguishing what is and is not a testament. These are:

1. historical retrospective reviewing each patriarch's life (*T. Ash.* is the only exception),
2. ethical exhortation, and
3. prediction of the future.[261]

On this analysis, Collins concludes that only a small number of works are rightly designated testaments, namely, *T. 12 Patr.*, the *Testament of Job* (*T. Job*), and the *Testament of Moses* (*T. Mos.*).[262] Nevertheless, he acknowledges that there are testaments embedded in works of other genres which correspond to the definition offered above, chiefly Tob. 14, 1 Macc. 2.49–70, *Jub.* 21, 36, *Bib. Ant.* 19, 23–24, 33, and *2 Bar.* 43–47.[263]

Von Nordheim argues that the authors of testaments argue their case for an ethical lifestyle not by imposing precepts on the audience but by persuasive argument drawn from the example of the speaker and his life-experience (e.g., *Jub.* 20–21, *T. Jud.* 14–17, 19, *T. Sol.* 26, *T. Job* 27), the order to be observed in nature (e.g., *T. Naph.* 2, *T. Zeb.* 9), and from observations of the positive or negative consequences of the life-style choices of other people (e.g., 1 Macc. 2.51–64, *T. Iss.* 5, *T. Gad* 3–4, *T. Benj.* 4–6).[264] To this one might add the persuasive dynamic of revelation (e.g., *T. Levi* 2–3) and ancestral tradition (e.g., *T. Levi* 9–10). Not only does the Testament contain the moral exhortation of one who, at the end of his life, is able to draw lessons from the whole scope of that life but he is one of the great ones of the past whose authority and right to exhort is already accepted by the addressees.[265]

Berger's analysis of the constituent features of the testament emphasizes a number of characteristics significant for the PE.[266] He observes that testaments are closely connected with the Jewish concept of tradition and make provision for the transmission of the sage's teaching and moral exhortation. He gives *T. Sim.* 7.3 as an example. Having exhorted his children to be obedient to Levi and Judah because God will raise up a savior from them, the patriarch adds:

> For this reason I command these things to you and you command them to your children, so that they may observe them in their successive generation (ὅπως φυλάξωσιν αὐτὰ εἰς τὰς γενεὰς αὐτῶν).[267]

The use of φυλάσσω here finds several parallels in the PE in which the verb is used five times.[268] While 2 Tim. 1.14 and 4.15 are not relevant to our discussion, the first two of the five instances (i.e., 1 Tim. 5.21; 6.20) refer to Timothy's charge to "guard" what has been entrusted to him.[269] The third, 2 Tim. 1.12, places confidence in God's commitment to guard the deposit.

Berger also observes that testaments juxtapose the sage's life and teaching. This is a prominent theme in the PE, as noted above in the discussion in the previous section of the example of suffering offered by the assumed author as the evidence of his value and worth as a model of the Christian life and ministry. But this feature of the testament may take the form of a negative life-example, as in many of the *T. 12 Patr. T. Reub.* 1 and *T. Sim.* 2 contain two such instances.

The third of the features Berger underscores is the warning against falling away from the teaching being imparted or the traditions commended as tantamount to loss of salvation. This is exemplified in *T. Levi* 10 in which the faithlessness of Levi's children with respect to the law will result in the destruction of Jerusalem and their being scattered among the nations.

While Collins contends that there are no examples of the testament genre in the NT, there are indisputable examples of farewell addresses which rightly belong to the genre as defined by von Nordheim. Among these are John 13–17 and Acts 20.18–35. Berger also classes the Last Supper narrative in Luke 22.7–38 as testamentary.[270] Each provides the last words of the speaker in the face of impending death, focuses on the manner of life of the speaker, anticipates the dangers to come for the members of his "family," and features moral exhortation for the hearers.

According to Acts 20.25 and v. 38, Paul knows he will not see the Ephesians again. Though he does not know for certain what will befall him in Jerusalem, he does know that the Spirit has been testifying in every city that imprisonments and afflictions await him (v. 23). He testifies to his manner of life as a minister (vv. 18–21, 24, 26–27). His exhortation to the leaders of the Ephesian church in v. 28, though brief, is reminiscent of similar material in the PE:

> προσέχετε ἑαυτοῖς καὶ παντὶ τῷ ποιμνίῳ, ἐν ᾧ ὑμᾶς τὸ πνεῦμα τὸ ἅγιον ἔθετο ἐπισκόπους, ποιμαίνειν τὴν ἐκκλησίαν τοῦ θεοῦ, ἣν περιεποιήσατο διὰ τοῦ αἵματος τοῦ ἰδίου.[271]

His prediction of the coming of false teachers—"fierce wolves" (v. 29) whose intent is to prey on the "flock"—can be paralleled in any number of early Jewish testaments. *T. Mos.* 3–8, the bulk of the book in its extant form, is given over to a detailed account of the coming of external threats to the people of God while under the leadership of Joshua. *T. Levi* 14–16 perceives the threat to the people coming from within.[272]

2 Bar. 78–87 is presented as a letter. Book 5 of *1 Enoch* (chs. 91–

107) has been commonly regarded as a letter. Testamentary features are present in both, especially in the material of *2 Baruch*. Accordingly, my attention here will be devoted to *2 Bar*. 78–87.

Baruch writes his letter/testament to the nine and a half tribes to console them in their midst of their suffering. A narrative of the sufferings occasioned by the destruction of Jerusalem (chs. 79–80) gives way to a tone of consolation and assurance of divine mercy, with a concomitant underscoring of divine vengeance on the enemies of the people of God (81–83).[273] The exhortation of chapter 84 centers on learning God's "mighty commandments." While Baruch is still living ("before I die"), he reminds them of the fulfilment of Moses' warnings concerning the scattering of the people should they transgress the law. But now, Baruch exhorts them in 84.8–10, they should remember

> Zion and the Law and the holy land and your brothers and the covenant and your fathers, and do not forget the festivals and the sabbaths . . .

Moreover, if they

> pass on this letter and the traditions of the Law to your children as also your fathers handed down to you . . .

and if they ask for mercy, they can expect to receive it from God when he remembers the integrity of their fathers. Consequently, Baruch reminds them of the examples set by their faithful ancestors. There is a considerable eschatological urgency in the exhortations of this chapter.

Finally, in ch. 86 Baruch directs that the letter be read to the assemblies of the people as a means of facilitating their memory of him, just as in the writing of it he has remembered them. The comparison with similar injunctions in Col. 4.16 and 1 Thess. 5.27 is noteworthy. The NT passages demonstrate, at least with respect to these two letters, that Paul's parousia is conveyed in the reading of these letters, as it is in the case of Baruch's. Paul's letters represent what he, as apostle, wants to say to the assembled believers. These are not private communications. In like manner, the regular reading of the letter of Baruch preserves his exhortation and warning for generations to come.

Johannes Munck's survey of the relevant texts in the NT demonstrates that 1 and 2 Timothy, as well as 2 Peter, might be classed in the testament genre, though they are first and foremost letters.[274] Munck notes the following testamentary characteristics common to 1 and 2 Timothy.[275] These are:

1. definitive imparting of apostolic teaching,
2. moral exhortation,
3. the author as model of faithful Christian witness, and
4. prediction of the coming of false teachers.

I intend examining in turn each of these points briefly, though my analysis will concentrate on 2 Timothy almost exclusively.

Imparting apostolic teaching. In the light of his impending death,[276] 2 Timothy depicts the apostle preparing to take his leave of his close associate, his "son." He reminds him of his responsibility to guard what has been entrusted to him for his own ministry and to transmit this to trustworthy men for generations to come (see 2 Tim. 2.2).[277] The content of this tradition is not explicitly spelled out in 2 Timothy or in the other PE. However, it almost certainly includes what I have termed the Pauline legacy, or the Pauline παραθήκη, as constituted by the letters of Paul, including the PE, the collection of the πιστοὶ λόγοι, and the church order—in short the teaching, moral examples, and ecclesiastical order the Pastor commends.[278]

Moral exhortation. As the "child" and "son" of the apostle, Timothy is exhorted to perseverance and sharing in the suffering that has marked the assumed author's exercise of his ministry. While the moral exhortation of the PE has been examined in some detail in the previous section of this chapter, it might be summarized as a confirmation of the tradition of moral convention encountered in Greco-Roman psychagogy. This is not to say that the moral exhortation of the PE has surrendered all claim to be distinctively Christian. We have had cause to note the considerable appeal to remembering the saving deeds of God in the Christ-event as providing motivation for the exhortation which, by and large, follows traditional content.

The author as model. The Paul of the PE presents himself as a model of faithful witness. Wolter draws attention to the example of Abraham in

Jub. 21.1–6.[279] Abraham declares his lifelong aversion to idols, testifies to his commitment to doing the will of God, and recommends that Isaac follow his example (v. 5). This bears comparison with the Pastor's exhortations:

2 Tim. 3.10–12
σὺ δὲ παρηκολούθησάς μου τῇ διδασκαλίᾳ, τῇ ἀγωγῇ, τῇ προθέσει, τῇ πίστει, τῇ μακροθυμίᾳ, τῇ ἀγάπῃ, τῇ ὑπομονῇ, τοῖς διωγμοῖς, τοῖς παθήμασιν, οἷά μοι ἐγένετο ἐν Ἀντιοχείᾳ, ἐν Ἰκονίῳ, ἐν Λύστροις, οἵους διωγμοὺς ὑπήνεγκα· καὶ ἐκ πάντων με ἐρρύσατο ὁ κύριος. καὶ πάντες δὲ οἱ θέλοντες εὐσεβῶς ζῆν ἐν Χριστῷ Ἰησοῦ διωχθήσονται.

2 Tim. 4.7
τὸν καλὸν ἀγῶνα ἠγώνισμαι, τὸν δρόμον τετέλεκα, τὴν πίστιν τετήρηκα.

In the discussion of the PE as letters of moral exhortation in the previous section of this chapter, I have already acknowledged the function and significance of "Paul's" sufferings. In his persecutions, deprivations, and, above all, in his resolute endurance, he advertises his moral and vocational worth as an explicit example for his "son" and an implicit one for the leaders of the churches to follow.

Prediction of false teachers to come. Testaments invariably warn their audience of the coming of false teachers, or the falling away of the hearers.[280] Hence, much of the moral exhortation of the testament genre derives its persuasive dynamic from the "predictions" of the sage. In 2 Timothy Paul predicts the arising of false teachers who will be opponents of his teaching (3.1–9). Indeed, many have already fallen away (1.15; 2.17–18; 4.10). In this present emergency and in the crises to come, Paul exhorts Timothy to "train" himself, to guard the deposit, and to continue in what he has learned (3.14–17). Paul is confident that in aptitude, training, and spiritual gifts Timothy is well-placed to continue attending to his responsibility.

As a testamentary pseudepigraphon 2 Timothy combines the sanction accorded to "last words" with the claim of the authority and persuasive dynamic of the apostle in whose name the writer speaks his words of encouragement and exhortation. These, I believe, are significant observations for understanding 2 Timothy and also the other

PE with which 2 Timothy is intimately associated, and the manner in which the Pastor argues his case for continued faithfulness to the Pauline legacy and opposition to the false teachers who would undermine it.

SUMMARY

This extensive examination of the PE's participation in the Greco-Roman and early Jewish traditions of moral exhortation reveals, at a number of significant points, just how comfortably the PE fit into that tradition.[281] The fact that the PE presents ethical ideals which are fully in accord with the conventions of moral exhortation enhances the epistolary analogies that can be perceived. This is not to say that the PE must be assessed exclusively from this point of view. Nevertheless, the fact that the PE are at face value concerned with exhortation invites the kind of comparison I have undertaken.

Moreover, the function of Paul in the PE, or, rather, the image of the apostle constructed by the Pastor, accords with the psychagogic tradition encountered in the Greco-Roman letters. The fact that the Pastor can speak of "Paul's" endurance under suffering, and can depict his settled and confident demeanor as he faces death, demonstrates that he was well aware of the powerful persuasive appeal his portrait of Paul possessed for his intended audience.

The Pastor received a deposit of Pauline tradition which he seeks to commend to his addressees in the face of a perceived threat to the Pauline legacy from false teachers. This chapter has examined the persuasive strategies employed in the PE as letters of moral exhortation in which the paraenetic mode of address predominates. It was in this form that the Pastor actualized that tradition and commended it to his audience.

Having investigated the PE as letters of moral exhortation employing persuasive strategies which were recognizable and literate, the task now at hand is to investigate the presence in the PE of strategies commended in the rhetorical handbooks and applied primarily to speeches, i.e., to oral discourse, rather than letters.

NOTES

1 τὸ μέρος τοῦ διαλόγου. Demetrius, *On Style*, 223.

2 See *Bible Studies* (Edinburgh: T. & T. Clark, 1901), 4. Cf. *Light from the Ancient East* (Grand Rapids: Baker, 1978 [repr. of the 4th ed.]), 228 (hence *LAE*). Deissmann's discussion can be followed on 3–59 of the former book, and on 146–251, esp. 227–51, of the latter.

3 *Bible Studies*, 9, 20. Cf. *LAE*, 229: "An epistle is an artistic literary form, a species of literature, just like the dialogue, the oration, or the drama."

4 *Bible Studies*, 43–45. Here Deissmann is drawing a comparison between contingent papyrus letters and the letters of Paul. Contingent letters—whether written by semi-literate Egyptians, Paul, Aristotle, or Epicurus—are "real" letters.

5 *Bible Studies*, 53–55. He does not give precise reasons for his classification of the PE.

6 *Bible Studies*, 44.

7 *LAE*, 241: "All the traces of systematization that are found here and there in him are proofs of the limitation of his genius; the secret of his greatness lies in religion apart from system." Cf. his *Paul: A Study in Social and Religious History* (2nd ed.; London: Hodder & Stoughton, 1926).

8 See Stanley K. Stowers, *Letter Writing in Antiquity* (Philadelphia: Westminster, 1986), 17–20; William G. Doty, "The Classification of Epistolary Literature," *CBQ* 31 (1969), 183–99, *Letters in Primitive Christianity* (Philadelphia: Fortress, 1973); and Klaus Thraede, *Grunzüge griechisch-römischer Brieftopik* (München: Beck, 1970), 1–4. See also John L. White, "Saint Paul and the Apostolic Letter Tradition," *CBQ* 45 (1983), 434–5.

9 See, e.g, Doty, "Classification," 183–9; *Letters*, 24–26.

10 Stowers, *Letter Writing*, 19.

11 "Classification," 191.

12 "Classification," 193.

13 "Classification," 197. On 198 he proposes to class the letters of Paul "and his

school" as belonging to the "more private" type of letter. Hebrews, on the other hand, "has so little relation to private correspondence as to omit epistolographic conventions."

14 Heikki Koskenniemi, *Studien zur Idee und Phraseologie des griechischen Briefes bis 400 n. Chr.* (Helsinki/Wiesbaden: Suomalaien Tiedakatamie/Otto Harrassowitz, 1956), 35–47. Koskenniemi also criticizes Deissmann's differentiation between letters and epistles. He observes no such distinction operating in the epistolary theorists. See *Studies*, 50–53.

15 See *Grundzüge*, 95–106. The passages are 1 Thess. 2.17, 1 Cor. 5.3–5, and Col. 2.5. He concludes that the apostle's word conveyed by the letter is the representation of his presence (παρουσία) with them. See the discussion of 1 Cor. 5.3–5 on 99–100: "Es ist also nicht mehr nur von einer im Brief nur bezeugten Verbundenheit die Rede, sondern von einer völligen Identität des Briefes mit dem 'Spruch' des Apostels. Das macht den Brief in den Händen der Gemeinde zu einem verbindlichen Urteil."

16 White, "Letter Tradition," 435–6.

17 See Abraham J. Malherbe, *Ancient Epistolary Theorists* (Atlanta: Scholars Press, 1988), 3 (hence *AET*).

18 *AET*, 2–4.

19 The LCL translator, W. Rhys Roberts, has an extensive discussion of the attribution of the work to Demetrius of Phalerum. The attribution originates in a manuscript of the tenth or eleventh century. Roberts argues in his introduction that in its present form the work derives from the latter half of the first century C.E. and that Demetrius of Tarsus was the author. See *On Style* (LCL vol. 199; London: Heinemann, 1927), 271–8. Moreover, he argues on 278–81 that Paul was deeply influenced by the tradition of "literary study," which is exemplified by both this Demetrius, the Stoic Archedemus of Tarsus (fl. 130 B.C.E.), and the later rhetorician Hermogenes of Tarsus (fl. 170 C.E.). Paul's letter-writing and the rhetorical effectiveness of his speech to the Areopagus (Acts 17.22–31) *inter alia* are claimed as evidence of his exposure to this influence. While Roberts' theory regarding the authorship of *On Style* has not met with enthusiastic response, he is correct to point out the excellent educational opportunities from which Paul might have benefited in Tarsus. Nevertheless, the actual contours of that education, whether in Tarsus or in Jerusalem, where it was possible to gain an acquaintance with the Greek cultural tradition, are by no means clear. See Edwin A. Judge, "St. Paul and Classical Society," *JAC* 15 (1972), 29, 32; Abraham J. Malherbe, *Social Aspects of Early Christianity* (Philadelphia: Fortress, 1977), 33–35; and Helmut Koester, *Introduction to the New Testament* (Philadelphia/Berlin and New York: Fortress/Walter de Gruyter, 1982), 2.97–99.

20 See Malherbe, *AET*, 2. Koskenniemi, *Studien*, 24–29 argues that the digression in Demetrius might possibly represent the epistolary theory of Artemon, the publisher of Aristotle's posthumous letters.

21 For discussion of "plain" style, see §§36–37 and §§190–239. The other three styles are the "elevated" (μεγαλοπρεπής), "elegant" (γλαφυρός), and "forcible" (δεινός).

22 *On Style*, 223. Cf. Seneca, *Letters*, 75.1–2 ("I prefer that my letters should be just what my conversation would be if you and I were sitting in one another's company or taking walks together,—spontaneous and easy."); Cicero, *Letters to Atticus*, 12.53 ("Though I have nothing to say to you, I write all the same, because I feel as though I were talking to you"). Cf. *Letters to Atticus*, 9.10.1; 12.30.1.

23 *On Style*, 224.

24 *On Style*, 225. Demetrius' criticism of Aristotle is apparently directed to the content and style of the extant frag. 615 in the 1831 edition of the fragments of Aristotle (see *AET*, 17; Roberts, *On Style*, 440 n. [a]). See V. Rose (ed.), *Aristoteles Fragmenta* (Stuttgart: Teubner, 1966 [repr. of the 1886 edition]).

25 *On Style*, 235.

26 Demetrius, *On Style*, 232. On the point of ornamentation and embellishment, cf. Philostratus of Lemnos, *On Letters*, 2.257,29–258,28 (for text see *AET*, 42–43); Gregory Nazianzus, *Ep*. 51.5–7; Pseudo-Libanius, *Epistolary Styles*, 48; Julius Victor, *The Art of Rhetoric*, 27; Malherbe, *AET*, 14.

27 Demetrius, *On Style*, 228. According to Philostratus, clarity of style is persuasive: ἐρῶντες ῥᾷον πείσομεν. Cf. Gregory of Nazianzus, *Ep*. 51.4 (*AET*, 59).

28 Demetrius, *On Style*, 232. Note the distinction between letters written in the formal and in the familiar style drawn by the Socratic writer in the introduction to letter 33 in Abraham J. Malherbe (ed.), *The Cynic Epistles* (Missoula: Scholars Press, 1977), 300–01. In this regard, the editor draws attention to Cicero's precept in *ad Fam*. 2.4.1.

29 Demetrius, *On Style*, 233. Aristotle uses the word "proof" (πίστις) to refer to an argument which is based on reason, ethos, or emotion. See also ch. 3 n. 14.

30 Demetrius, *On Style*, 234.

31 Cf. Cicero, *Letters to his Friends*, 16.16.2 ("All of you was revealed to me in your letter"); Seneca, *Letters*, 40.1 ("I thank you for writing to me so often; for you are revealing your real self to me in the only way you can"). Cf. Thraede, *Grundzüge*, 23: "[I]m Brief spiegelt sich die Persönlichkeit eines einzelnen Verfassers selbst."

32 Demetrius, *On Style*, 228. For the definition of the "period," see George A. Kennedy (ed.), *Aristotle: On Rhetoric* (New York/Oxford: Oxford University Press, 1991), 239 commenting on Aristotle's *Rhetoric*, 3.9.3. See also the discussion in Demetrius, *On Style*, 10–19. Cf. Philostratus of Lemnos, *On Letters*, who considers "periods" rhetorically far too impressive even for longer letters (see text in *AET*, 42–43).

33 Demetrius, *On Style*, 229. Cf. Seneca, *Letters*, 75.1–2: " . . . [M]y letters have nothing strained or artificial about them. . . . Even if I were arguing a point, I should not stamp my foot, or toss my arms about, or raise my voice; but I should leave that sort of thing to the orator."

34 This point can best be illustrated in the tradition of letters of moral exhortation. In the NT, Galatians is an excellent example of a letter which appears to use overtly the techniques which derive directly from the oratorical tradition. See also Fiore, *Personal Example*, 43–44.

35 See Malherbe, *AET*, 4–5, 6–7. See especially the Bologna Papyrus of bilingual epistolary exercises of Egyptian provenance (for text see *AET*, 44–55). The evidence of the letters of antiquity demonstrates that their style changes little over the centuries. The evidence of the copious papyrus letters from Egypt, many of them aiming at educated style, also suggests that letter-writing was part of the educational syllabus.

36 See Deissmann, *Bible Studies*, 13; Doty, *Letters*, 6–7; John L. White, *Light From Ancient Letters* (Philadelphia: Fortress, 1986), 189–90; Malherbe, *AET*, 6–7, and "Hellenistic Moralists and the New Testament," *ANRW* II.26.1 (1992), 283; Thraede, *Grundzüge*, 23–24; Fiore, *Personal Example*, 108–10. These exercises were called *prosopopoeia*. It has been proposed that pseudonymous letters were written deceitfully to be palmed off to competing libraries (see, e.g., Deissmann, *Bible Studies*, 13 n. 1). However, see M. Luther Stirewalt, Jr., "Forgery and Greek Epistolography" in *Studies in Ancient Greek Epistolography* (Atlanta: Scholars Press, 1993), part 2 (27–42). Stirewalt contends that it is more likely that some of the letter collections attributed to philosophers emanated from their schools in the debates between their later followers and their opponents. The legacy of a school's founder was re-cast in the form of a letter collection.

37 See Malherbe (ed.), *Cynic Epistles*, 2–3; Stirewalt, *Studies in Ancient Greek Epistolography*, part 2. Malherbe suggests that the Cynic epistles have been neglected, in part because they were reckoned mere rhetorical exercises. On the letters of Socrates and the Socratic letters as propaganda against more rigid Cynics, see Fiore, *Personal Example*, 116–7. For a brief discussion of the production of pseudepigrapha in the philosophical schools, see Speyer, *Das literarische Fälschung*, 34–35. He draws an interesting comparison between the school collections and the production of the Gospels of Mark and Luke, both of which, he contends, were school products. He cites Tertullian, who, though he is aware that

Mark and Luke wrote the Gospels that bear their names, ascribes both to apostles (Peter and Paul respectively). See *Against Marcion*, 4.5: "And it may well seem that the works which disciples publish belong to their masters."

38 See Quinn, *Titus*, 6–9; Donelson, *Pseudepigraphy*, ch. 1 (pps. 7–66). Cf. the thesis of R. A. Culpepper's book *The Johannine School* (Missoula: Scholars Press, 1975).

39 See Meade, *Pseudonymity and Canon*, 9–10. See also the recent survey by A. G. Patzia, "The Deutero-Pauline Hypothesis: An Attempt at Clarification," *EvQ* 52 (1980), 27–42, especially 32–34. Patzia does not commit himself to the position that there was a school. However, see the more confident arguments of H. -M. Schenke, "Das Weiterwirken des Paulus und die Pflege seines Erbes durch die Paulus-Schule," *NTS* 21 (1975), 505–18.

40 Schenke, "Das Weiterwirken," 516.

41 See Malherbe, *AET*, 4–5.

42 For the text of *Epistolary Types*, see Malherbe, *AET*, 36–37. The advisory type of letter is no. 11 in Pseudo-Demetrius' catalogue.

43 Text in Malherbe, *AET*, 32–33.

44 Cf. 1 Tim. 3.14–15 (my italics): ταῦτά σοι γράφω, ἐλπίζων ἐλθεῖν πρὸς σὲ ἐν τάχει· ἐὰν δὲ βραδύνω, *ἵνα εἰδῇς πῶς δεῖ ἐν οἴκῳ θεοῦ ἀναστρέφεσθαι*, ἥτις ἐστὶν ἐκκλησία θεοῦ ζῶντος, στῦλος καὶ ἑδραίωμα τῆς ἀληθείας.

45 See Malherbe, *AET*, 5. Another manuscript tradition attributes the work to Proclus.

46 See Malherbe, *AET*, 5.

47 Pseudo-Libanius, *Epistolary Styles*, §5. For text, see Malherbe, *AET*, 68–69: παραινετικὴ μὲν οὖν ἐστι δι᾽ ἧς παραινοῦμέν τινι προτρέποντες αὐτὸν ἐπί τι ὁρμῆσαι ἢ ἀφέξεσθαί τινος. ἡ παραίνεσις δὲ εἰς δύο διαιρεῖται, εἴς τε προτροπὴν καὶ ἀποτροπήν.

48 For text, see Malherbe, *AET*, 68–69. The example Pseudo-Libanius gives involves conflicting advice in the matter of going to war.

49 See the discussion of the views of Dibelius in n. 87 below.

50 Stowers, *Letter Writing*, 95.

51 See his *Letter Writing*, 94.

52 See the comments of D. E. Aune, *The New Testament in Its Literary Environment* (Philadelphia: Westminster, 1987), 158, 160–1. On 158 Aune writes that "rhetoric

had a profound effect on all genres of literature including letters. A knowledge of ancient rhetorical theory, therefore, can contribute to understanding letters written by ancients (like Paul and Ignatius) who had more than a basic education." Cf. Stowers, *Letter Writing*, 34: "In contrast to our own culture, linguistic skill focused on oral speech; the written word was secondary, derived from primary rhetoric." Although letter-writing was never fully integrated into rhetorical theory, he continues: "The rules for certain types of speeches, however, were adapted for use in corresponding letter types."

53 *Grundzüge*, 23.

54 See, e.g., Koskenniemi, *Studien*, 38–42; J. L. White, "Epistolary Literature," *ANRW* II.25.2 (1984), 1739–50; Quinn, *Titus*, 60.

55 See "The Apostolic *Parousia*: Form and Significance," in W. R. Farmer, C. F. D. Moule, and R. R. Niebuhr (eds.), *Christian History and Interpretation: Studies Presented to John Knox* (Cambridge: University Press, 1967), 249–68.

56 See H. Koester, "I Thessalonians—Experiment in Christian Writing," in F. F. Church and T. George (eds.), *Continuity and Discontinuity in Church History* (Leiden: Brill, 1979), 33–44; Malherbe, "Hellenistic Moralists and the New Testament," 304.

57 See also n. 186 below.

58 See Schenke, "Das Weiterwirken," 516. Not only must the Pastor have knowledge of the Pauline letters if he is to bring Paul's message to speech, he must also have an awareness of Paul's claim to absolute authority "so dass, wenn im Paulinismus der Gedanke der apostolischen Tradition aufkommt bzw. in ihn eindringt, man, wie die Pastoralbriefe zeigen, die Tradition allein durch den Apostel Paulus vermittelt sieht."

59 Doty, *Letters*, 27, and the extended discussion on 27–47. Cf. White, "New Testament Epistolary Literature," 1739–51.

60 "New Testament Epistolary Literature," 1739.

61 For the influence of the Pauline letter on the other letters of the NT see White, "New Testament Epistolary Literature," 1751–5; "Saint Paul and the Apostolic Letter Tradition," 442–4.

62 See, e.g., the two essays in A. T. Hanson in *Studies in the Pastoral Epistles* (London: SPCK, 1968). In the first, "Elements of a Baptismal Liturgy in Titus" (78–96), Hanson argues that the authors of Titus, Ephesians, and 1 Peter each knew a "long baptismal prayer or act of praise" which they adapted independently of each other. Elements of it occur in Tit. 3.4–7//1 Pet. 1.3–5; Tit. 2.11–14//1 Pet. 1.13b–19//Eph. 5.25b–27; Tit. 3.3–8//Eph. 2.1–10. In the second, "Eucharistic References

in 1 and 2 Timothy" (96–109), Hanson contends that comparison with the explicit statements in the *Didache* 9 and 10 regarding the eucharist suggests that 1 Tim. 4.1–5 and, less directly, 2 Tim. 1.10 also contain references to the eucharist.

63 White, "St. Paul and the Apostolic Letter Tradition," 439.

64 See the convenient tables in O. Roller, *Das Formular der paulinischen Briefe* (Stuttgart: Kohlhammer, 1933). The κατ' ἐπιταγήν formula is only found in the NT in the Pauline corpus (see 1 Cor. 7.16; 2 Cor. 8.8; Rom. 16.26; 1 Tim. 1.1; Tit. 1.3). Cf. the use of θέλημα in the superscriptions of 2 Tim. 1.1; 1 Cor. 1.1; 2 Cor. 1.1; Gal. 1.4; Eph. 1.1; Col. 1.1.

65 See Quinn, *Titus*, 19–21, 50–51. The Muratorian Canon implies the order Titus, 1 Timothy, 2 Timothy.

66 See Rom. 1.1; Phil. 1.1. Note the use of δοῦλος in the superscripts of James 1.1 (κυρίου 'Ιησοῦ Χριστοῦ); 2 Pet. 1.1 ('Ιησοῦ Χριστοῦ) and Jude 1 ('Ιησοῦ Χριστοῦ). On the use of δοῦλος and its Hebrew Bible background, see G. Saß, "Zur Bedeutung von δοῦλος bei Paulus," *ZNW* 40 (1941), 24–32. Saß argues, correctly in my opinion, that Paul's self-designation has its counterpart in the call of a prophet for the task of fulfilling some task, often with respect to his saving initiative, assigned by God. See also Quinn, *Titus*, 62 who points out that the self-designation articulates "total commitment to another person." Yet, he continues, "the confession has grown out of the realization of one's total dependence on that person. If the slave must obey the master who has dispatched him with his word, it is with the satisfaction that the master has put his trust in him." See also Klaus Berger, "Apostelbrief und apostolische Rede/Zum Formular frühchristlicher Briefe," *ZNW* 65 (1974), 215. Berger notes the use of δοῦλος in Baruch's letter to Jeremiah in the first or second century C.E pseudepigraphon *4 Bar.* 6.19 (*Paraleipomena Jeremiou*) as the closest parallel to Paul's use. The work is extant in Greek as well as other languages.

67 φιλήμονι τῷ ἀγαπητῷ καὶ συνεργῷ ἡμῶν. Cf. 3 John 1: Γαΐῳ τῷ ἀγαπητῷ.

68 Fiore, *Personal Example*, 161 draws attention to Socratic Letter 6.9–11 for the familial relationship between philosopher and his students. For text see Malherbe (ed.), *Cynic Epistles*, 237–9. Cf. John L. White, "The Ancient Epistolary Group in Retrospect," *Semeia* 22 (1981), 8–9. See also the use of τέκνον in the adscripts of papyrus letters cited in MM 628, s.v. τέκνον.

69 They are more analogous with the greetings of Jude 2 (ἔλεος ὑμῖν καὶ εἰρήνη καὶ ἀγάπη πληθυνθείη) and *Mart. Pol.* prescript (ἔλεος, εἰρήνη και ἀγάπη). Cf. Ign. *Smyrn.* 12.2 (χάρις ὑμῖν, ἔλεος, εἰρήνη, ὑπομονὴ διὰ παντός).

70 Cf. 2 John 3: ἔσται μεθ' ἡμῶν χάρις ἔλεος εἰρήνη παρὰ θεοῦ πατρός, καὶ παρὰ 'Ιησοῦ Χριστοῦ τοῦ υἱοῦ τοῦ πατρός, ἐν ἀληθείᾳ καὶ ἀγάπῃ; Jude 2: ἔλεος ὑμῖν καὶ εἰρήνη καὶ ἀγάπη πληθυνθείη.

71 See also Dibelius and Conzelmann, *Pastoral Epistles*, 131. They note that ἔλεος is added in some manuscripts of Titus. See also the discussion of ἔλεος in the greeting formulae in Judith M. Lieu, "Grace to you and Peace," *BJRL* 68 (1985), 171–3.

72 Cf. James, 2 Peter, and Jude among the remainder of the NT epistolary corpus.

73 J. Murphy-O'Connor, *Paul the Letter-Writer: His World, His Options, His Skills* (Collegeville: Liturgical Press, 1995), 103; White, "New Testament Epistolary Literature," 1753. White argues similarly for Ephesians.

74 See M. Kiley, *Colossians as Pseudepigraphy*, 69. Kiley argues that the author of 2 Thessalonians, heavily dependent on 1 Thessalonians, has included the fuller "the grace of the Lord Jesus Christ be with you all" under the direct influence of 1 Thess. 5.28.

75 See Hanson, *Pastoral* Epistles, 116. Dibelius and Conzelmann, *Pastoral Epistles*, 93 n. 35 ascribe to copyists the emendation to the singular. See also Roller, *Das Formular*, 148. Roller notes that the formality of 1 Timothy and Titus is due to the fact that "[d]ie beiden Briefe sind eben nicht in erster Linie für die Empfänger bestimmt, sondern in noch höherem Maße auf die Gemeinden berechnet, an denen die beiden Empfänger als Vertreter des Apostels in höchst offiziellem Auftrage wirken sollten." See also Roloff, *Der erste Brief an Timotheus*, 48, who notes a triangular relationship between the author (of 1 Timothy) and the assumed addressee (Timothy) and actual audience (the community): "Die spezifische Kommunikationsstruktur dieses Briefes ist dadurch bestimmt, daß neben Absender und Adressat als weitere Größe die Gemeinde in Erscheinung tritt." Quinn, *Titus*, 269 aptly characterizes the letter (Titus) as a "personal letter with a public function." I contend that the same could be said for all three PE.

76 See Paul Schubert, *Form and Function of the Pauline Thanksgivings* (Berlin: Töpelmann, 1939), 8. Cf. Peter T. O'Brien, *Introductory Thanksgivings in the Letters of Paul* (Leiden: Brill, 1977), 2. O'Brien declines to treat 1 Tim. 1.12–17 and 2 Tim. 1.3ff. not only because of the question of authorship but also on the ground that they "do not contribute anything of significance to our study." Note, however, the response of Prior, *Paul the Letter Writer*, 189–90 n. 3.

77 With 2 Tim. 1.3–5 and 1 Tim. 1.12–17 in mind, Schubert, *Form and Function*, 8 writes: "Their value from the point of view of form-criticism is that, genetically speaking, they are vestiges of the original and complete Pauline pattern." On 183–4 Schubert argues that the more detailed thanksgivings of Philemon, 1 Thessalonians, Colossians and Philippians "characterize the more elaborate, intimate and personal letters of Paul," while the simpler thanksgivings belong to the less personal and more formal of the letters (Romans, 1 Corinthians, 2 Thessalonians). The εὐλογητός formula of the proemium of 2 Corinthians substitutes for the thanksgiving. This letter was written against the backdrop of Paul's strained relationships with that church. The suppression of the thanksgiving altogether in

Galatians is evidence of Paul's judgment that this church has broken with him and his gospel.

78 *Form and Function*, 9.

79 "The Transition from Opening Epistolary Thanksgiving to Body in the Letters of the Pauline Corpus," *JBL* 82 (1963), 348–62.

80 Sanders, "Transition," 353. See, e.g., 1 Cor. 1.10; 1 Thess. 4.1; 2 Thess. 2.1.

81 Sanders, "Transition," 353. See, e.g., Rom. 1.8; Phil. 1.12; Col. 2.1.

82 δι' ἣν αἰτίαν ἀναμιμνήσκω σε ἀναζωπυρεῖν τὸ χάρισμα τοῦ θεοῦ. However, note the use of the formula in 2 Tim. 3.1 (τοῦτο δὲ γίνωσκε, ὅτι . . .).

83 Τούτου χάριν ἀπέλιπόν σε ἐν Κρήτῃ, ἵνα . . .

84 See Sanders, "Transition," 349–54. Cf. 1 Tim. 2.1; 4.11; 5.7; 6.3, 13, 17; 2 Tim. 3.1; Tit. 3.8. Cf. White, "New Testament Epistolary Literature," 1743–4.

85 See Keck, *Paul and his Letters*, 22.

86 *From Tradition to Gospel* (New York: Scribners, 1965). See especially 238–44.

87 *From Tradition to Gospel*, 238. Dibelius only nominates the "first section" of the *Didache*. Presumably he had *Did.* 1–6 in mind. Interestingly, 7–16 are manifestly specific and occasional. The work is, therefore, an example of "mixed" general and specific paraenesis. For further discussion, see, e.g., Victor P. Furnish, *Theology and Ethics in Paul* (Nashville/New York: Abingdon, 1968), 72–75; W. Schrage, *Die konkreten Einzelgebote in der paulinischen Paränese* (Gütersloh: Mohn, 1961), e.g., 102–09.

88 See Stowers, *Letter Writing*, 23.

89 See *Paul the Apostle*, 69–74. See also the helpful survey in the excursus "paraenetic discourse" in Verner, *Household of God,* 112–25.

90 See Keck, *Paul and his Letters*, 22. Keck notes that the moral exhortation of the Pauline letters is usually somewhat conservative, and that Paul drew on "traditions of moral counsel which touch a range of topics."

91 "New Testament Epistolary Literature," 1739.

92 See *Heirs of Paul*, 40–41.

93 See Malherbe, *Moral Exhortation*, 121; R. Vetschera, *Zur griechischen Paränese*

(Smichow: Rohlicek & Sievers, 1912), 3–5; Fiore, *Personal Example*, 41.

94 Vetschera, *Paränese*, 6. Cf. 7: "Paränese ist ein Literaturerzeugnis, das nach seiner Anlage und seinem Zwecke eine Sammlung von Vorschriften darstellt, die sich durchwegs auf die praktische Lebensführung beziehen, bestimmt, die, die es angeht, zu fördern und zur Tugend zu führen." See also the survey of protreptic address in A. D. Nock, *Conversion* (Oxford: University Press, 1933), ch. 11 (164–86). The contours of the protreptic mode of address were never defined, apparently, in the ancient world.

95 Vetschera, *Paränese*, 7.

96 Seneca, e.g., lists the following varieties of paraenesis (*monitio*) in *Letters*, 94 and 95. Under the category of *monitio* he places consolation (*consolatio*), warning (*dissuasio*), encouragement (*adhortatio*), censure (*objurgatio*), and praise (*laudatio*) (94.39; "Omnia ista monitionum genera sunt"), and, by implication, protreptic exhortation (*exhortatio*) (95.65). For text, see the LCL edition of Seneca's *Epistulae Morales*, vol. 3. See also Appendix A in LCL 3.452.

97 See Stowers, *Letter Writing*, 107–08.

98 Vetschera, *Paränese*, 10–11. Cf. Isocrates, *To Nicocles*, 43.

99 For the question of the influence of Ancient Near Eastern wisdom on Greek thought, see H. Thyen, *Der Stil der Jüdisch-Hellenistischen Homilie* (Göttingen: Vandenhoeck & Ruprecht, 1955), 86.

100 For text, see James H. Charlesworth (ed.), *Old Testament Pseudepigrapha* (New York: Doubleday, 1985), 2.574–82. For extensive discussion and commentary, see P. W. van der Horst, *The Sentences of Pseudo-Phocylides* (Leiden: Brill, 1978).

101 See *Theognidis et Phocylidis fragmenta: et adespota quaedam gnomica* (Berlin: de Gruyter, 1978). The fragments of Chiron can be accessed in the LCL edition of Hesiod, 71–74.

102 See chiefly his *Paul and the Thessalonians: The Philosophical Tradition of Pastoral Care* (Philadelphia: Fortress, 1987); "Hellenistic Moralists and the New Testament," 301–04.

103 Stowers, *Letter Writing*, 92.

104 Stowers, *Letter Writing*, 107.

105 See further on the "species" of rhetoric in ch. 3 section B.

106 The affinities should not be pressed, however. See Stowers *Letter Writing*, 93. Exhortation, Stowers explains, was more often treated by philosophers in their ethics, not by rhetoricians.

107 See Stowers, *Letter Writing*, 92. He adduces the example of 1 Thessalonians.

108 See Fiore, *Personal Example*, 39–40 for affinities between various types of rhetoric. He adduces Quintilian, *Institutes*, 3.8.28 in support.

109 Stowers, *Letter Writing*, 94.

110 See Stowers, *Letter Writing*, 91–92.

111 For discussion, see Nock, *Conversion*, 175; Stowers, *Letter Writing*, 92–93. For reconstructed text, see I. Düring, *Aristotle's Protrepticus: An Attempt at Reconstruction* (Göteborg: Elanders, 1961). Aristotle penned his *Protrepticus* as a response to Isocrates' paraenetical works. See Düring, *Aristotle's Protrepticus*, 19–24.

112 Frag. 50. See Düring, *Protrepticus*, 68–69.

113 Frag. 51. See Düring, *Protrepticus*, 68–69. Cf. frag. 96 (Düring, *Protrepticus*, 86–87): "Therefore all who can should study philosophy, for this is either complete good life, or of all single things most truly the case of good life in souls."

114 Frag. 53 (Düring, *Protrepticus*, 70–71): διὰ δὲ φρόνησιν μηδὲν πονεῖν μηδὲ δαπανᾶν.

115 For text, see Malherbe (ed.), *Cynic Epistles*, 46–51. Cf. *Letter*, 6 ("To the son of a king"): "You have flutes and a purse, but I have arrows and bows. Therefore, with good reason you are a slave, but I am free. And you have many enemies, but I have none. But should you be willing to throw away your money, to carry bows and a quiver, and to live as a free citizen with the Scythians, then these same conditions will obtain for you." Text in Malherbe (ed.), *Cynic Epistles*, 42–43. The collection of letters written in Anacharsis' name date from the third century B.C.E. Anacharsis was a sixth century Scythian prince who visited Athens seeking wisdom. For further detail, see Malherbe (ed.), *Cynic Epistles*, 6. The theme of the "disease" of those who, in the eyes of the philosopher, are enslaved to desire and possessions is also found in the letter of Pseudo-Pythagoras, *Letter to Hiero*, ll. 15–16. "Do not summon Pythagoras to come and live with you," the writer concludes, "because doctors do not want to be infected by their patients" (my trans.). See also *Pseudo-Melissa to Nikostrate*, l.4 in which jealousy is likened to sickness. Texts in A. Städele, *Die Briefe des Pythagoras und der Pythagoreer* (Meisenheim: Anton Hain, 1980).

116 For text, see Diogenes Laertius, *Lives of Eminent Philosophers*, 10.6; C. Bailey, *Epicurus: The Extant Remains* (Westport: Hyperion, 1979), 128–9.

117 For text, see Diogenes Laertius, *Lives of Eminent Philosophers*, 10.122–35; C. Bailey, *Epicurus*, 82–93. Cf. Epicurus' letter to his mother in which the philosopher expresses the hope that one day she will reverse her rejection of his philosophy and, having "knocked at the doors of philosophy," enter the Epicurean community. For text, see Stowers, *Letter Writing*, 115–6.

118 See Diogenes Laertius, *Lives of Eminent Philosophers*, 10.131; Bailey, *Epicurus*, 88–89: ὅταν οὖν λέγωμεν ἡδονὴν τέλος ὑπάρχειν, οὐ τὰς τῶν ἀσώτων ἡδονὰς καὶ τὰς ἐν ἀπολαύσει κειμένας λέγομεν . . . ἀλλὰ τὸ μήτε ἀλγεῖν κατὰ σῶμα μήτε ταράττεσθαι κατὰ ψυχήν.

119 See Diogenes Laertius, *Lives of Eminent Philosophers*, 10.135; Bailey, *Epicurus*, 92–93. In Epicurus' picture of the philosophical life, the student follows the example not just of Epicurus but seeks to conform his life to that set by the gods. They are themselves without trouble (οὐθὲν γὰρ ἀτάκτως θεῷ πράττεται, 10.134). Indeed one becomes a god by the pursuit of the Epicurean ideal (ζήσεις δὲ ὡς θεὸς ἐν ἀνθρώποις, 10.135). Cf. Pseudo-Pythagoras' *Letter to Hiero*, l.8 in which the writer claims that in contrast to the self-indulgent life-style of the addressee, Pythagoras' pursuit of the goals of ἀσφάλεια and αὐτάρκεια leads him closer to God (ἐγγυτάτω θεοῦ).

120 "Come now (ἄγε νῦν)," the writer challenges Diognetus in 2.1, "and look not only with your eyes but with your intelligence (ἴδε . . . τῇ φρονήσει)." Compare the use of ἄγε νῦν in James 4.13; 5.1. Cf. Epicurus, *To Pythocles* (frag.), παιδείαν δὲ πᾶσαν, μακάριε, φεῦγε . . . ("Blessed one, flee from every form of culture"). Text in Bailey, *Epicurus*, 128–9.

121 Cf. the passages discussed at n. 119 above in Epicurus, *Letter to Menoeceus* and Pseudo-Pythagoras, *Letter to Hiero*.

122 *Formgeschichte des Neuen Testaments* (Heidelberg: Quelle & Meyer, 1984), 217.

123 See *Formgeschichte*, 217–8: "In Rom 1–11 geht es um den christlichen Weg des Glaubens an Jesus Christus, in dem trotz der Vorrangstellung des Judentums der jüdische Weg 'aufgehoben' ist."

124 *Formgeschichte*, 218.

125 *Formgeschichte*, 218–20. Cf. the exhortation to accept suffering in 2 Tim. 3.10–13.

126 *Formgeschichte*, 220.

127 See *Personal Example*, 56–57.

128 Cf. Cicero, *To his Brother Quintus*, 1.24. Cicero regards the greatest possible happiness of the governed as the test of the integrity and worth of his brother's actions as propraetor of Asia.

129 Cf. *Demonicus*, 7. Virtue is better than riches. It makes "possible what is for others impossible; it supports with fortitude that which is fearful for the multitude."

130 This was the advice proffered the rebellious Sicilian prince Dionysius in Pseudo-Plato *Letters*, 7 (332D). The author reflects that he and Dion (Dionysius' father) had sought to maintain by argument that this is the way "every man will save both himself and all those under his leadership." See also Seneca, *Letters*, 11 which counsels emulating the virtuous, and *Letters*, 62 which commends the value of keeping good company. Cf. the citation of Menander in 1 Cor. 15.33: φθείρουσιν ἤθη χρηστὰ ὁμιλίαι κακαί. Note also the letter of Zeno to Antigonus. Antigonus had requested his attendance at his court in order that he (Zeno) might train the king in virtue. Because of the infirmity of old age Zeno sends some associates. If you associate with these, he writes, "you will in no way fall short of the conditions necessary to perfect happiness" (for text, see Diogenes Laertius, *Lives of Eminent Philosophers*, 7.9). See also Cicero, *To his Brother Quintus*, 1.18 in which Cicero urges his brother to be careful in the choice of his close associates.

131 Cf. Cicero, *To his Brother Quintus*, 1.21–22.

132 Cf. Pseudo-Isocrates, *Letters*, 7.5 and the exhortation to ruling with gentleness (πράως). See further Pseudo-Plato, *Letters*, 7 (336C–337E) in which the author rehearses, for the sake of the friends of the assassinated Dion of Sicily, similar precepts of mastery over self in the exercise of statecraft. Moreover, they should restrain themselves from seeking vengeance. Only by showing themselves superior both in their attitude to pleasures and in their readiness to abide by the laws will strife be banished from the state (337A). See also Cicero, *To his Brother Quintus*, 1.7: "For what trouble is it to control those whom you rule, if you control yourself?"

133 Cf. Antigonus to Zeno in Diogenes Laertius, *Lives of Eminent Philosophers*, 7.7: "[I]t is obvious that whoever instructs the ruler of Macedonia and guides him in the paths of virtue will also be training his subjects to be good men." The PE value σωφροσύνη highly. See the use of the term and its cognates in 1 Tim. 3.2, 9, 15; 2 Tim. 1.7; Tit. 2.2, 4, 5, 6, 12.

134 For σεμνότης see 1 Tim. 2.2; 3.4; Tit. 2.7. For σεμνός see Phil. 4.8; 1 Tim. 3.8, 11; Tit. 2.2.

135 Isocrates judges Hesiod, Theognis, and Phocylides as the best teachers and advisers (σύμβουλοι τῷ βίῳ τῷ τῶν ἀνθρώπων, §43).

136 *Letters*, 94.32–35.

137 See, e.g., 1 Thess. 4.2; Ign. *Eph.* 4.1; *Trall.* 2.2. For further discussion, see Malherbe, "Hellenistic Moralists and the New Testament," 280–2, 286–7.

138 See D. G. Bradley, "The *Topos* as a Form in the Pauline Paraenesis," *JBL* 72 (1953), 240–1. Cf. T. Y. Mullins, "Topos as a New Testament Form," *JBL* 99 (1980), 542–3. Both scholars note the use of ethical τόποι in the NT paraenetic materials.

139 §15: ἡγοῦ μάλιστα σεατῷ πρέπειν κόσμον αἰσχύνην, δικαιοσύνην, σωφροσύνην. Cf. Seneca, *Letters*, 11 (modesty); 116 (self-control).

140 See also Cicero, *To his Brother Quintus*, 1.13. Cf. Col. 3.8.

141 For "self-control," Pseudo-Isocrates uses the term ἐγκράτεια. Cf. Cicero, *To his Brother Quintus*, 1.5, 7, 8; Tit. 1.8.

142 Cf. Seneca, *Letters*, 83. See also Anacharsis, *Letters*, 3 (text in Malherbe [ed.], *Cynic Epistles*, 40–41); Crates, *Letters*, 10 (text in Malherbe [ed.], *Cynic Epistles*, 60–61). Cf. Eph. 5.18; 1 Tim. 3.8; Tit. 2.3.

143 Cf. Pseudo-Isocrates, *Letters*, 7.12. Though the addressed is not a member of his school, the author has heard reports that he resembles his best students. See further Pseudo-Plato, *Letters*, 10 (358C): "You exhibit the most philosophic disposition."

144 See Verner, *Household of God*, 122–4; Stowers, *Letter Writing*, 94–95. Stowers reminds the reader of Pseudo-Libanius' example of a paraenetic letter (see Malherbe, *AET*, 74–75). Cf. Pseudo-Isocrates, *Letters*, 7.8 and the example of a good king, like Cleomnis of Methymna. See also Pseudo-Plato, *Letters*, 4 (320D–E) which adduces the example of the character and statecraft of both Lycurgus and Cyrus. In the seventh letter, the murdered Dion is presented by the author as an example of virtue to his friends now endeavoring to rule in the stead of the manifestly ill-fitted Dionysius, who functions as a negative example. Cf. Cicero, *To his Brother Quintus*, 1.10 in which Cicero praises Quintus' advisers, one of whom, Tubero, a historian, is especially commended because he has access in research and in writing to many commendable examples from the past. Cf. 1.23 (Xenophon's laudatory portrayal of Cyrus).

145 See LCL edition of the *Moralia*, Vol. 10 which includes the other relevant treatises, namely, *Old Men in Public Affairs* and *Precepts of Statecraft*.

146 A. S. Hunt and J. Gilbart Smyly (eds.), *Tebtunis Papyri, Vol. 3 Part 1* (London: Humphrey Milord, 1933), 66–102. In this period, a *dioecetes* was a minister of finance. See White, *Light From Ancient Letters*, 225. For further discussion of this papyrus, see Fiore, *Personal Example*, 81–83.

147 Cf. *To Nicocles*, 40; *To Demonicus*, 44. Cf. Rom. 15.14–15; 1 Cor. 4.17; 1 Tim. 1.3–7; Tit. 1.5.

148 Lines 270–7.

149 For an extensive examination of the use and function of example in the letters of Socrates and the Socratic letters, see Fiore, *Personal Example*, 101–63.

150 Cf. the maxim: "Train the soul, flee pleasure" attributed to Aristotle (frag. 34), and preserved in Arabic. For text, see D. Gutas (ed.), *Greek Wisdom Literature in Arabic Translation: A Study of the Graeco-Arabic Gnomologia* (New Haven: American Oriental Society, 1975), 172–3. See also Pseudo-Socrates, *Letters*, 5.2 ("To Xenophon"): " . . . let us be better men than others . . . and know that both of these virtues are especially necessary for war; both patient endurance (καρτερία) and contempt for riches (ἀφιλοχρηματία)." For text, see Malherbe (ed.), *Cynic Epistles*, 230–1. The interest in Socrates as an ethical example is particularly developed in letter 6.

151 A similar sentiment is expressed in the paraenetic letter P. Oxy. 3069 (third or fourth century C.E.) in which the writer, who styles himself as a philosopher, commends continued perseverance of pursuit of virtue through ascetic denial.

152 Another letter in the Pythagorean corpus, *Theano to Eubule*, bears comparison with the PE with respect to the duties of mothers with their children. For a discussion of the *Haustafeln* and 1 Peter, see David L. Balch, *Let Wives be Submissive: The Domestic Code in 1 Peter* (Atlanta: Scholars Press, 1981). Balch argues that this teaching stems from the Platonic-Pythagorean tradition of instructing wives. He writes, "The common Greco-Roman demand that wives be submissive to their own husbands was addressed to Christian wives" (121). Cf. Verner, *Household of God*, 71–79; Kidd, *Wealth and Beneficence*, 78–80. Also relevant is the more extensive discussion of household duties in the second century C.E. epitome of Hierocles. See especially excerpts 36f and 36g in Malherbe, *Moral Exhortation*, 97–104 and "Hellenistic Moralists," 304–13.

153 See LCL edition of Pliny's correspondence, Vol. 2, 72 n. 1.

154 Pliny, *Letters*, 8.24.1. See also *To Nicocles*, 40 (cf. *To Demonicus*, 45). Cf. Pseudo-Plato, *Letters*, 10 (358C); Cicero, *To his Brother Quintus*, 1.7; see also 1 Thess. 4.1–2, 9; 5.2; 2 Tim. 3.14; *1 Clem*. 53.1; Ign. *Eph*. 14.1; *Trall*. 3.2.

155 James D. G. Dunn suggests Heb. 6.9 and Ign. *Trall*. 3.2–3 as analogies. See *Romans 9–16* (Waco: Word, 1988), 857.

156 Cf. Isocrates, *To Nicocles*, 24.

157 Stowers, *Letter Writing*, 99. Cf. H. Cancik, *Untersuchungen zu Senecas Epistulae morales* (Hildesheim: Georg Olms Verlagsbuchhandlung, 1967), 78: "Für Seneca ist die Erziehung wie die Freundschaft eine Äusserung philosophischen Lebens."

158 With respect to Seneca's letters and epistolary theory and practice, see Cancik, *Untersuchungen*, 46–58. Cancik notes, e.g., how Seneca's letters serve as self-

presentations of his character.

159 See also the helpful commentary in Cancik, *Untersuchungen*, 62–63.

160 See Fiore, *Personal Example*, 90–97. Cf. 1 Cor. 4.16; 11.1; Phil. 3.17; 4.9; 1 Thess. 1.6; 2 Thess. 3.7, 9; cf. 2 Tim. 3.10–15.

161 *Letters*, 52.8.

162 Cancik, *Untersuchungen*, 32: "Nicht umsonst hat Seneca in §4 so nachdrücklich die Bedeutung der Freundschaft herausgestellt; durch den Zuspruch seines Freundes Seneca wird Lucilius seinerseits die Hilfe der Freundschaft erfahren."

163 On this subject in general, and in the Corinthian letters in particular, see the excellent monograph by John T. Fitzgerald, *Cracks in an Earthen Vessel: An Examination of the Catalogues of Hardships in the Corinthian Correspondence* (SBLDS 99; Atlanta: Scholars Press, 1988), especially ch. 3 entitled: "The Hardships of the Sage."

164 Fitzgerald, *Cracks in an Earthen Vessel*, 76–79 draws attention to other relevant passages in Seneca. These include *Of Providence*, 4.7: "God tests those he loves" (cf. Heb. 12.5–11). In 4.12 Seneca observes that there is no easy proof of virtue, except through suffering. Indeed, only the truly blessed of God suffer. God has not removed the hardships that strike good men so as to cause their true worth to be advertised to all (see further ch. 6).

165 On the athletic imagery of this letter, see Cancik, *Untersuchungen*, 33–35. On 33 n. 52 she draws attention to Paul's similar use of the imagery in 1 Cor. 9.25.

166 *Letters*, 91.15. Cf. 92.2. In 92.18 he proposes that disaster, losses, and wrongs "have only the same power over virtue that a cloud has over the sun." See also *Of Providence*, 5.

167 *Letters*, 2.6. Cf. 1 Tim. 6.6; 2 Tim. 4.13.

168 Cf. Lucius Lucceius' rebuke to Cicero, *Letters to his Friends*, 5.14 (text in LCL *Letters to his Friends*, vol. 1). The writer reproaches Cicero for withdrawing from public and social life in Rome to the isolation of his country estate (at Astura) as though he were the only one affected by political events in Rome. Cicero replies that he is deeply disturbed by the turn of political events and his waning political influence (5.15). Caesar appeared to be seeking the crown. Moreover, Cicero's daughter had recently died in childbirth. Note also the subtle reproach in Cicero's *Letter to his Brother Quintus*, 1.38. Having praised his brother's virtue—"all who come from the province dwell on your virtues" (§37)—he adds that they say that he (Quintus) is the most pleasant person in the world as long as he keeps his temper (§38).

169 See Roloff, *Der erste Brief an Timotheus*, 48; Wolter, *Die Pastoralbriefe als Paulustradition*, 157–61.

170 See 1.1: "Welcoming your godly mind which is fixed as if on immovable rock . . ." *Cf.* the examples from Pseudo-Isocrates and Pseudo-Plato in n. 143 above.

171 Ign. *Pol.* 7.3: εἰδὼς ὑμῶν τὸ σύντονον τῆς ἀληθείας, δι᾽ ὀλίγων ὑμᾶς γραμμάτων παρεκάλεσα.

172 Cf. 2 Tim. 4.5: σὺ δὲ νῆφε ἐν πᾶσιν. See also the similar use of νήφω in 1 Thess. 5.6, 8; 1 Pet. 1.13; 4.7; 5.8.

173 Cf. 2 Tim. 2.3–4 in which suffering and military service are also linked.

174 See, e.g., *Letters*, 78. Cf. 1 Cor. 9.24–27 and, of course, 2 Tim. 4.7 (τὸν δρόμον τετέλεκα).

175 μᾶλλον τοὺς λοιμοτέρους ἐν πραότητι ὑπότασσε. See also the use of the variant πραΰτης in the similar context of 2 Tim. 2.25 (cf. Ign. *Trall.* 3.2).

176 *Formgeschichte*, 121. "Die Funktion paränetischer Reihen ist daher die Erinnerung an allgemeine Verhaltensnormen."

177 See the extensive discussion in *Formgeschichte*, 124–54.

178 See the excellent discussion of Timothy and Titus as Paul's co-workers in W.-H. Ollrog, *Paulus und seine Mitarbeiter* (Neukirchen-Vluyn: Neukirchener Verlag, 1979), 20–23 and 33–37 respectively.

179 See Victor P. Furnish, *II Corinthians* (Garden City: Doubleday, 1984), 103–04. Furnish also suggests that Paul may have been influenced by the requirement of Deut. 19.15, which stipulates that two or three witnesses are required to sustain testimony.

180 See the arguments for knowledge of Acts in Hanson, *Pastoral Epistles*, 13–14, 148–9. Brox, *Pastoralbriefe*, 72–74 and Trummer, *Die Paulustradition*, 132 are not as confident. Dibelius and Conzelmann, *Pastoral Epistles*, 119 are not persuaded that the Pastor knew Acts.

181 See Roloff, *Apostolat*, 239; O. Knoch, *Die "Testamente" des Petrus und Paulus* (Stuttgart: KBW Verlag, 1973), ch. 4.

182 See Trummer, *Die Paulustradition*, 131: "Es entspricht durchaus der schriftstellerischen Technik der Past, daß sie solche authentischen, historischen Nachrichten erweitern und konkretisieren." These "reports" Trummer locates in sources, not necessarily in Acts, known also to the author of the *Acts of Paul*.

183 See, e.g., the incidents which involved Paul and Timothy in Philippi, Thessalonica, and Corinth recorded in Acts 16–18.

184 Brox, *Pastoralbriefe*, 73–74. Cf. Beker, *Heirs*, 64; *The New Testament: A Thematic Introduction*, 92–93; and discussion of Acts 14.4, 14 in G. Lüdemann, *Early Christianity according to the Traditions in Acts: A Commentary* (Minneapolis: Fortress, 1989), 159.

185 1 Cor. 4.17; 16.10; Phil. 2.19; 1 Thess. 3.2, 6.

186 See Schrage, *Die konkreten Einzelgebote*, 108: "Gerade als geistlicher Vater kann Paulus von seinen Kindern, die er in Christus Jesus durch das Evangelium gezeugt hat (1 Kor 4,15), Gehorsam verlangen, was er denn auch ohne alle Umschweife klar und unmißverständlich tut . . ." Schrage continues, "Daß aber nicht die geistliche *Vaterschaft* dem Apostel seine Vollmacht zur paränetischen Weisung gibt, sondern der hinter ihm stehende *Herr*, zeigen die Mahnungen an Gemeinden, die Paulus selbst nicht gegründet hat (Rom, Kolossae), wie Paulus ja auch allermeist seine Mahnungen unter ausdrücklicher Berufung auf sein apostolisches 'Amt' gibt."

187 See Abraham J. Malherbe, *Paul and the Thessalonians: The Philosophical Tradition of Pastoral Care* (Philadelphia: Fortress, 1987), 75; "'Gentle as a Nurse': The Cynic Background to 1 Thessalonians 2," in *Paul and the Popular Philosophers* (Minneapolis: Fortress, 1989), 35–48 (originally published in *NovT* 12 [1970], 203–17. For objections to Malherbe's reading of 1 Thess. 2.7 (ἐγενήθημεν ἤπιοι ἐν μέσῳ ὑμῶν. ὡς ἐὰν τροφὸς θάλπῃ τὰ ἑαυτῆς τέκνα), see S. E. Fowl, "A Metaphor in Distress: A Reading of ΝΗΠΙΟΙ in 1 Thessalonians 2.7," *NTS* 36 (1990), 469–74. Fowl prefers the reading νήπιοι ("infants"). He argues that in 2.1–7 Paul wants to remind the Thessalonians of the lack of self-serving and deceit that characterized his ministry to them. He and his associates were like "infants," with respect to their lack of guile. However, in view of the fact that infants can be demanding, Paul changes metaphor in v. 8 to that of the nurturer. Fowl's argument is not persuasive.

188 For discussion, see Hans D. Betz, *Galatians* (Philadelphia: Fortress, 1979), 233–5 and B. R. Gaventa, "The Maternity of Paul: An Exegetical Study of Galatians 4:19," in R. T. Fortna and B. R. Gaventa, *The Conversation Continues: Studies in Paul and John in Honor of J. Louis Martyn* (Nashville: Abingdon, 1990), 189–201. Gaventa also draws attention to other maternal nurturing imagery used by Paul of his own nurturing role in 1 Cor. 3.1–4.

189 See *TDNT* V, 638–9; Fiore, *Personal Example*, 178–80; Quinn, *Titus*, 72; P. T. O'Brien, *Commentary on Philippians* (Grand Rapids: Eerdmans, 1991), 324. Quinn draws attention to a number of relevant Qumran passages, namely, 1QH 7.20–21 where the Righteous Teacher says, "Thou hast made me a father to the sons of grace, and as a foster father to men of marvel; they have opened their mouths like little babes . . . ," CD 2.14 ("Hear now, my sons, and I will uncover your eyes that

you may see and understand the works of God . . . "); CD 13.9 ("[the Guardian] shall love them [the members of the community] as a father loves his children . . . ") (trans. Vermes).

190 See 1 Tim. 1.2 (γνήσιον τέκνον, cf. τέκνον Τιμόθεε, v. 18); 2 Tim. 1.2 (ἀγαπητὸς τέκνον, cf. τέκνον μου, 2.1); Tit. 1.4 (γνήσιον τέκνον).

191 See Dibelius and Conzelmann, *Pastoral Epistles*, 13.

192 See Quinn, *Titus*, 72. Cf. Roloff, *Der erste Brief an Timotheus*, 58; Kelly, *Pastoral Epistles*, 40–41.

193 μηδείς σου τῆς νεότητος καταφρονείτω.

194 Cf. 2 Tim. 2.22 (τὰς δὲ νεωτερικὰς ἐπιθυμίας φεῦγε). For commentary, see Roloff, *Der erste Brief an Timotheus*, 251, and n. 146. Anyone under 40 years old was considered young.

195 See Furnish, *II Corinthians*, 100, 170. Furnish notes that in addition to Titus in 2 Cor. 2.13, Epaphroditus is styled ἀδελφός in Phil. 2.25, as is Onesimus in Phlm. 16. Only a handful of other co-workers are so designated. For precise details, see *II Corinthians*, 100.

196 See also Rom. 16.3, 9, 21; Phil. 2.25; 4.3; Phlm. 24.

197 See Ollrog, *Paulus und seine Mitarbeiter*, 34–37. Ollrog argues persuasively that Titus, as a Gentile Christian accepted by the Jerusalem "Urgemeinde," represents the unity of Jew and Gentile in the one church.

198 See Furnish, *II Corinthians*, 171.

199 The verb ἐπιποθέω is used of Paul's desiring to see the addressees of a number of his letters (Rom. 1.11; 1 Thess. 3.6; cf. Phil. 1.8; 2.26). See also 2 Tim. 1.4.

200 See Beker, *Paul the Apostle*, 331–2. The collection heralds the unity of Jew and Gentile in the one church.

201 Brox, *Pastoralbriefe*, 269 rightly notes the implied contrast between the behavior of Demas and that of Crescens and Titus, both of whom continue faithful to Paul (see 2 Tim. 4.10).

202 Cf. Donelson, *Pseudepigraphy*, 58–59. Donelson speaks of the "aura of friendship among Paul, Timothy and Titus" created in the PE.

203 Cf. P. Oxy. 528 (second century C.E.).6–9: γινόσκειν σε θέλω ἀφ' ὡς ἐξῆλθες ἀπ' ἐμοῦ πένθος ἡγούμην νυκτὸς κλέων ἡμέρας δὲ πενθῶν ("I want you to know that

ever since you left I have been in mourning, weeping by night and lamenting by day").

204 This is a particularly significant passage for W. Stenger, "Timotheus und Titus als literarische Gestalten," *Kairos* 16 (1974), 252–67. Building on R. W. Funk's article "The Apostolic Parousia: Form and Significance," Stenger (see especially 261, 267) argues that by invoking the *topos* of the apostolic parousia (cf. 1 Cor. 4.17) the author means to claim the presence of the apostle in the traditions and teachings already in place in the church.

205 Cf. the practice of the apostle in 1 Cor. 16.5–6: ἐλεύσομαι δὲ πρὸς ὑμᾶς ὅταν Μακεδονίαν διέλθω, Μακεδονίαν γὰρ διέρχομαι· πρὸς ὑμᾶς δὲ τυχὸν παραμενῶ ἢ καὶ παραχειμάσω, ἵνα ὑμεῖς με προπέμψητε οὗ ἐὰν πορεύωμαι. This sentiment is clearly echoed in several respects in Tit. 3.12–13.

206 Cf. P. Tebt. 703.258–61.

207 See the discussion in Roloff, *Der erste Brief an Timotheus*, 88–90; Quinn, "The Holy Spirit in the Pastoral Epistles," in D. Durken (ed.), *Sin, Salvation, and the Holy Spirit* (Collegeville: Liturgical Press, 1979), 348.

208 This word is used in Mark 16.17 (of the signs that will accompany those who believe). However, individuals are the subject of the verb in Luke 1.3 (the evangelist) and 1 Tim. 4.6 and 2 Tim. 3.10 (Timothy). Cf. 2 Macc. 9.27.

209 Note Brox's remark on this passage in *Pastoralbriefe*, 257. Timothy is the ideal church leader ("Timotheus dieses Ideal verkörpert"), as long as he keeps before his eyes the image of Paul.

210 Note Paul's insistence in 1 Cor. 11.2–16 that in church a woman should wear "authority on the head" (a head covering, see v. 10) while she exercises a ministry of public prophecy in the congregation. For all Paul's concern for social propriety, theologically expressed, that ministry is not taken away. For further discussion, see H. Conzelmann, *1 Corinthians* (Philadelphia: Fortress, 1975), 184–6, 191; Antoinette Clark Wire, *The Corinthian Women Prophets: A Reconstruction through Paul's Rhetoric* (Minneapolis: Fortress, 1990), 130–4.

211 See the concluding comments of part 2 of MacDonald's, *Pauline Churches*, 157–8.

212 See MacDonald, *Pauline Churches*, 16–18, 204, 234.

213 See MacDonald, *Pauline Churches*, 170–180.

214 *Bürgerliches Christentum im Neuen Testament?: Eine Studie zu Ethik, Amt und Recht in den Pastoralbriefen* (ÖBS 4; Klosterneuberg: Verlag Österreichisches Katholisches Bibelwerk, 1983).

215 *Bürgerliches Christentum?*, 120.

216 *Bürgerliches Christentum?*, 120. He cites Eccl. 4.6; Prov. 11.12; 17.1; Sir. 28.16.

217 *Bürgerliches Christentum?*, 121.

218 Cf. 2 Tim. 4.5: σὺ δὲ νῆφε ἐν πᾶσιν, κακοπάθησον, ἔργον ποίησον εὐαγγελιστοῦ, τὴν διακονίαν σου πληροφόρησον. Cf. Ign. *Pol.* 1.3: γρηγόρει ἀκοίμητον. See also White, "New Testament Epistolary Literature," 1755–6, who notes that the traditional summons to responsibility (μὴ ἀμέλει τοῦ ἐν σοὶ χαρίσματος) occurs just this once in the NT, while μέλω and ἀμελέω occur frequently in the hortatory literature. See also Roloff, *Der erste Brief an Timotheus*, 255 and the parallels in the papyri he notes in n. 170. Wolter, *Die Paulustradition*, 185–9 draws attention to the similar use of ἀμελέω in P. Tebt. 703 as well as to its use in the hortatory literature (see especially 188).

219 See his article "Topos as a New Testament Form," *JBL* 99 (1980), 541–7.

220 See his *Let Wives be Submissive*, 51–59. Cf. Verner, *Household of God*, 13–26; Kidd, *Wealth and Beneficence*, 78–93.

221 See Dibelius and Conzelmann, *Pastoral Epistles*, 39–41. "Here, as in Luke-Acts, the ethics of good citizenship serve to regulate the time until the parousia, which is no longer felt to be imminent" (40).

222 Dibelius and Conzelmann, *Pastoral Epistles*, 40.

223 See 2 Tim. 3.12: πάντες δὲ οἱ θέλοντες εὐσεβῶς ζῆν ἐν Χριστῷ Ἰησοῦ διωχθήσονται. See also the discussion of 2 Tim. 1.8–12 and 4.16–17 in MacDonald, *Pauline Churches*, 205.

224 It is highly likely that proto-Gnostic emancipationist tendencies are at work in the congregations of the PE. See also L. W. Countryman, *The Rich Christian in the Church of the Early Empire: Contradictions and Accommodations* (New York/Toronto: Edwin Mellen Press, 1980), 153, and the discussion of the attraction that the Marcionite and other heretical movements of the second century had for the entrepreneurial wealthy. Cf. Verner, *Household of God*, 166–71.

225 See, e.g., the discussion in Dibelius and Conzelmann, *Pastoral Epistles*, 45–49 in which other early Christian and Greco-Roman materials are discussed; and Kidd, *Wealth and Beneficence*, 85. In Aristotle's discussion of the household he was under no illusion that men were fitted to rule over women in the household (see his *Politics*, 1259a37ff.).

226 See further ch. 3 n. 118.

227 See Kidd, *Wealth and Beneficence*, 85–86; Verner, *Household of God*, 186.

228 See the discussion in J. Thurén, "Die Struktur der Schlußparänese 1. Tim. 6, 3–21," *ThZ* 26 (1970), 247. Thurén rightly draws a comparison between the generous disposition expected of Timothy and the rich, and contrasts the greed implied of the false teachers in vv. 3–10.

229 See, e.g., Am. 2.6–8; Prov. 11.24–28.

230 See Kidd, *Wealth and Beneficence*, 83–85 who cites Verner's study with approval. See also Countryman, *Rich Christian*, ch. 5.

231 Quinn, *Titus*, 88–89: "The church is a family in which God is Father; a bishop is compared to a man, often a slave, who administered the property of the head of the house" (88).

232 See Kidd, *Wealth and Beneficence*, 61–66. The work of Edwin A. Judge, *The Social Pattern of Christian Groups in the First Century* (London: Tyndale Press, 1960) has been crucial in explicating this aspect of the early mission of the church (see especially 57–61).

233 See the brief discussion of *1 Clem.* 44 and life-long tenure of the clergy in Countryman, *Rich Christian*, 154.

234 See Verner, *Household of God*, 149; Countryman, *Rich Christian*, 165–6; Kidd, *Wealth and Beneficence*, 77, 136–7.

235 See Countryman, *Rich Christian*, 162–6. The wealthy, according to Countryman, would have expected the shape of their role as members of the church to conform to those they enjoyed as members of Greco-Roman clubs.

236 Cf. the example of Jesus given in Ign. *Pol.* 3.2: "Wait for him who is above seasons, timeless, invisible, who for our sakes became visible, who cannot be touched, who cannot suffer, who for our sakes accepted suffering, who in every way endured for our sakes."

237 See discussion in Fiore, *Personal Example*, ch. 8 (191–231), who notes not only the use of positive and negative examples in the PE but also their use in the Pauline and the Socratic letter corpora.

238 *Cracks in an Earthen Vessel*, especially ch. 4.

239 See, e.g., 47 n. 4 on the catalogue of 2 Tim. 2.6; 167 n. 141 on the "ignoble" vessels in 2 Tim. 2.20.

240 Fitzgerald, *Cracks in an Earthen Vessel*, 203.

241 See the discussion of the Greco-Roman background in Fitzgerald, *Cracks in an*

Earthen Vessel, 90.

242 See Brox, *Pastoralbriefe*, 229: "Sehr wichtig ist die enge Verknüpfung des 'Zeugnisses für den Herrn' mit der Person des Apostels."

243 Fitzgerald, *Cracks in an Earthen Vessel*, 96 draws attention to Epictetus' remarks in *Discourses*, 1.1.22–25 and 1.30.7 on the philosopher remembering his training in times of adversity.

244 Fitzgerald, *Cracks in an Earthen Vessel*, 60 notes the observation in Plato, *Phaedo*, 60E to the effect that of all people philosophers find death least alarming. The prospect of death reveals not only the true philosophers but also reveals the false, the "lovers of the body," like Demas (2 Tim. 4.10).

245 Prior, *Paul the Letter-Writer*, 161 interprets the present imperatives in 2 Timothy 2—see, e.g., vv. 22–23 (my italics) (τὰς δὲ νεωτερικὰς ἐπιθυμίας *φεῦγε*, *δίωκε* δὲ δικαιοσύνην, πίστιν, ἀγάπην, εἰρήνην μετὰ τῶν ἐπικαλουμένων τὸν κύριον ἐκ καθαρᾶς καρδίας. τὰς δὲ μωρὰς καὶ ἀπαιδεύτους ζητήσεις *παραιτοῦ*)—as indications that "there is something seriously astray in Timothy and in his presentation of the Gospel." In 2 Tim. 2.14 (ταῦτα ὑπομίμνῃσκε, διαμαρτυρόμενος ἐνώπιον τοῦ θεοῦ μὴ λογομαχεῖν), Prior argues (158–62) that it is Timothy again who is the problem, not the false teachers (cf. Brox, *Pastoralbriefe*, 245–6). Prior has misread the significance of the present imperatives. See N. Turner, *A Grammar of New Testament Greek, Vol. III: Syntax* (Edinburgh: T. & T. Clark, 1963), 74–75. On Turner's analysis of the distinction between the present and aorist imperative, either nothing specially significant can be read into the use of the present (n.b. the inexplicable switch to the aorist in 2.15), or that the use of the present is "less pressing, less rude, less ruthless, than the aorist" (75). It should also be noted that the present is the preferred tense of the imperative in the paraenetic discourses of Isocrates. See, e.g., *To Demonicus*, 13: "First of all, then, show devotion to the gods" (πρῶτον μὲν οὖν εὐσέβει τὰ πρὸς τοὺς θεούς); 32: "avoid drinking parties" (εὐλαβοῦ τὰς ἐν τοῖς πότοις συνουσίας). See also Ign. *Pol.* 4.3: "Do not be haughty [to slaves]" (μὴ ὑπερηφάνει) and 5.1: "Flee from evil arts" (τὰς κακοτεχνίας φεῦγε).

246 Cf. Ign. *Pol.* 2.3 in which the prize for sober diligence in the task (of being a bishop) is "immortality and eternal life" (τὸ θέμα ἀφθαρσία καὶ ζωὴ αἰώνιος).

247 See Dibelius and Conzelmann, *Pastoral Epistles*, 88 (baptism or ordination); Kelly, *Pastoral Epistles*, 141–2 (baptismal confession).

248 See Quinn, "The Holy Spirit," especially 359–63.

249 Quinn, "Holy Spirit," 359 ("no trite formula").

250 See, e.g., Seneca, *Letters*, 78.1, 4; Pliny's letter to Geminus (advice about the recipient's illness drawn from personal experience), *Letters*, 7.1 (107 C.E.); P. Tebt. 315.32 (second century C.E.): μὴ ἀμελήσῃς σαυτοῦ.

251 See Baur, *Pastoralbriefe*, 24–25; Kelly, *Pastoral Epistles*, 128–9; Dibelius and Conzelmann, *Pastoral Epistles*, 80–81.

252 See Jeremias, *Die Briefe an Timotheus und Titus*, 58.

253 For discussion of this and another possible identification (cf. Acts 19.33), see Hanson, *Pastoral Epistles*, 160.

254 See Brox, *Pastoralbriefe*, 274: "Der 1 Tim 1,20 genannte Alexander wird kein anderer als der hier erwähnte sein. Es ist gut denkbar, daß eine historische Gestalt, und zwar ein prominenter Ketzer, hinter diesem Namen steht."

255 See "Testaments," in Michael E. Stone (ed.), *Jewish Writings of the Second Temple Period* (Philadelphia/Assen: Fortress/ Van Gorcum, 1984), 325.

256 For the terms of the wills of philosophers, see Diogenes Laertius, *Lives of Eminent Philosophers*, 3.41–43 (Plato), 5.11–16 (Aristotle), 5.51–57 (Theophrastus), 5.61–64 (Strato), 69–74 (Lyco), and 10.16–22 (Epicurus, including a brief letter to Metrodorus). All these are concerned with the disposal of property, not with moral exhortation as in the Jewish testaments. However, the note in Lucian, *The Passing of Peregrinus*, 41 concerning the letters Proteus wrote before his death is enigmatic and suggestive of exhortatory concerns: φασὶ δὲ πάσαις σχεδὸν ταῖς ἐνδόξοις πόλεσιν ἐπιστολὰς διαπέμψαι αὐτὸν, διαθήκας τινὰς καὶ παραινέσεις καὶ νόμους. Other Greek writers are reported to have written διαθῆκαι, namely, Apollonius of Tyana (*Life*, 7.35) and Menippus (*Lives of Eminent Philosophers*, 6.101).

257 *Personal Example*, 161–3.

258 See, e.g., *2 Bar.* 44, *Bib. Ant.* 33 (law), *Jub.* 21 (idolatry), and *T. Reub.* 1 (sexual sins). Cf. the Letter of Jeremiah (Bar. 6). Though it has no epistolary prescript or postscript, it is introduced as a letter ('Αντίγραφον ἐπιστολῆς, ἃς ἀπέστειλεν Ιερεμιας πρὸς τοὺς ἀχθησομένους αἰχμαλώτους εἰς Βαβυλῶν . . .). The bulk of the document is a polemic against idolatry. Like much of the early Jewish testamentary deposit, therefore, Ep. Jer. stresses loyalty to Moses in difficult times. For discussion of other early Jewish letters, see Berger, "Apostelbrief und apostolische Rede," 190–231, and P. S. Alexander, "Epistolary Literature," in Stone (ed.), *Jewish Writings of the Second Temple Period*, 579–96.

259 See his helpful summary in *Die Lehre der Alten* (Leiden: Brill, 1980), 1.229–42.

260 *Die Lehre der Alten*, 1.233. Consequently, von Nordheim has no difficulty in assigning Acts 20.17–38 to the genre, even though it is not recorded that Paul dies. See his remarks on this passage on 238–9.

261 See "Testaments," 325. Cf. G. W. E. Nickelsburg, *Jewish Literature Between the Bible and the Mishnah* (Philadelphia: Fortress, 1981), 232.

262 Collins, "Testaments," 326–9 discusses other works bearing the title "Testament." *T. Abr.* is not a testament at all, since it does not purport to report the final words of Abraham. *T. Sol.* does not describe the narrative context and death of Solomon. *T. Adam*, a composite work whose parts are only loosely related to each other, bears only a slight relationship to the testament genre as defined by Collins. The same could be said of the Testaments of Isaac and Jacob. By contrast, von Nordheim's more flexible definition allows more documents to be classed as testaments including *T. Sol.*, *T. Adam*, *T. Abr.*, *T. Isaac*, *T. Jacob* (the last three are regarded as one work, *T. 3 Patr.*) and 4QAmram.

263 Collins, "Testaments," 329.

264 *Die Lehre der Alten*, 1.233–4. The character of the moral exhortation, von Nordheim writes, "tritt nicht gesetzlich auf, selbst wenn sie in Imperativen einhergeht, sondern sie will überreden, überzeugen, einsichtig machen. Da ein Testament also seine Lehren nicht aufzwingen will, bleibt nichts anderes übrig, als sie mit Argumenten zu belegen, um sie so den Lesern nahezubringen."

265 Von Nordheim, *Die Lehre der Alten*, 1.238.

266 *Formgeschichte*, 75–80.

267 Cf. *T. Levi* 10.1: "And now, my children, observe the things which I commanded you (νῦν οὖν φυλάξασθε ὅσα ἐντέλλομαι ὑμῖν), since what I have heard from my ancestors I have told you."

268 1 Tim. 5.21; 6.20; 2 Tim. 1.12, 14; 4.15.

269 1 Tim. 5.21 (διαμαρτύρομαι . . . ἵνα ταῦτα φυλάξῃς χωρὶς προκρίματος); 1 Tim. 6.20 (ὦ Τιμόθεε, τὴν παραθήκην φύλαξον).

270 See *Formgeschichte*, 78–79.

271 See Roloff, *Apostolat*, 239. Roloff also draws attention to other parallels between this passage and the PE, such as Acts' account of Paul's ministry of teaching in Acts 20.20 (cf. 1 Tim. 2.7; 2 Tim. 1.11) and the certainty of the coming of false teachers in 20.29–30 (cf. 1 Tim. 4.1–3; 2 Tim. 3.1–9; 4.3–4). See also Knoch, *Die "Testamente,"* chs. 4 (on Acts 20.18–35) and 5 (on 2 Timothy).

272 See, e.g., the warning concerning false teachers in 14.4: "You will bring down a curse on our nation, because you want to destroy the light of the Law which was granted to you for the enlightenment of every man, teaching commandments which are opposed to God's just ordinances."

273 Cf. the alternate consolations and woes in *1 Enoch* 94–104.

274 See also Wolter, *Die Pastoralbriefe als Paulustradition*, 222. Nevertheless, he, like J. Munck (see "Discourses d'adieu dans le Nouveau Testament et dans la littérature biblique," in *Aux sources de la tradition chrétienne: Mélanges offerts à M. Maurice Goguel* (Neuchatel: Delachaux & Niestlé, 1950), 155–70), perceives testament-like elements in 2 Timothy. See his analysis on 222–41. By and large, he concurs with von Nordheim's delineation of the genre.

275 "Discourses d'adieu dans le Nouveau Testament," 155–70. See especially 163. In 2 Peter the characteristics are the same except for (iii)—the author as model of faithful Christian witness. In 2 Peter the assumed author claims to be a witness of the transfiguration.

276 Prior's thesis in his *Paul the Letter-Writer* to the effect that 2 Timothy is not a "farewell letter," is unpersuasive and defies the context of the letter as a whole. His reading of 2 Tim. 4.6–8 is totally forced. Had he given more attention to the scholars who have attempted to define the genre, he might have not dismissed the views of those who have attempted to read 2 Timothy as a testament. As it is, Prior repeatedly charges falsely that those who take this view have not defined what they mean by a testament.

277 See Wolter, *Die Pastoralbriefe als Paulustradition*, 235 for parallels from *T. Sim.* 7.3, *T. Dan* 6.9, *T. Benj.* 10.3–4, *2 Bar.* 84.9, and *T. Adam* 6.9–10. The German translation of the latter can be found in von Nordheim, *Die Lehre der Alten*, 1.173–4. This section of the later manuscript tradition of the *T. Adam* has been excluded from Charlesworth's edition of the Old Testament Pseudepigrapha (see *OTP*, 1.xxvi).

278 See Knoch, *Die "Testamente,"* 53–55.

279 See *Die Pastoralbriefe als Paulustradition*, 232–3.

280 See, e.g., *T. Levi* 10; *T. Iss.* 6.

281 Cf. Stowers, *Letter Writing*, 97; Fiore, *Personal Example*, 190; Quinn, "Paraenesis and the Pastoral Epistles," in M. Carrez, J. Doré, and P. Grelot (eds.), *De la Tôrah au Messie* (Paris: Desclée, 1981), 495–501; Wolter, *Die Pastoralbriefe als Paulustradition*, 134.

CHAPTER THREE

THE PE AND THE RHETORIC OF SPEECHES

Chapter two focused on the PE as letters of moral exhortation in which the Pauline tradition received by the Pastor was commended to the actual addressees. My attention in this chapter will be the Pastor's use of the strategies approved in the classical and Greco-Roman rhetorical handbooks, chiefly those of Aristotle (384–322 B.C.E.) and Quintilian (ca. 35–ca. 100 C.E.) as representative of the Greek and Roman rhetorical traditions respectively.

It is not my intention to offer a reading of the individual PE according to one or other of the species of oratory and the schema (τάξις) appropriate for it. None of the PE, in my opinion, are susceptible to the kind of reading that scholars have recently proposed for Galatians, 2 Thessalonians, or 2 Peter and Jude.[1] The PE do not belong to the forensic, deliberative, or epideictic species of oratory. They are letters, not speeches. However, I hope to show that the PE can be better understood not just as letters employing the kinds of persuasive strategies used in the letter writing tradition of moral exhortation but as letters owing much to the tradition of oratory as it was analyzed by the rhetorical theorists and practised by the orators.

Accordingly, I will begin by outlining briefly the role of oratory in the ancient world. Subsequently, I will examine the PE against the background of the species of rhetoric, before proceeding to an investigation of the PE and the three "proofs," namely, appeals to reason (arguments grounded in the persuasive appeal of logic in the speech), ethos (arguments grounded in the persuasive appeal of the trustworthy character of the speaker), and pathos (arguments grounded in the persuasive appeal to emotion in the hearers). These studies will be supplemented with appropriate comparisons drawn from other classical theorists, examples from classical oratory, and comparisons with the other letters of the Pauline corpus in addition to analysis and comment from modern commentators. Finally, I propose analyzing the Pastor's disposition towards his audience as an attempt to account for the function of the PE in the ecclesiastical situation as far as that can be fairly ascertained from the letters themselves.

A. Rhetoric in the Ancient World

Rhetoric has been called the "art of speaking well": i.e., the art of speaking persuasively.[2] As such, it is an essential prerequisite of those who function in settled public life—politicians and lawyers in particular. It would be impossible to over-estimate the significance of rhetoric in the Greco-Roman world in the realms of political and judicial discourse, education, and literature. In Greek society, with its stress on public speaking, it had been recognized by the middle of the fifth century B.C.E., at least, that there were persuasive strategies that could be emulated and taught, and, moreover, used for powerful effect in the public arena and in literary enterprise, including the production of letters, as we have already seen in chapter two.

The rhetorical craft appears to have been reduced to a system and practised first in Sicily as a tool for training speakers in the law courts.[3] The craft was brought to Athens by the sophist Gorgias in 427 B.C.E. The preeminence of rhetoric in public discourse by the beginning of the fourth century was not without challenge. Gorgias' arrival and subsequent effect on political life in Athens provoked a vigorous response from Plato, whose dialogue *Gorgias* is a particularly spirited attack on the integrity of rhetoric.[4] Plato, much exercised by questions of rhetoric's perceived lack of virtue, argued that it was merely a species of flattery (κολακεία), and that the orator was more concerned with being pleasant and entertaining than with questions of truth.[5] The skilled but unscrupulous practitioner could persuade his audience by flattery that something untrue was in fact true, or that a course of action considered unwise or unjust should be followed instead of one which was inherently wise and just.[6] Crucial for understanding Plato's implacable opposition to rhetoric is the fact that Socrates, Plato's revered teacher and mentor, had roundly condemned sophists before succumbing to the fate of being judicially murdered in 399 B.C.E.

However, the rhetorician and educator Isocrates (436–338 B.C.E.), a pupil of Gorgias, sought to counter Plato's weighty arguments. He contended that the way to overcome the problem of unscrupulous use of the craft of rhetoric was to provide training in the art as a preparation for political life. By this means one might be able to inculcate a sense of what is right and honorable in those being trained for public life. In his famous speech, the *Antidosis*, Isocrates laid the foundations of Greek rhetorical education (*paideia*) by arguing that while no one is able to implant honesty and justice in depraved people, they can become better if they devote themselves to the task of speaking well and being able to persuade their hearers (τοῦ πείθειν δύνασθαι τοὺς ἀκούοντας). This is so because the person who desires thus to be persuasive will not be negligent of the matter of character.[7]

Isocrates established the first rhetorical school in Athens in 390 B.C.E.[8] Thereafter rhetoric formed the curriculum of the most advanced of the three stages of Greco-Roman education.[9] It was a remarkably long-lived and widespread phenomenon, extending its influence through the medieval and renaissance eras into modern times.[10] In the Greek democracies persuasive speaking was essential to the judicial and political process.[11] The study of rhetoric was therefore regarded as essential for operating in the vocal political life that obtained. Moreover, the early theoreticians, such as Isocrates and Aristotle, were remarkably influential throughout the Greco-Roman era. Cicero and Quintilian in their treatments of the subject pay homage to their forebears in the rhetorical tradition, Aristotle in particular. They saw themselves as those who built on the earlier foundation.[12]

This is not to say, however, that Aristotle's rhetorical theory was followed in every respect. J. Wisse shows that the Aristotelian system with its distinctive role of the three proofs as organizing principles is not to be encountered in the handbooks again until Cicero's *de Oratore*.[13] The kind of rhetorical theory operating in Aristotle's day, constructed according to the arrangement of the parts of a speech, viz., *proemium*, narration, proofs, and epilogue, was intentionally superseded by Aristotle. His *Rhetoric* is grounded on the three proofs, namely, arguments grounded in appeals to reason, ethos, and pathos.[14] However, the extant handbooks between Aristotle and *de Oratore* revert to the older pattern. This is not to say their authors did not discuss the proofs. They simply chose to structure their theory differently.[15]

Aristotle, himself Plato's pupil, while acknowledging the danger of rhetoric in the hands of the mere flatterer or sham, contended, nevertheless, that those speaking the truth have an obligation to be persuasive since rhetoric, to be effective, operates at the level of what is recognized by the audience as ethically or generally true.[16] He proceeded to analyze the craft as an art (τέχνη) with its own set of principles and rules, paying due regard to the need of the speaker to understand his audience.

The differences between Plato and the rhetoricians, including Aristotle, are quite profound. Aristotle, while allowing dialectic as it had been practised by Socrates, saw its shortcomings in public life. Philosophical dialectic presented arguments which most could not follow and which did not sway and move their hearers for all the philosophers' devotion to investigating the truth (see n. 2). Aristotle saw the possibilities of persuasive speech in the public arena, particularly in matters of truth and justice. Moreover, he increasingly came to concentrate his attention on the fields of practical knowledge, rhetoric included, and less on matters involving "theoretical knowledge" (ἐπιστήμη) of the transcendent world of the ideas, access to which Plato and his school confidently asserted.[17] The Platonists looked down on the rhetorical arena in which debate largely consisted in what was possible or probable. For them the pursuit of "proof" (πίστις) was a pursuit after an inferior knowledge based on mere "opinion" (δόξα) and altogether inferior to ἐπιστήμη.[18] However, Aristotle contended that the quest for πίστις was an entirely proper aim of public discourse. He wrote his *Rhetoric* out of the conviction that the responsible orator had an obligation to persuade (πείθω) his audience in matters of truth and justice where differences of opinion required deliberation and debate.

Rhetorical manuals were produced from the second quarter of the fifth century.[19] Aristotle's *Art of Rhetoric*, though not really a manual for public speakers, is a treatise devoted to careful analysis for speakers of how the minds of listeners work.[20] In many ways its influence was pervasive throughout antiquity and the medieval era. It represents, in the words of one commentator, the first systematic hermeneutic of the everydayness of being with another.[21]

The work is marked by supreme confidence in the goodness of the orator and in his ability to move his audience to the right decisions about good and just courses of action. The *Rhetoric* is the handbook *par excellence* of the statesman intimately concerned with the political life of the city-state.

Although rhetorical theory is only clearly systematized and enunciated in the fifth century, it is evident that effective rhetorical practice is to be encountered and appreciated as early as Homer. One presumes that the later conventions of rhetorical discourse were deduced from the earlier literary models. Although by the standards of later fully-fledged Greek oratory the speeches in Homer are lacking somewhat in inventive artistry when compared with later classical practice, there is, nonetheless, an awareness of persuasive strategy. The speaker in Homer, Kennedy observes, "relies heavily on his personal authority."[22] This is to be seen, e.g., in the debate between Agamemnon and Odysseus in the first book of the *Iliad*. The poet shows that he is aware of the effect of the persuasive and credible impression given by the speaker, an argumentative strategy based on what Aristotle termed the ethos (ἦθος) of the speaker. In the example from Homer, the gods actually enhance the speaker's poise and dignity. Persuasion is also effected by emotion (πάθος) in Homer, the most memorable example of which is Priam's speech to Achilles in the *Iliad*, book 24.[23] There are also examples of the use of what Aristotle would later call non-artistic or "extrinsic" proofs, such as Odysseus' design to rouse Achilles to action by quoting Achilles' father's words to his son concerning the need to save the Achaeans (see *Iliad*, book 9).[24]

In the PE, the ἦθος of Paul the apostle stands behind the author in much the same way that the gods enhance the persuasive effectiveness of Homer's Greek heroes. To invoke the name of the revered apostle in his manifesto against the heretics of his day and for the maintenance of the Pauline heritage in the church was to enlist Paul's undeniable apostolic authority as the weight behind his message. That authority was presumably recognized and esteemed by the audience. In turn, as the author of the PE underscores, God himself guarantees the message of the assumed author (1 Tim. 1.11–12; 2.7; 6.3; 2 Tim. 1.11–12).

This observation does not imply that the PE are exclusively oriented to classical and Greco-Roman modes of persuasion. Certainly, Kennedy argues, *reflection* on the art of rhetoric was foreign to Hebrew culture. This does not mean, however, that persuasive technique was not significant.[25] He notes signs of "oral, persuasive intent" in the literature of the Hebrew Bible and early Judaism which should be acknowledged in the study of early Christian rhetoric.

But, observes Kennedy, the essential quality of biblical rhetoric in Judaism is not the self-conscious use of the persuasive strategies of reason, ethos and pathos but the assertion of authority. That authority derives from God's assertive speech—the law being his final word in the realm of personal and public conduct.[26] Divine authority can also be accorded to agents—prophets in particular—who speak not on their own but on God's behalf with a sure and authoritative word. Authority is somewhat analogous to the function of the persuasive power of the ethos of the orator in Greco-Roman rhetoric. This is so because persuasion depends on knowledge of the character of God whose assertive speech the prophet mediates. Nevertheless, in the Hebrew Bible the assertion of divine authority appeals to something other than the orator's ability to craft a credible and ordered presentation of a case and invent appropriate persuasive strategies. Moreover, miracles play a large part in confirming or establishing the authority of the speaker.[27] Aristotle might have classed miracles, along with prophetic oracles, as extrinsic rather than intrinsic to the speech, i.e., they pre-exist the speech and, to paraphrase him, are used by the speaker not invented by him.[28]

A. N. Wilder highlights a further difference between the rhetoric of the classical Greek tradition and that of the Bible. He observes that the "rhetorics" of the Hebrew Bible take their rise from the response of the people of God to his already existing deeds and speech. The word of God elicits the response of praise which in turn summons the hearers to make the praise of God their own.[29] Kennedy himself argues that public discourse in early Christianity is characterized by proclamation, with its attendant stress on authoritative and assertive speech, and not by persuasion. With special reference to Mark 13.9–13 and 1 Corinthians 1–2, this thesis is argued for the NT writings in his book *Classical Rhetoric and its Christian and Secular Tradition from Ancient to Modern Times*.[30] However, in his 1984 book, *New Testament*

Interpretation through Rhetorical Criticism, he refines his position. He now argues that it is possible to investigate most NT texts from the standpoint of Greco-Roman rhetoric. However, discourse which relies on assertion rather than reasoned argument he now terms "radical Christian rhetoric."[31] Paul's stated position in 1 Corinthians regarding his avoidance of rhetorical eloquence is still taken at face-value by Kennedy.

However, Kennedy's understanding of the rhetoric of the NT has been recently challenged by John R. Levison.[32] Pointing out Kennedy's change of mind over the matter of the disjunction of Greco-Roman rhetoric and NT rhetoric, i.e., in so far as the NT relies on assertion of authority not persuasion, he makes a case for interpreting Paul's comments in 1 Cor. 1–2 as those of the εἴρων—the ironical person. He argues that Paul avoids not the conscious crafting of his message—there are rhetorical *tours de forces* in the Corinthian correspondence—but the extravagances of the rhetorically literate "super-apostles" which induce the Corinthian audience to compare unfavorably Paul's rhetorical ability with theirs (see 2 Cor. 10.10).[33] It is a comparison in which the "super-apostles" also seem to have been boastfully engaged (see 2 Cor. 10.12; 11.12).

Despite Kennedy's commitment to the distinctive qualities of the rhetoric of the Hebrew Bible, he finds an analogy to the function of pathos in Greco-Roman rhetoric in the Bible's clear delineation of divine salvation-historical initiatives on Israel's behalf as a spur to heeding the divine word in the present. Deuteronomy is especially relevant in this regard. At one level the appeal is to heed the message because of divine achievement on Israel's behalf in the past. The stress is also on future punishment if that word is not heeded now—Deut. 26–28 is particularly instructive here. Similar to the manner of deliberative rhetoric in which the focus is on the advantages and disadvantages of a course of action under consideration, Moses advises that failure to heed now will have disastrous disadvantageous consequences for the future felicity of the nation, while obedience will reap untold benefits. Consequently he urges a decision to be made in the present that will avert national catastrophe and guarantee salvation.[34]

Much closer links than those argued by Kennedy for the Hebrew Bible, indeed links of influence, between Hellenistic rhetoric and the legal deposit of the later Rabbinic era have been posited by David Daube.[35] He argues that the Rabbis, following the lead of Hillel, whose teachers, according to the Talmud, were the Egyptian proselytes Shemaiah and Abtalion, interpreted scripture in ways that bear out close analogy with rhetorical practice, especially in forensic rhetoric.[36] This is evidenced, as Daube shows, in Hillel's seven norms of interpretation of the scriptural deposit, especially in the Rabbis' approach to *lacunae* in scriptural law. As in the rhetorical theory of Cicero, they argued that a point of law not written might be derived by analogy from what is written.[37] Moreover, according to the Rabbis, the lawgiver, in this case Moses, foresaw the interpretation of his statutes, and, accordingly, did not legislate on all matters because they were deducible from general precepts. Once again parallels in Cicero are cited by Daube.[38] Lest one think that only diaspora Jews would have encountered the tradition of Greek rhetoric, Hengel is able to demonstrate that Gadara, in Palestine, was a center of Hellenistic *paideia*.[39]

B. The PE and the Species of Rhetoric

Different occasions and kinds of audiences require the speaker to employ different rhetorical strategies. Beginning with Aristotle, the manuals and treatises speak of at least three species of rhetoric relative to the occasions and kinds of audiences addressed.[40] Aristotle classifies his three species and the subjects proper to each as "judicial"—dealing with what is just (δίκαιον), "deliberative"—with what is expedient (συμφέρον), and "epideictic"—with what is honorable (καλόν).[41]

Judicial (τὸ δικανικόν)

This species of rhetoric, sometimes called "apologetic" or "forensic," was the type of rhetoric suited to the law-court where the speaker seeks to bring about a judgment concerning events of the past. The hearers function as the jury. The speaker seeks to persuade his hearers with respect to matters of justice and injustice. Aristotle observes that there are two kinds of judicial speech—accusatory (κατηγορία) and defensive (ἀπολογία).[42] Kennedy calls this species of rhetoric "the most characteristic form of Greek oratory" because litigants were required by Athenian law to speak on their own behalf.[43] Many accomplished rhetoricians, like Antiphon, Lysias, Isaeus, and Andocides, wrote speeches for litigants to deliver.[44] Typically such a speech gained the attention of the hearers in a *proemium*, set out the facts relevant to the case, offered proof with the meeting of objections, and concluded with a succinct epilogue which sometimes included polemic against one's opponent(s), and a final, often emotion-laden, appeal to the jury.[45]

In the NT, the book of Acts includes a number of judicial speeches, the most extensive of these being Paul's defences before Felix (24.10b–21) and Agrippa and Festus (26.1–23), the former being preceded by an accusatory speech by Tertullus (24.2b–8).[46] More contentious as far as identification of genre is concerned is the case of Galatians. Hans D. Betz, first in an article and later in an extensive commentary on the letter, contends that the presentation of the argument in Galatians can be explained in the same terms as a judicial speech, the apostle defending himself and his message before the Galatian church as jury.[47] Betz accounts for the structure of the letter according to the rhetorical conventions of the handbooks. His thesis has been challenged by a number of writers.[48] Joop Smit, as we shall see below, argues that Galatians is a deliberative speech.

Deliberative (συμβουλευτικόν)

This species of rhetoric, the rhetoric of parliamentary debate, concerns itself with a course of action to be taken in the immediate future, and appeals to the hearers' perception of what is advantageous or disadvantageous for them. Aristotle argues that there are two forms of deliberative speech: exhortation or persuasion (προτροπή) and dissuasion (ἀποτροπή).[49] The hearers are in a position to be won over by the speaker to his way of thinking and to his vision of the future. This species of oratory might be concerned with finances, war and peace, defence, imports and exports, the framing of laws, and religious ritual (ἱεροί).[50]

Typically the deliberative speech followed a similar course to that outlined above for the judicial speech, although Aristotle observes that there was little need for a *proemium* since the audience usually already knew the issues to be addressed.[51]

Much of the New Testament and early Christian literature, including the PE, has affinities with this category of persuasion. This is because many of the documents of the NT are seeking to inculcate in their respective audiences the need to be diligent concerning their continued commitment to the Christian life-style.[52] In chapter 2 we noted the obvious analogies of such letters with deliberative rhetoric. In my examination of the epistolary tradition I sought to show that the theorists regularly defined paraenetic letters as communications concerned with exhortation (προτροπή) and dissuasion (ἀποτροπή). Persuasion or dissuasion is often accompanied by warning and rebuke, lest the believers fail to set their minds to working out the moral and relational implications of their salvation. The point is made particularly clearly by James H. Moulton in a discussion of the unusual use of μή with the present imperative in Eph. 5.18 (μὴ μεθύσκεσθε), Col. 3.9 (μὴ ψεύδεσθε), and Jas. 5.12 (μὴ ὀμνύετε). Such commands, Moulton insightfully observes,

> were very practical indeed . . . [T]he apostles were not tilting at windmills, but uttering urgent warnings against sins which were sure to reappear in the Christian community or were as yet only imperfectly expelled.[53]

In the same way, the exhortations of the PE seek to persuade or dissuade. We have observed that a number of different persuasive strategies are at work in these letters. The Pastor underscores the past saving events and the eschatological events to come as motivation for godly living. He appeals to conventional morality, social expectation, the Hebrew Bible, and Jewish tradition (see 1 Tim. 2.11–15) as a means of excluding women from teaching in the congregation. Elsewhere, in his endeavor to direct the discussion on the subject of the conduct of and prerequisites for congregational leaders, and the proper use of wealth, he presents a paradigm of the suffering, but patient, apostle—content even in hardship.

The letter to the Galatians, a fruitful source of investigation for scholars of Greco-Roman rhetoric, has been assessed as a deliberative speech by Joop Smit.[54] Smit argues that the apostle writes not so much to defend his apostleship but to persuade the Galatians to remain true to him and his message. The choice facing them, he writes, is whether they should

> cling to the religious practice they learned from Paul or whether they should make the changes advocated by the opponents.[55]

The choice for the Pauline gospel has moral implications which are set out in chapters five and six. Paul clearly delineates the advantages of remaining loyal to his gospel. He is equally adamant that to change their loyalty will prove disadvantageous to them. In like manner, the PE have a decided deliberative function since the Pastor is concerned to inculcate a particular image of Paul the apostle and to commend his concept of the shape of ecclesiastical and Christian life. He is seeking to demonstrate that his image of Paul as the worthy apostle is the only valid one, possibly in the face of challenge from other professed guardians and keepers of the heritage of the apostle. The assumed author of the PE underscores his apostolic authority and right to sanction ecclesiastical and moral order in the church.

Epideictic (ἐπιδεικτικόν)

This species of rhetoric, the oratory of display,[56] seeks assent to a particular value or virtue, or invites the apportioning of blame and censure. Once again Aristotle divides the species into two categories. The audience is summoned to affirm the praise (ἔπαινος) or blame (ψόγος) offered by the speaker.[57] Existing qualities in things and in people are the focus of this species (*Rhetoric*, 1.3.4). The chief way forward in constructing such a speech, Aristotle advises, is to amplify the characteristics—whether praise- or blameworthy—of the subject (1.9). Thus in a speech of praise (or *encomium*) the presence of virtues such as justice, courage, self-control, magnificence, liberality, gentleness, prudence, and wisdom are to be amplified, whereas in a speech of blame their absence is to be underscored.[58] The arrangement of such a speech resembles the format of the judicial and deliberative species. The orator underscores what the audience already values and esteems.[59]

The NT also knows this kind of speech and the rhetorical strategies appropriate to it. Paul uses epideictic strategies in 2 Corinthians in a justly famous parody of them in chs. 10–12 as he struggles for the affections of the Corinthians against the rhetorically pretentious "super-apostles." In 11.22–12.10 he allows himself equality with the latter in respect to γένος (11.22), but proceeds to advertise his "superior" achievements which amount to a parading of his weaknesses, ignominies, and griefs as an apostle willing to be spent in the service of the churches.[60] He can even speak of his "courage," one of the virtues regularly amplified in epideictic speeches, in his frightened escape down the wall of Damascus (11.32–33).[61]

The hymnic and liturgical materials of the NT belong broadly to this species of rhetoric. In his survey of the characteristics of the Pauline letters William Doty observes that Paul writes to the congregations in his care not merely to maintain friendly relations with them but

> to bring his addressees into richer experiences of the new religion, to move them to new heights of action and response.[62]

For this reason, Doty implies, the letters

> incorporate elements of the ongoing life of the churches such as liturgical materials, sacred institutions, legal and moral guidelines, and sayings.[63]

Liturgical materials are my interest here. Why, precisely, do the letters of the Pauline corpus, and other NT letters for that matter, include this material? One answer is that they function epideictically, i.e., they are reminders of what the addressees already and regularly affirm in their meetings.

Building on B. Malinowski's understanding of language's capacity to establish "phatic communion," i.e., rapport between people, George B. Caird terms this function of language "cohesive."[64] Small talk regularly performs the function of setting people at ease, creating "a sense of mutual trust and common ethos."[65] But rapport can also be created, Caird observes, by less trivial language, including appeals to traditions, like scripture, or other authorities revered in common, and by the language of worship.[66]

In the PE rapport, or "cohesion," between the Pastor and his audience is established by at least four kinds of material:

1. The "faithful sayings" (πιστοὶ λόγοι) function as authoritative statements which are part of the transmitted Pauline tradition, and which, I surmise, were held in undiminished esteem by the Pauline congregations of the PE. These sayings underscore what for the audience constitutes, in part, the body of self-evident truth. They have the effect of affirming the teaching and ethics of the PE, and, in the case of 1 Tim. 3.1, the ambitions of those who would be leaders in the congregation.

2. The Pastor and his audience share a partially overlapping understanding of what constitutes proper social behavior. While writer and members of his audience might not unanimously agree, perhaps, on the universal applicability of these standards to church life, the author can at least appeal to certain moral and social conventions and proprieties which are both valued in society and sanctioned by tradition. Where there might be disagreements, such as over the role of the wealthy men in the congregations, the Pastor appeals to the unquestioned authority of Paul as an ethical model to underscore what is proper conduct for them in the church. With respect to the role of women teaching men in the congregation, the Pastor argues from the potent mix of social convention, early Jewish tradition, and scriptural warrant.

3. The literary conventions of the Pauline letter are reproduced in the PE. The PE commend themselves to their audience as Pauline letters. The letters' stylized prescripts and postscripts, their modicum of Pauline *personalia*, their evocation of the apostolic parousia, their presentation of the apostle who suffers and endures yet who sanctions and guides the believers still in his care through his emissaries, and their echoes of the Pauline corpus and Pauline theology all commend this assessment. The PE plead their faithfulness to Pauline traditions, and are redolent of the apostle's own mode of operating with his congregations. In doing so, the Pastor is writing "cohesively," appealing to traditions about Paul held in common by the congregations.

4. The Pastor cites liturgical and hymnic materials to establish rapport with his audience. All believers share this language in the churches of the PE. Moreover, this strategy of citing liturgical material enables the Pastor to enlist his addressees' support in confirming the paraenesis offered in the letters. Thus, as Verner argues, 2 Tim. 2.11–

13, a hymnic formulation (which is also a πιστὸς λόγος), serves as the climax to the argument in which believers are urged to endure suffering in their service in the sure knowledge that Jesus, who suffered and died and was raised, will not forsake them.[67]

The case of the "Christ-hymn" of 1 Tim. 3.16 warrants special attention. Here is an undeniable hymnic fragment. However, its function in its context is disputed. The significance of that context, both for the letter and the PE as a whole, has often been noted. For example, Lock argued that 3.14–16 was the "heart of the Epistle," 3.15 encapsulating the purpose of the PE.[68] Stephen E. Fowl also regards the hymn of great significance.[69] He associates the passage with the theological argument which follows in 4.1–5, arguing that

> the teaching about Christ's appearance in the earthly realm and subsequent vindication [affirmed and proclaimed in the hymn] supports the claim (in 4.1–5) that God's creation is good.[70]

Verner, however, contends more persuasively that the hymn really accompanies the argument in 3.14–15, the hymn climaxing the discussion of the centrality of the church in the purposes of God as "the church of the living God, the pillar and foundation of the truth" (ἐκκλησία θεοῦ ζῶντος, στῦλος καὶ ἑδραίωμα τῆς ἀληθείας, v. 15).[71] For Verner, the majesty affirmed in the hymn neatly supplements the greatness of the household of God. The Pastor is appealing to his audience to affirm his vision of the household. The exalted and cosmic focus of the hymn invests living as members of the household, whatever one's status, with utmost seriousness and responsibility. Verner himself concludes:

> The way one conducts oneself as a member of the Christian community is a matter of the highest significance.[72]

Furthermore, the definition of "the mystery of godliness" (τὸ τῆς εὐσεβείας μυστήριον, 3.16a) is a significant issue for understanding this passage. The term μυστήριον clearly has reference to the disclosure of saving events captured in the hymn.[73] Εὐσέβεια, "religious duty," was one of the cardinal virtues everywhere affirmed. In the context of the PE, one would therefore expect the term to have a decided Godward reference, and, moreover, given the confessional nature of v. 16, to be a synonym for the objective sense of "the mystery of faith" (τὸ μυστήριον τῆς πίστεως) the Pastor has in mind in 3.9.[74]

However, it is arguable that the term also has to do with the quality of life within the household of God which is in view in 3.14–15. This would mean that right behavior in the household is designated as εὐσέβεια. According to this argument, εὐσέβεια functions both as a designation of the confessional statement of divine saving achievement (in 3.16) and as the virtue which denotes what has been brought into being in the household and which is manifesting itself among believers in the godly household.[75] The saving events, the subject of the Christ hymn, have their analogy in the church's life. Salvation leads to εὐσέβεια. In this way, the Pastor buys into the debate concerning the contours of εὐσέβεια in the congregation by presenting Paul, the assumed author, as the ultimate guide and exemplar of what is appropriate behavior in the household of God.

This discussion of the rhetoric of praise in the PE shows that what the Pastor affirms the audience also affirms. Yet, as we have seen in the discussion of 1 Tim. 3.14–16 in particular, the Pastor directs his appeals to changed behavior and perceptions on the basis of what is already held in common and affirmed by both writer and audience.

C. The PE and Aristotle's Three "Proofs"

Aristotle argues that there are two kinds of proof (πίστις): one extrinsic to the speech, and the other intrinsic to the speech.[76] The former, already discussed briefly above in the first section of this chapter, pre-exist the speech and are merely used by the speaker, not "invented" by him. Aristotle gives as examples witnesses to an event, evidence of slaves taken under torture, and contracts.[77]

By contrast, proof intrinsic to a speech is created by the speaker. Books 1 and 2 of his *Rhetoric* are devoted to the means of persuasion available to the orator, and which are invented by him. These are three in number: (i) reason, (ii) ethos, and (iii) pathos. Solmsen notes that Aristotle raised the proofs of ethos and pathos to a status on par with reason, and made proofs no longer a part of the taxonomy of a speech, as in many extant contemporary speeches, but a "function of the speech" as a whole. This means that for Aristotle the use of proofs was appropriate throughout the speech, not confined, as in contemporary rhetorical practice, to that one section only (namely, the proof section following the *proemium* and the *narratio*).[78]

The persuasive force of the appeal to reason in a speech resides in the content of the speech itself, i.e., in the logic of the arguments employed. Their persuasive power derives from the truth as generally understood, or the apparent truth of what is said, as perceived by the hearers (1.2.6).[79] By ethical proof Aristotle means the persuasive force of the trustworthy character—the ethos—of the speaker which lends credibility to the case he is making (1.2.4). The persuasiveness of appeals to pathos resides in the speaker's ability to arouse the emotions and dispose his audience to hearing him favorably (1.2.5).

Reason (λόγος)

Aristotle detects two categories of persuasive technique which are used in this category of rhetorical proof. These are inductive and deductive arguments. The former take the form of examples or paradigms. Aristotle denotes an argument by deduction a rhetorical syllogism. The differences between the two are addressed briefly in *Rhetoric,* 1.2.9.[80] In inductive mode the speaker attempts to show from many instances that something is true. In employing rhetorical syllogism—Aristotle calls this the enthymeme—the speaker is hoping to demonstrate deductively what is true via the medium of the speech.

Discussion of the rhetorical paradigm is taken up again in 2.20. The paradigm, an especially useful device in deliberative oratory, can take two forms. The speaker can refer to things that have happened, and he can invent his own paradigms. Into this latter category fall metaphor or comparison (παραβολή) and fable (λόγος). Their use, counsels Aristotle, is particularly helpful when it is difficult to find historical incidents by which to argue one's case. It is necessary, e.g., that the orator show the existence of the analogy between the fable he inserts into his speech and present day conditions (2.20.7). Nevertheless, historical illustrations are more valuable if they are at hand, since "future events will be like those of the past" (2.20.8). Finally, urges

Aristotle, if one does not have a "supply of enthymemes, one should use paradigms as demonstration" (2.20.9). However, if the speaker does have enthymemes, paradigms are helpful as illustrations and witnesses of the truth of the enthymeme. At the end of an argument, paradigms are especially powerful. Moreover, few are needed at the end of an argument, whereas if one begins inductively a larger number is needed.

The persuasive power of paradigms is well-illustrated in Plutarch's *Lives* in which the praiseworthy deeds and accomplishments of great ones from the past are held up as examples to be emulated in the present. The *encomia* of the "faithful ones" (πιστοί) in Heb. 11 and the "famous men" in Sir. 44–50 function similarly.

In Greco-Roman oratory, two speeches by Isocrates—*On the Peace* and *Areopagiticus*—illustrate the use of paradigms in support of enthymemes. The former speech was published in Athens in 355 B.C.E. during the Social War in an attempt to persuade Athens to sue for peace with her former confederates. In support of the contention that a state's happiness and prosperity depend on its commitment to religious duty (εὐσέβεια), moderation (σωφροσύνη), justice (δικαιοσύνη), and virtue (ἀρετή), Isocrates argues that Athenians will attain to this character if they "stop setting their hearts on the empire of the sea."[81] Using the example of disastrous Athenian ventures during the Peloponnesian War, he demonstrates that nothing has been learned by his audience in their present attempt to emulate the "recent follies" of their ancestors. Indeed, in more recent times they criticized the Spartans for seeking to exercise such an hegemony.[82]

In the *Areopagiticus*, another deliberative speech addressing the Athenians, delivered at the conclusion of the Social War in the same year (355 B.C.E.), Isocrates appeals for a restoration of the powers of the aristocratic Areopagus as a means of checking the extravagances of demagoguery, which only contributes to mismanagement of foreign policy. He observes:

> Nothing can turn out well for those who neglect to adopt a sound policy for the conduct of their government as a whole.[83]

In support of this statement, Isocrates instances the recent Athenian experience. The city destroyed its own hegemony among the Greeks in the ruinous Social War because there was no proper political machinery in place to deal with Athenian internal affairs (§12). Those who govern their states "nobly and wisely," he continues, are visited with success (§13). To this end, Isocrates proposes restoring the contours of the democracy that was instituted by Solon and re-established by Cleisthenes (§16). The strongest proof, he argues, that this constitution was right for Athens lies in the fact that those who lived under it

> wrought many noble deeds, won the admiration of all mankind, and took their place, by the common consent [not by coercion] of the Hellenes, as the leading power of Hellas.[84]

On the other hand, the present sorry state of constitutional affairs has produced a great many internal and foreign indignities, as well as evils (§§17–18). The remainder of the speech is replete with a large number of examples enlisted to prove the truth of the above contention.

In the discourses and letters of moral exhortation examined in chapter 2 there are many instances of the use of examples to demonstrate the point being made by the author. In Seneca's correspondence with Lucilius, e.g., the author on occasion proffers himself as an example for his *protégé* in the interests of furthering his moral guidance.[85] In letter 6 Seneca comments on the value of examples as a helpful means to inculcating virtue. Precepts, on their own, slow the process down.[86]

The use of examples in the PE has also received attention in chapter 2. The examples found in the PE are both negative and positive. The latter are aimed at setting up models of ministry and Christian living which are recognizably Pauline in their orientation. They function as persuasive adjuncts to the exhortations delivered by the author, underscoring their reasonableness. Whether the examples are Jesus, Paul, Timothy, Titus, or Onesiphorus, all these are embodiments of the vision the Pastor has for life and leadership in the church. By contrast, the negative examples afforded by Demas, Alexander, Phygelus and Hermogenes, Hymenaeus and Philetus, and Jannes and Jambres, serve to underscore the perils awaiting those who trifle with the apostolic faith.

Persuasion derived from rhetorical deduction, i.e., the enthymeme, receives greater attention in Aristotle than inductive paradigm. Having introduced the subject in *Rhetoric*, 1.2.8–22, Aristotle devotes a considerable section of book 2 (chs. 21–25) elaborating the use and effectiveness of the enthymeme. The reason for his more extensive treatment resides in his conviction that speeches using enthymemes are more persuasive than those using paradigms alone (1.2.10).

Enthymemes are persuasive because they are deduced from premises which are or seem true to the audience (1.2.11). In Lysias' speech *On the Murder of Eratosthenes*,[87] the case hinges on the syllogism:

1. The law condemns adulterers to death,
2. Eratosthenes was an adulterer, therefore
3. Eratosthenes deserved to die.

A further matter in this speech is also being debated in the court. This issue might be expressed syllogistically as follows:

1. The law allows the wronged husband the satisfaction of killing the man who committed adultery with his wife,
2. The husband killed Eratosthenes, who had committed adultery against him, therefore,
3. The husband did not break the law by killing Eratosthenes.

Indeed, the premises may be left unstated by the speaker to be supplied by the audience in cases where the premise is self-evident (*Rhetoric*, 1.2.13).[88]

Enthymemes are derived from the cumulative evidence of paradigms, and also from two other sources. These are what Aristotle calls "probabilities" (εἰκότα) and "signs" (σημεῖα) (1.2.14). By "probabilities" he means statements or observations which are generally true, though not necessarily true in individual instances.[89]

When Aristotle speaks of "signs" in rhetoric he means premises which bear a relationship to what is signified. Aristotle subdivides "signs" into those that evidence a "necessary" and an "unnecessary" relationship to the signate (1.2.17). Necessary "signs" (τεκμήρια) are those which are logically irrefutable and from which might be derived a logically valid syllogism. However, while an "unnecessary sign" (σημεῖον ἀνώνυμον)—like a "probability" (εἰκός)—yields only a "probable conclusion," the "unnecessary sign" (σημεῖον ἀνώνυμον) exhibits "a stronger probability pointing toward the specific signate than a probability" (εἰκός).[90] Both the "probable" statement and the "unnecessary sign" are subject to refutation. The "necessary sign," however "indicates a constant and unchanging relationship between sign and signate," and is not subject to refutation.[91]

In book 2 of the *Rhetoric* Aristotle deals extensively first with maxims and then with the strategies that can be employed in framing enthymemes. A maxim (γνώμη), he argues, is an assertion (2.21.2). The conclusion of enthymemes are maxims, as are the premises (when one omits the full syllogism). He observes that those who tend to speak in maxims are the elderly. They speak from the authority of a life-time of experience. On the other hand, those who indulge in maxims, but are in-experienced, only demonstrate their foolishness. Country folk, Aristotle surmises, are inordinately given to uttering maxims, showing themselves off as they do so (2.21.9).

Aristotle is persuaded that maxims make a significant contribution to speeches especially when the hearers are uncultivated. The persuasiveness of the speech is rendered more so by the speaker who, by his maxims, affirms opinions the hearers already hold to be self-evidently true (2.21.15). Moreover, if the speaker's maxims commend what is morally good, the estimate of his character (ἦθος) is enhanced (2.21.16).

Kennedy's observation respecting the appropriateness of the use of maxims in religious discourse is apposite.[92] In such discourse the authoritative teacher can offer unsupported maxims. These are effective and persuasive because in many cases the authority of the teacher has been established on grounds that are extrinsic to the discourse such as portents, miracles, or oracles. The religious history and literature of Israel, with its succession of prophets speaking authoritatively in God's name, furnishes many examples of this kind of rhetoric. The NT is not without its successors of the prophets of Israel who speak in this way.[93]

However, we have observed that moral exhortation in the Greco-Roman tradition as well as in the PE is often concretized. It proceeds on the basis of appeal to what is regarded as traditional or conventional, or can be demonstrated by logic, as we saw in the brief analysis of some of the *topoi* of 1 Timothy in the previous chapter. In these the Pastor does not lay out bare, unsupported maxims.

Lewis Donelson has argued that the Pastor's argumentative strategy is based on the kind of deductive reasoning that is encountered in Aristotle's theory of the enthymeme, i.e., on reasoning based either on self-evident truth or truth that can be demonstrated.[94] The truths to which the orator appeals should accord with the world-view of the orator, and for maximum effect, should be shared by the audience. Donelson demonstrates that the ethical injunctions of the PE are not simply imposed on the audience, but flow from three sources. These are (a) salvation statements, (b) the character of the religious life, and (c) the entrusted traditions.[95] A number of brief examples of deductive reasoning from each of Donelson's three categories follow.

(a) The conviction that Jesus came into the world to save sinners (see 1 Tim. 1.15) is followed by the statement that Paul regards himself as the "worst of sinners." Therefore, Jesus is able to save him (see vv. 13, 16). In 1 Tim. 4.7b–8, the exhortation to "train yourself for godliness" can be expressed enthymetically. As godliness leads to life, and training can produce godliness, so, if one wants life, one should train oneself in godliness.[96]

(b) What is proper behavior for women is argued on the basis of the character of the religious life as understood by the Pastor and sanctioned by societal convention (see 1 Tim. 2.9–15). Likewise, widows are exhorted to act properly on the basis of the Pastor's sense of what is appropriate (1 Tim. 5.5–8). In both instances, the argument is sound, Donelson observes, if the audience accepts as self-evident the truths to which the Pastor appeals. 2 Tim. 3.17 is an excellent example of an enthymeme—a man of God should do good works, scripture equips a person for good works, therefore, the Pastor appeals to his audience, study scripture.[97]

(c) If the bishop/overseer adheres to the "sound word," i.e., the entrusted traditions, it is argued that he will be able to give sound instruction and refute his opponents (Tit. 1.9). This conclusion is derived from an implied major premise—a bishop is God's steward set over the household of God for its good order and progress in godliness.[98]

Ethos (ἦθος)

Persuasive strategies based on the speaker's portrayal of the trustworthiness of his character are called ethical by Aristotle. The definition extends to the speaker's evocation of the personality and character of others, perhaps his opponents or allies.[99]

An extensive discussion of this πίστις occurs in *Rhetoric*, 2.1.5–7 and 2.2.12–17. In the former, Aristotle observes that speakers are persuasive not only on the strength of their use of reason (see the discussion of enthymemes above) but also if they convince the hearers that they (the speakers) are endowed with practical wisdom (φρόνησις), virtue (ἀρετή), and good-will (εὔνοια) towards the audience (2.1.5). As we saw in the discussion of Isocrates' defence of rhetoric against Plato's charges that it was merely a species of flattery, the existence of wisdom and virtue in the rhetorician was presupposed by Aristotle. Persuasion is the product, at least in part, of affirming in the minds of the audience the prevailing sense of what is morally appropriate and just.

The use of ethical persuasion is well-illustrated in three speeches of Lysias. In *On the Murder of Eratosthenes,* the speaker, accused of setting a trap to murder his wife's lover, portrays himself as a trusting, though naïve, husband. The death of Eratosthenes by his hands is justified, he argues, in the light of ancestral custom, which ceded such a right to the husband. The frank and engaging glimpses into the home-life of the accused is crafted to portray the accused as a man of simple and innocent habits, admitting even to the accusation by his wife that he has made improper advances, while drunk, to the maid. The character of the dead man, on the other hand, is that of the habitual adulterer.

Something of the same persuasive frankness is evident in the speech *Against Simon*. Here the defendant, a middle-aged man caught up in an embarrassing amorous rivalry with the accuser Simon for a young boy, is accused of wounding Simon with intent to kill. The defendant portrays himself as a peace-loving citizen, the victim of Simon's repeated outrageous, violent, and jealous attacks. While Simon desired to force the boy's favor, the accused showed him kindness. While on the one hand Simon's violent temperament was already evident in his military service as well as in his relentless harassment of the accused and the boy, the accused, on the other hand, has long been a model citizen.

In the speech *Before the Council: In Defence of Mantitheus at his Scrutiny*, Mantitheus is accused of siding with the oligarchs in the crisis of 404–03 B.C.E. in Athens. Now under scrutiny before he can take his place in the Council in the restored democracy, he portrays himself as a supporter of the existing constitution, and as one whose private life is exemplary. Although impoverished in the wake of the death of his father, he has bestowed two sisters in marriage with not inconsiderable dowries, and settled the larger part of the estate on his younger brother. In public affairs, he observes that the best proof of his character lies in the fact that his younger contemporaries, who spend all their time drinking or playing dice, are all feuding with him. He instances his bravery in a number of foreign campaigns. The speech ends with an admission of and an apology for his precocity in speaking in the Council. He declares his respect for the service rendered by his ancestors as councillors and for the members of the present administration, who furnish him with the proper models for public service.

In the PE the most persuasive of the strategies employed by the actual author is the presentation of the ethos of Paul. He is no mere example, but a model, a paradigm, of Christian life and leadership. He models self-less, faithful service. On the basis of his life of faithfulness, encapsulated in the passages like 2 Tim. 3.10–12, Paul can exhort with supreme authority. Moreover, this can only be the case if the audience already subscribes in considerable degree to the contours of the ethos of Paul generated by the Pastor.

Here the personal details recorded in 2 Tim. 4.6–22 and Titus 3.12–15 come into their own.[100] They function as contemporary vignettes of the kind of ethos Paul has always projected. Paul makes do without a cloak for the time being, until it is necessary in the approaching winter (2 Tim. 4.13a; cf. 1 Tim. 6.8). Contentment (αὐτάρκεια) marks his life-style (1 Tim. 6.6). Unlike the wealthy, who might be tempted to ruinous love of luxury, he is not inured to excess and self-indulgence (cf. 1 Tim. 6.7–10). He continues to work, requesting manuscripts and parchments (2 Tim. 4.13b), and, as is implied in 2 Timothy, continues to write and conduct his apostolic brief from prison (2 Tim. 4.10b, 12). His first defence became a further opportunity for him to exercise his apostolic ministry to the Gentiles, declaring the gospel fully for them to hear (2 Tim. 4.17). Yet, he is fully confident, even in the midst of suffering, that he will be kept for the Lord's heavenly kingdom (2 Tim. 4.18). As the suffering apostle, he is presented in terms reminiscent of the worthy philosopher, facing death calmly without bitterness and threat.[101] His thoughts are only for his colleagues (2 Tim. 4.15; Tit. 3.13) and the churches languishing at the hands of false and unscrupulous teachers who are seeking to undo the apostle's legacy (Tit. 3.14). He is the model of divine grace. Once the chief of sinners, he is now above reproach. He is the good and faithful teacher: the enduring apostle.

The personal details, therefore, function as paradigms of Christian life and leadership.[102] Paul, Donelson argues, is the prototype of the gracious servant (i.e., congregational leader) of God.[103] Paradoxically, he is also the prototypical heretic as well as the rebuker of heretics. He is, moreover, the prototype of the abandoned, but faithfully enduring, church leader.

Aristotle's *Rhetoric*, 2.12–17 is devoted to the classification of various types of audience and the kind of ethical strategies the speaker should adopt in speaking to each. Coming after his examination of ethos (2.1.5–7) and pathos (see 2.2–11), this section has implications for constructing both ethos and pathos arguments.[104] As it stands in the *Rhetoric*, this section aids the speaker to adopt the appropriate manner of speaking to audiences, which are presented according to well-defined "characters."[105] Aristotle's investigation is suggestive for the study of the ways in which the Pastor addresses his audiences and the ethos he assumes for each.

The young (2.12), Aristotle observes, are impulsive. Their wants are sharply felt and quickly satisfied. They long for victory more than honor. They are the least lovers of money. They are also guileless, filled with good hopes, and are sensitive to shame.

Something of the ethos of the young, as Aristotle presents it, is reflected in Paul's appeal to Timothy to flee youthful passions (τὰς δὲ νεωτερικὰς ἐπιθυμίας φεῦγε, 2 Tim. 2.22). Titus is bidden to urge the young men of his charge to control themselves (Tit. 2.6).[106] Young widows, and young women in general, are also addressed in the PE (see 1 Tim. 5.11–15; Tit. 2.4–5) as inherently impulsive, unstable in their commitment to Christ, and apt to forget their household duties.

The elderly (*Rhetoric*, 2.13), on the other hand, are, for the most part, the opposite of the young. They think they know everything. They are cynical and suspicious. Worn down by life, they are small-minded, expect the worst, live in their memories of the past and by calculation.

The Pastor advises his emissaries not to rebuke an older man but rather to treat him as a father, and to treat older women as mothers (1 Tim. 5.1–2). On the other hand, the exhortation in Tit. 2.2–4 with respect to the character of the elderly implies cause for rebuke.

Those in the prime of life (2.14) combine the best and worst of the characters of the young and elderly. Those of good birth (2.15) are rather ambitious because those born with advantage seek to add other benefits to it. They are contemptuous, even to those who share their rank and whose achievements rank alongside their own. They are fixated by the deeds of their ancestors. The Pastor also alerts the young Timothy to be on guard lest he become the object of contempt.[107]

Aristotle rather dismisses the well-born, likening them to the harvest from the old stock which sometimes brings forth what is good and sometimes produces a degenerate harvest. The wealthy (2.16) are insolent, arrogant, ostentatious, and pretentious. They think that they deserve to rule, believing that their possession of money makes them worthy. The *nouveaux riches* have all the vices of those with old wealth only to a greater degree because they lack the education to use their money well. The powerful (2.17) are ambitious, aiming at deeds they have the means to accomplish. They are earnest because of their responsibilities, and grave and reserved because of their prominence in society. Those blessed with good fortune, concludes Aristotle (2.17.5–6), though often arrogant and insolent, are, nonetheless, "lovers of the gods" (θιλόθεοι) and stand in a special relationship to them.

The PE set great store by the wealthy men in the congregation. 1 Tim. 6.18 finds them being urged to be rich in good deeds, liberal, and generous. As Countryman has argued, these men would probably have expected to be leaders in the congregation by virtue of their wealth, after the manner of the exercise of leadership in their clubs.[108] However, although the leadership will come from their ranks, since they too are heads of households (1 Tim. 3.4, 12), they are charged not to be haughty (μὴ ὑψηλοφρονεῖν, 6.17). Significantly, wealth is absent as a prerequisite for congregational leadership. The Pastor seems fully aware of the potential dangers presented to the church by the ethos of the wealthy.

In this subsection on ethos arguments, some comments on the rhetoric of polemic or invective in the PE are warranted. In speeches, polemic can arouse emotions of hostility against the targets of the orator. Polemic belongs to the genre of the rhetoric of blame. In epideictic speeches, therefore, it consisted of the studied reversal of the topics used in the rhetoric of praise. However, the function of polemic in the PE has more to do with the need to contrast the ethos of the speaker with the ethos constructed by the Pastor of the false teachers.

Paul also uses the language of polemic. For example, Rom. 16.17–18, with its warning of the coming of false teachers (cf. Acts 20.29–30), anticipates the more sustained attacks on them in the PE, especially in 1 Timothy (1.9–10 contains a list of particularly gross moral lapses) and Titus. The polemic of the PE has been likened to the traditional vilification of sophists by philosophers.[109] Robert J. Karris, however, seeks to demonstrate that one can learn a little about the specifics of the teaching of the false teachers from the polemic of the PE. He perceives both the traditional schema in the PE and the evidence of more specific charges made against their teaching.[110]

Unfortunately, the results of his investigation are meagre, as Karris himself acknowledges.[111] Once one removes the traditional vilification contained in the vice lists and the stock polemic,[112] and when the charges distinctive of the three letters are tabulated, there remains the following picture of the teachers. They desire to become "teachers of the law" (1 Tim. 1.7), are fixated by genealogies (1 Tim. 1.4; Tit. 3.9),[113] forbid marriage, and teach abstinence from certain foods (1 Tim. 4.3). They also teach Jewish myths (Tit. 1.14; cf. 1 Tim. 1.4).[114] As for their origin, some, at least, are Jewish (μάλιστα οἱ ἐκ τῆς περιτομῆς, Tit. 1.10).

The Ephesian false teachers of 1 and 2 Timothy might be further defined, over against the Cretan false teachers, as proto-Gnostics (1 Tim. 6.20). They argue that the resurrection has already occurred (2 Tim. 2.18), and hold ascetic notions concerning marriage and food (1 Tim. 4.3), views not specified of the Cretans. The Cretan false teachers are given a more specific Jewish persona, as indicated by Tit. 1.10, 14. As far as the actual situation of the letters is concerned, I conclude hesitantly that the false teachers on Crete are either not precisely identical with those in Ephesus or the writer had only a rudimentary understanding of them. There are emancipationist tendencies in evidence in 1 Tim. 2.11–15 (with respect to women teaching men), as well as in 6.2 (with respect to slaves' attitude to their believing masters). I think it likely that these tendencies were the fruit of the false teachers' activity.[115] Although there is very little that can be asserted of the false teachers with any confidence, this does not mean, however, that there is no actual crisis being faced by the Pastor[116] or that the polemic of the Pastor is almost exclusively beholden to traditional vilification.

Furthermore, the polemic of the PE takes concrete form in the following two examples. In Tit. 1.11–14 Paul vilifies the Cretans among whom his emissary labors. In v. 12 he asserts that Cretans are liars. He adduces "one of their own prophets" (Epimenides) as witness to his claim. As Jerome Quinn observes, Paul the apostle legitimates the word of the Cretan "prophet." No further argument, with the Cretans or against Paul, on this matter is possible.[117]

In 1 Tim. 2.13–15 a devastatingly powerful argument is brought to bear against the practice of women teaching men in the congregation. Not content with evoking the traditional code regarding female dress and submissive decorum (vv. 9–11; cf. Tit. 2.5), the Pastor argues what amounts to a potent and polemically charged case against women engaging in teaching (διδάσκειν) or having authority (αὐθεντεῖν, v. 12) over men. Primacy belongs to men. It was so in the order of creation. Moreover, Eve was "deceived" (ἡ δὲ γυνὴ ἐξαπατηθεῖσα, v. 14), not the man. Consequently, a woman is unfitted for the role of teaching and exercising leadership in the congregation. Furthermore, it is more than possible that the reference to Eve's being deceived evokes early Jewish tradition to the effect that she was actually sexually seduced by the serpent.[118] Women, therefore, by their very nature, are simply unable to muster the sexual self-mastery required for the exercise and ministry of teaching and leadership in the congregation. In other words, the Pastor implies that women are sexual predators who need to be mastered by men. That is why he denies women opportunities to teach and exercise leadership in the congregation. Consequently, commensurate with her guilt, a woman's salvation is integrally bound up with performing her womanly duty to her husband as a submissive child-bearer.[119] In few other passages in the NT is the traditional view that women are inherently lacking in self-mastery more pronounced. Gender roles and stereotypes, subverted by Paul in passages like Gal. 3.28, are here reinforced and underscored. Women are to be passive; men are to master them.

Why is the author of the PE so dependent on the schema of the polemic of the philosophers' attacks on the sophists? Karris' answer is surely on target. The author regards his teaching as the true philosophy; that of the false teachers is false wisdom.[120] What gives such a mode of presentation so much persuasive force, I would add, is the portrayal of Paul the apostle as the worthy one who suffers and endures. The picture recalls the description of the perseverance of the true sage. Since the audience of the PE already accords honor and authority to Paul, the Pastor knows that the audience will hear him, draw the proper analogies with their own situation, and affirm the polemic of their "founder" against the false teachers.[121]

Little has been said of the situation of 2 Timothy. Here, as Karris notes, there is little polemic, and what little there is, is stock.[122] However, in his study of the letter, Luke T. Johnson contends that the polemic in the PE should not be treated as a mine from which to quarry evidence that enables us to construct the general contours of the teaching of the false teachers.[123] He argues that the shrill polemic directed at the opponents' moral failings is not to be understood to refer to the false teachers' actual moral lapses (a position to which Karris in his dissertation seems to subscribe[124]) even when allowances are made for polemical exaggeration,

However, his account of the function of the polemic in the PE is really little different from that of Karris. Johnson contends that the polemical language is meant to advertise by means of contrast the soundness of the teaching that is in accord with Paul and his emissaries. The polemic addressed to the false teachers serves as an antithesis to the healthful and saving teaching of the apostle. We have already encountered this use of antithesis in the Greco-Roman letters of moral exhortation.[125] In other words, the polemic of the PE serves the rhetorical and paraenetical purpose of contrasting the ethos of Paul with the ethos of the opponents. Whereas Karris argues that the false teachers are teachers of false doctrines because they are immoral, I would argue that the teaching of errorists is false because it is not in accord with Paul's (as that is understood by the Pastor). Their morals are scored in traditional polemical fashion because that is the ethos that fittingly attends perverted teaching.[126]

Pathos (πάθος)

The mode of persuasion called "pathos" by Aristotle is extensively discussed in book two of his *Rhetoric* in which he focuses on techniques of arousing emotion on the audience. The persuasive speaker must not only seem to be a certain type of person but must put the audience in a frame of mind to be favorably disposed towards the speaker and his purpose in speaking.[127]

In *Rhetoric*, 2.12–17, an excursus relevant also to ethical argument and which has received considerable attention in the discussion above on the subject of ethos, Aristotle devotes considerable attention to the kinds of emotions most apposite to certain types of character, with the implication that one should tailor one's speech to take account of these. Given the close connection between pathos and the disposition of speaker and audience, I am reserving detailed comment on pathos until the section below (D) on the matter of being well-disposed to one's audience.

Nevertheless, some comments relevant to pathos can be made here. I have already drawn attention to the manner in which Aristotle structured his *Rhetoric* around the three proofs. Generally, however, the rhetorical tradition reserved its pathos arguments for the *proemium* and the epilogue of speeches. This can be demonstrated in a speech we have already examined, namely, Lysias' *On the Murder of Eratosthenes*.

The speech opens with an appeal to the audience/jury to consider how heinous all societies regard the crime of adultery, a truth evident to all insofar as the crime is penalized, whether the guilty party is well-born or low-born, with utmost rigor (§§2–3). He appeals to the disgrace the crime brings on a family, and the outrage all wronged by the crime feel (§§4–5). Convinced of the guilt of the murdered Eratosthenes, the speaker concludes the *proemium* asserting that all he has to do is to tell his story to the members of the jury (§5). He knows that they too will share his outrage, and judge accordingly. In the epilogue, the speaker claims not to be acting solely in his own interests but in the interests of the whole city (§47). Acquittal for him will send a powerful message to those who might be inclined to trespass against their neighbors (ἧττον εἰς τοὺς ἄλλους ἐξαμαρτήσονται, §47), since they will see that the jury upholds the view that adulterers deserve death. If he is found guilty, however, the laws might as well be erased and the innocent in these matters punished by the guilty (§48). The speech concludes on one final note of pathos. The speaker, who considers that in taking Eratosthenes' life he was in the right in the sight of the law, argues that in obeying the laws of the city he now finds himself in the anomalous position of risking his life and all his property if found guilty by his peers (§50).

In the NT, Galatians features a particularly powerful conclusion to the argument against the Judaizers. In 5.7–12, sometimes termed the *indignatio*,[128] Paul sums up his case against the Judaizers with a number of arguments designed to appeal to the emotions (as well as to the ethos of the addressees). The Galatians were "running well" (cf. 2 Tim. 2.5; 4.7) but have been tripped up, as it were, and deceived (Gal. 5.7). Moreover, they have all but abandoned the gospel (v. 8; cf. 1.6). The circumcisers, Paul implies, are acting out of desire to avoid persecution (v. 11). Paul, on the other hand, remains faithful to the gospel even to the extent of suffering persecution. He concludes the section by sarcastically suggesting that the circumcisers should go the whole way and "mutilate themselves" (ὄφελον καὶ ἀποκόψονται . . . , v. 12).

Pathos arguments are common in the PE. This is particularly so in the case of 2 Timothy with its pronounced testamentary features. The Pastor encapsulates Paul's final word, his dying wish, as it were, bequeathed to his posterity (i.e., his "son" Timothy). Paul is in physical need as well as in immediate danger. The prospect of his martyrdom faces him daily. His death is undeserved. He is a transparently good man. His worth is evident by his endurance under trial and suffering. Although he has encountered threats from enemies (2 Tim. 4.14) and desertions of colleagues (2 Tim. 1.15; 4.10a, 16) he has run the race and kept the faith (2 Tim. 4.6–8). He is the very model of the perseverance he enjoins on his addressees, Timothy and Titus, even though such perseverance may result in sharing the sufferings of the apostle. In fact, no believer who seeks to live a godly life can avoid suffering (2 Tim. 3.12). All things can be endured, the Pastor confidently implies, because Paul has gone before and found the Lord faithful, his promises true, and his reward certain (2 Tim. 1.12; 2.11–13; 4.7, 8).

D. Being Well-Disposed: The Pastor and his Audience

Aristotle acknowledges that the speaker may fail in his task because he not only does not possess practical sense (φρόνησις) in being able to say what people believe to be true but also does not lend his moral support to the opinions he has enunciated as commendable and true for people (*Rhetoric*, 2.1.6). As far as virtue is concerned, lack of good-will towards the audience can destroy the impression of excellence of character that otherwise he might have been able to convey.

Aristotle's *Rhetoric*, 2.2–11 is actually an examination first and foremost of the state of mind of various types of audience. Kennedy aptly calls these chapters "the earliest systematic discussion of human psychology."[129]

While I am not suggesting that the Pastor knew Aristotle, or any other rhetorical handbook for that matter,[130] the rhetoricians suggest a set of starting points from which to investigate the Pastor's disposition to the actual audience. Behind the address of the assumed author to the assumed addressees of the PE, the disposition of the actual author as one writing to commend Pauline tradition to the leadership of contemporary churches standing in the Pauline tradition can be encountered.

Disposition, as an aspect of persuasive strategy, is not an issue foreign to this book. In the hortatory literature examined in the previous chapter, I noted that reminding the addressee of the content of what was being exhorted was designed to complement him/her and give assurance of the author's goodwill. The addressee already knows, the author affirms, what is expected in terms of conduct and moral orientation. What is delivered by way of exhortation, therefore, serves by way of a reminder, not a rebuke for negligence or wilful ignorance. In speeches and in the hortatory discourses this can also be observed, especially in the opening remarks. Aristotle, however, addresses the question of the disposition of the speaker in more ways than the *captatio benevolentiae* most often encountered in the *proemium*. Not all the dispositions he examines are relevant to the PE.[131] The following, however, are.

In the first of the dispositions treated, namely, anger (ὀργή), Aristotle's discussion concludes with the comment that the speaker may need to put his audience into an angry frame of mind. The orator might need to show that one's opponent has indeed been responsible for things which cause anger, or has himself dealt with the audience in anger by treating them with contempt by insulting them or being spiteful towards them (*Rhetoric*, 2.2.27). Demosthenes' speech *Against Meidias* reveals not only the orator's sense of outrage but anger in the face of the accused's public and repeated insults. Meidias, he reminds the audience, is an overbearing bully whose insults inflict injury not just on Demosthenes but on the whole citizenry (§7). Indeed Meidias is represented as a man whose hatred of the orator is bound to result in his death if Meidias is acquitted (see §§219–25).

We have already seen that polemic can have this function. In the PE, polemic is used to arouse a feeling of antipathy towards the false teachers. Given the urgency that can be glimpsed of the situation confronting the Pastor and the Pauline churches (see, e.g., 1 Tim. 1.3–11), such polemic gains in vitriol.

The second disposition examined in the *Rhetoric*, namely, gentleness (πραότης), is the opposite of anger. Those manifesting this disposition, writes Aristotle, are prepared to forgive those who repent, and are calm towards those who regard themselves as they themselves do. They are humble towards them as though admitting themselves to be inferior.[132] They are calm towards those speakers who do not treat them with contempt, or who do not belittle others, and towards those whom they fear and respect. The accused in Lysias' speech *Against Simon* discussed in the previous section (C) provides a good example of the calm man. Here is a man accused of inflicting bodily harm, and who, though repeatedly harassed by Simon, did not choose to bring charges against him though he was well within his rights to do so.

In the PE, leaders are exhorted to be gentle (see 1 Tim. 6.11; 2 Tim. 2.24–25; Tit. 3.2). 2 Tim. 2.24–25 prescribes the following:

> δοῦλον δὲ κυρίου οὐ δεῖ μάχεσθαι, ἀλλὰ ἤπιον εἶναι πρὸς πάντας, διδακτικόν, ἀνεξίκακον, ἐν πραΰτητι παιδεύοντα τοὺς ἀντιδιατιθεμένους, μήποτε δώῃ αὐτοῖς ὁ θεὸς μετάνοιαν εἰς ἐπίγνωσιν ἀληθείας . . .

The use of ἤπιος recalls Paul's own perception of his disposition towards the Thessalonians (see 1 Thess. 2.11). The use of πραΰτης can be paralleled in the Pauline corpus also. It refers to the apostle's pastoral demeanor in 1 Cor. 4.21 and 2 Cor. 10.1. He exhorts his addressees to practise such an attitude towards one another in Gal. 5.23 and 6.1 (cf. Eph. 4.2; Col. 3.12). In 2 Tim. 2.24–25, some hope is held out that as a result of this demeanor some of those who have gone astray may, in fact, be reclaimed.[133] However, the exhortation to gentleness does not absolve Timothy from being "urgent in season and out of season" (2 Tim. 4.2) in his confrontation (ἔλεγξον, ἐπιτίμησον, παρακάλεσον) with false teachers.[134]

The dispositions of friendliness (φιλία) and hatred (ἔχθρα) are treated together by Aristotle in *Rhetoric*, 2.4. Those who love others, Aristotle observes, and who believe that a mutual relationship exists, are friendly towards those who are disposed to do good to others. They are friendly towards those who have the same enemies as they do. They honor the generous and the brave. Moreover, they are friendly towards those who are self-controlled (σωφρόναι). Furthermore, and here the close links between ethos and pathos are especially apparent, those orators who are morally good and are respected will elicit admiration from the audience. Those who are not critical of the faults of others and who are not contentious or quarrelsome are, likewise, received in a friendly way.[135] Friendliness is also engendered by those who do not harbor grudges and who are easily appeased. They look for the good in others and do not want to know bad things about their neighbors. The section on hatred (2.4.30–32) introduces a distinction between the hate that is directed towards a type of person (the thief and the sycophant are Aristotle's examples) and that directed against individuals. The orator has the power to demonstrate to his audience which people ought to be regarded as friends or as enemies. Greek orators frequently take it upon themselves to warn the audience, especially in judicial contexts, of the need to adjudicate in a way that upholds the laws and customs, and not to allow them to be undermined.[136]

The Greco-Roman and NT letter-writing tradition facilitates the enhancement of the friendship between author and addressee. In the PE, as noted in chapter two, there are ample testimonies to the relationship of friendliness between the assumed author and the addressee. Out of this relationship—a relationship of friendship between apostle and emissary—comes authority to prescribe and exhort.

There are several hints in the PE which take us behind the assumed author/addressee relationship to glimpse the Pastor seeking the goodwill of the actual audience. In Tit. 3.3, the Pastor, using the first person plural, writes (my italics):

> *ἦμεν* γάρ ποτε καὶ *ἡμεῖς* ἀνόητοι, ἀπειθεῖς, πλανώμενοι, δουλεύοντες ἐπιθυμίαις καὶ ἡδοναῖς ποικίλαις, ἐν κακίᾳ καὶ φθόνῳ διάγοντες, στυγητοί, μισοῦντες ἀλλήλους.

He continues with traditional material in vv. 4–5, again cast in the first person plural (my italics):

> ὅτε δὲ ἡ χρηστότης καὶ ἡ φιλανθρωπία ἐπεφάνη τοῦ σωτῆρος *ἡμῶν* θεοῦ . . . ἔσωσεν *ἡμᾶς*

and maintains this inclusive mode through vv. 6–7.

There are other uses of inclusive address in the PE, such as 1 Tim. 4.10 ("For this reason we toil and strive . . . "), 6.7–8 ("we brought nothing into the world"), Tit. 2.8 and 2.12–14. However, Tit. 3.3–7 is the longest and most sustained inclusive appeal to the audience. Like Tit. 2.12–14, this passage expresses the solidarity of writer and addressees in the common possession of life and salvation in Christ. By writing thus the Pastor places himself among the addressees as one who is also under obligation to live out faithfully the life of discipleship he exhorts others to follow.[137] Both passages in Titus occur in exhortation to all believers. Tit. 2.1–10 is addressed to the constituents of the household of God; 3.1–2 addresses all believers in their responsibility to be submissive to rulers and authorities, and to be in good fellowship with all.

Pity (ἔλεος) is defined by Aristotle in *Rhetoric*, 2.8.1 as a

> certain pain at an apparently destructive or painful evil happening to one who does not deserve it and which a person might expect himself or one of his own to suffer, and this when it seems close at hand . . .

This emotion is not discussed from the standpoint of how to arouse it in the audience, though, given Aristotle's treatment, the practical implications suggest themselves. Those things which make pity greater—Aristotle terms these "signs and actions"—are rhetorically effective.[138]

Pity is a common emotion evoked in Greek rhetoric. Perhaps the most famous example occurs, as I have noted earlier, in the last book of the *Iliad* where Priam pleads for the body of Hector. In the speech *Against Aphobus, I,* Demosthenes, appeals to the jury for pity. His whole fortune is at stake in the contest with the embezzlers of his inheritance. Young and inexperienced, he faces formidable opponents. He is, he confesses, "the most wretched of men" (ὁ πάντων ταλαιπωρότατος, §66). Should he lose the case, he will be forced to pay damages out of an already sadly depleted estate. Should he win, his opponents will pay damages out of the same estate. Moreover, the state demands taxes (rightfully, he adds). If impoverished, he is in danger of losing his civic rights.

In the PE, as I observed in the previous section, the personal notices with their portrait of the degraded and forsaken apostle are meant to elicit pity for Paul's situation for the purposes of winning the hearers to supporting his legacy in the church. Paul's difficulties are all the more pitiable and, therefore, all the more rhetorically effective, because he is a transparently good man suffering in the assumed present situation of 2 Timothy and not in the distant past.[139]

SUMMARY

The PE are not speeches. They are letters which fit the broad category of letters of moral exhortation. However, as letters they also participate in the tradition of classical, Hellenistic, and Greco-Roman oratory and rhetorical theory from which many of the persuasive techniques of letters derive. This opportunity to investigate the relationship between PE and the rhetorical tradition, especially that represented by Aristotle, has further enhanced our awareness of the literateness and effectiveness of the PE's persuasive strategies from an angle other than that provided by comparison with the corpus of letters of moral exhortation.

Of the three species of Aristotelian rhetoric, the PE have least in common with the judicial. However, deliberative rhetoric has much in common with the aims of moral exhortation since people exhort to persuade or dissuade. Moral exhortation can also be viewed from the perspective of epideictic rhetoric; the author/speaker affirming moral values and orientations which he/she would hope to see confirmed in the addressee(s). Furthermore, the use of liturgical materials in the PE prompted us to examine the way in which that language functions for the Pastor. By appealing to his image of Paul, and by citing liturgical and hymnic formulations, I infer that the Pastor was writing "cohesively."

Aristotle's three proofs also make their appearance in the PE. Logical deduction is to be encountered in the letters. It is based largely on what the Pastor holds to be credible presuppositions in the arenas of the saving significance of the Christ-event, the character of the Christian life, and the propositions contained in the entrusted tradition. However, logical induction through the use of paradigms and examples is perhaps more pervasive in the PE. This is so because of the powerful literary "presence" of the apostle as the paradigm of Christian life and leadership. Ethical argument in the PE is attuned to the positive ethos of Paul, not to mention Jesus and the emissaries themselves. However, there are also negative examples. They function as contrasting images of the vision of church order and leadership, and of the godly daily living and the sound teaching the Pastor commends.

The false teachers' failure to heed the teaching that accords with Pauline tradition (as understood by the Pastor) makes them the target of sustained and bitter polemic. This is directed at their presumed vices. The polemic serves to affirm the audience's assent to the positive image of Paul on the one hand and to create and increase aversion to the false teachers on the other.

Appeals based on pathos are closely linked to ethos arguments. In the PE, pathos arguments are particularly implicit in the *personalia* of the apostle in 2 Tim. 4.6–8 and Tit. 3.12–15. With its pronounced testamentary features, 2 Timothy provides the Pastor with considerable opportunities for pathos since Paul is on the point of martyrdom, all have deserted him, winter is approaching, yet the apostle's head is "bloody but unbowed."

Pathos arguments are linked to the disposition of the audience and the actual author. The Pastor seeks to arouse the feelings of his audience by evoking the image of the pastorally concerned yet suffering apostle. Moreover, the actual author commends himself to them as one who, like them, participates in the present in the saving achievement of God.

NOTES

1 See Hans D. Betz, *Galatians*; F. W. Hughes, *Early Christian Rhetoric and 2 Thessalonians* (JSNTSS 30; Sheffield: JSOT Press, 1989); Duane F. Watson, *Invention, Arrangement, and Style: Rhetorical Criticism of Jude and 2 Peter* (SBLDS 104; Atlanta: Scholars Press, 1988).

2 Plato has Gorgias say that rhetoric is the ability to persuade with speeches (τὸ πείθειν ἔγωγ' οἷον τ' εἶναι τοῖς λόγοις), see *Gorgias*, 452E. See also Isocrates, *The Antidosis*, 278; Aristotle, *Rhetoric*, 1.2.1; Cicero, *de Oratore*, 1.31; Quintilian, *Institutes*, 2.15.38. Cf. Kennedy, *The Art of Persuasion in Greece* (Princeton: Princeton University Press, 1963), 7: "Wherever persuasion is the end, rhetoric is present." However, Aristotle makes it clear that the art of rhetoric is not the ability merely to persuade but rather the ability "to see the available means of persuasion" for each case (1.2.1). The orator, he insists, is not to indulge in emotional chicanery (Plato's charge against the art) but to ensure the most persuasive articulation of truth and justice. Aristotle assumes that rhetoricians have knowledge (ἐπιστήμη) of the subjects they tackle. Rhetoric is like the process of dialectic encountered in Plato's dialogues in that the demonstration of truth is its concern. Unlike dialectic, however, rhetoric seeks to persuade audiences who are not able to appreciate the kind of rarefied reasoning that dialectic offered and who would otherwise remain unconvinced. Accordingly, rhetoric amounts to dialectic for the common person. The rhetorician, as least in Aristotle's mind, is like the philosopher-dialectician. He is concerned about the truth but is also concerned to persuade others of the truth in civic discourse (see 1.1.12). See further W. M. A. Grimaldi, *Aristotle, Rhetoric I: A Commentary* (New York: Fordham University Press, 1980), 24–27. Quintilian, like Aristotle, believes that the rhetorician must be a good person. However, according to Quintilian, the orator can bend the truth a little when confronted by "emergencies" of the security of the state (see *Institutes*, 12.1.36–45). He cites ancient and hallowed precedent for this "surprising" view. More blatant is the *Rhetorica ad Alexandrum*. In 1425b38, the writer proposes that *encomium* (a sub-category of epideictic oratory) has to do with the amplification of what is creditable in the subject and the attribution of qualities that do not exist.

3 See D. L. Clark, *Rhetoric in Greco-Roman Education* (New York: Columbia University Press, 1957), 25.

4 See especially *Gorgias*, 463E–466A.

5 *Gorgias*, 463B; 465A.

6 See Kennedy, *Art of Persuasion*, 14.

7 *Antidosis*, 274–8.

8 W. A. Smith, *Ancient Education* (New York: Philosophical Library, 1955), 142.

9 Clark, *Rhetoric*, 60. See his ch. 3, "The Schools" (59–66). Clark cites the second century C.E. poet Apuleius (*Florida*, 20) for the status of rhetoric in education. For education in antiquity, see H. -I. Marrou, *Histoire de l'éducation dans l'Antiquité* (2 vols.; Paris: Éditions de Seuil, 1948). See 1.291–306 and 2.87–96 for the teaching of rhetoric in the Greek and Latin schools respectively.

10 See Clark, *Rhetoric*, 60. He cites Juvenal, *Satires*, 15.10 for the evidence of the widespread geographical extent of interest in rhetoric.

11 W. Jaeger, *Paideia: The Ideals of Greek Culture* (3 vols.; New York: Oxford University Press, 1939), 3.51.

12 See Cicero, *de Oratore*, 1.55; 2.43; Quintilian, *Institutes*, 3.4.1.

13 See J. Wisse, *Ethos and Pathos from Aristotle to Cicero* (Amsterdam: A. M. Hakkert, 1989). The structure of Quintilian's *Institutes* follows a non-Aristotelian structure (that Wisse terms "contaminated"). He discusses the structure of the species of speeches, proceeding to "proofs," style, and ornamentation.

14 Wisse, *Ethos and Pathos*, 28. See Aristotle, *Rhetoric*, 1.1.9.

15 The relevant extant handbooks Wisse has in mind are *Rhetorica ad Alexandrum, Rhetorica ad Herennium*, and Cicero's *de Inventione*. The first two are anonymous works.

16 *Rhetoric*, 1.1.12: "our proofs (πίστεις) and arguments must rest on generally accepted principles" (διὰ τῶν κοινῶν). For this reason he is critical of the manuals produced up to that point because their authors were concerned only with the arts of persuasion in the law court, while neglecting attention to the truth as it is generally understood.

17 J. L. Kinneavy, *Greek Rhetorical Origins of the Christian Faith: An Inquiry* (New York/Oxford: Oxford University Press, 1987), 38.

18 See the gradation of kinds of knowledge in the *Republic*, 511D–E.

19 Kennedy, *Aristotle: On Rhetoric*, 8. Corax, a Sicilian, is credited with writing the first rhetorical manual. Some fragments of a handbook by Isocrates survive. On the existence of handbooks, see Plato, *Phaedrus*, 266C–269C, 271C; Isocrates, *Against*

the Sophists, 19; Quintilian, *Institutes*, 3.1.14.

20 Kennedy, *Aristotle*, ix.

21 Kennedy, *Aristotle*, ix citing Martin Heidegger.

22 *Art of Persuasion*, 37.

23 See ll. 486–506. Priam, bereft of all his sons now that Achilles has killed his sole surviving son Hector, has gone to the Achaean camp to request the body. He appeals to Achilles to remember his father, who, though beset by enemies, at least rejoices to know that his son still lives. The effect of the speech is to reduce Achilles to tears as he remembers his father and his dead friend Patroclus.

24 These examples are taken from Kennedy, *Art of Persuasion*, 37.

25 *Classical Rhetoric and its Christian and Secular Tradition from Ancient to Modern Times* (Chapel Hill: University of North Carolina Press, 1980), 121.

26 *Classical Rhetoric*, 121.

27 See Kennedy, *Classical Rhetoric*, 122. See, e.g., Exod. 4.1.

28 See Aristotle, *Rhetoric*, 1.2.1. Quintilian, *Institutes*, 5.11.36–37, 42–44 argues against the idea that authoritative sources are inartificial proofs, contending that they are "extrinsic" until the orator uses them artfully in his speech to support his case. See discussion in Watson, *Invention, Arrangement and Style*, 17 n. 143.

29 A. N. Wilder, *Early Christian Rhetoric* (London: SCM, 1964), 15. Cf. the discussion of the "imperative psalms" in C. Westermann, *Praise and Lament in the Psalms* (Atlanta: John Knox, 1981), 131–2.

30 See ch. 7 (121–60). Mark 9.9–13 counsels believers not to be concerned about eloquence in the face of arraignment before the courts. The Holy Spirit will provide the words to say. In 1 Cor. 1–2 Paul eschews rhetorical eloquence, and rejects the classical rhetorical tradition. For the rhetorical implications of preaching, see Kinneavy, *Greek Rhetorical Origins of the Christian Faith*.

31 *New Testament Interpretation through Rhetorical Criticism* (Chapel Hill: University of North Carolina Press, 1984), 7. See also his comments on the Gospel of Mark on 104–07.

32 "Did the Spirit Inspire Rhetoric?: An Exploration of George Kennedy's Definition of Early Christian Rhetoric," in D. F. Watson (ed.), *Persuasive Artistry: Studies in New Testament Rhetoric in Honor of George A. Kennedy* (JSNTSS 50; Sheffield: JSOT Press, 1991), 25–40.

33 See the discussion in Levison, "Did the Spirit Inspire Rhetoric?," 35–39.

34 Cf. Y Gitay, "Rhetorical Criticism and the Prophetic Discourse," in Watson (ed.), *Persuasive Artistry*, 13–24. The author seeks to demonstrate that an oracle like Jer. 14.2–15.9 is rhetorically effective in terms of the persuasive strategies of Greco-Roman deliberative rhetoric.

35 See his "Rabbinic Methods of Interpretation and Hellenistic Rhetoric," *HUCA* 22 (1949), 239–64.

36 Daube, "Rabbinic Methods," 240–1. On 241 he contends that while the historical accuracy of the identity of Hillel's teachers might be suspect, it is almost certain that "if they were natives of Alexandria, they studied and taught there long enough to go on using Egyptian measures even after settling in Palestine." On Hillel and his rhetorically literate descendants, see M. Hengel, *Judaism and Hellenism* (2 vols.; Philadelphia: Fortress, 1974), 1.77.

37 Daube, "Rabbinic Methods," 247. Daube cites Cicero, *de Inv.* 1.13.17. Cf. *ad Her.* 1.13.23.

38 Daube, "Rabbinic Methods," 248–9, see also 249 n. 33.

39 Hengel, *Judaism and Hellenism*, 1.83–84. The orator Theodore of Gadara instructed the young Emperor Tiberius. See also M. Hengel, *The "Hellenization of Judaea" in the First Century after Christ* (Philadelphia: Trinity Press International, 1989), 20. Note also the discussion of the influence of Hellenistic culture, especially rhetoric, in Kinneavy, *Greek Rhetorical Origins of the Christian Faith*, ch. 3 (56–91).

40 See *Rhetoric*, 1.3.1. Cf. Quintilian (*Institutes*, 3.4) who surveys theories that argue for a larger number of species than the Aristotelian three. *Ad Alex.* 2, e.g., argues for seven species.

41 See Aristotle, *Rhetoric*, 1.3.5. See also F. Solmsen, "Aristotelian Tradition in Ancient Rhetoric," in R. Stark (ed.), *Rhetorika: Schriften zur aristotelischen und hellenistischen Rhetorik* (Hildesheim: Georg Olms Verlagsbuchhandlung, 1968), 319. Solmsen remarks that the three species are concerned with the three cardinal virtues—what is just, good and honorable respectively.

42 *Rhetoric*, 1.3.3. Cf. Quintilian, *Institutes*, 3.9.1.

43 See *Art of Persuasion*, 126.

44 See Kennedy's survey of the speeches and style of these four late fifth-century Attic orators in *Art of Persuasion*, 126–49, concluding on 149–52 with a discussion of the most famous court-room scene, the trial of Socrates, in Plato's *Apology*.

45 See Aristotle, *Rhetoric*, 3.13–14, 16–19. Cf. Quintilian, *Institutes*, 3.9; *ad Alex.* 36 (1443b25ff.). Quintilian (*Institutes*, 6.2.1) contends that the epilogue in judicial speeches is important for appeals to the emotions. Lysias' brief speech for Euphiletus as a defence for the murder of Eratosthenes is typical of the genre: the *exordium* (§§1–5) gains the attention of the jury and states the defendant's purpose of refuting the charge; the *narratio* (§§6–26) states the facts of the case; the *propositio* (§§27–28) summarizes the facts just presented; the *probatio* (§§29–42) presents the proofs refuting the charge. The speech concludes with a brief epilogue appealing to the jury.

46 See the recent study of the speeches in Acts 24 by B. Winter, "The Importance of the *'Captatio Benevolentiae'* in the Speeches of Tertullus and Paul in Acts 24:1–21," *JThS* 42 (1991), 505–31. Note the appeals to favorable hearing in the *proemia* of both speakers (see Acts 24.2b–4; 10b).

47 "The Literary Composition and Function of Paul's letter to the Galatians," *NTS* 21 (1974–75), 353–79; *Galatians* (Philadelphia: Fortress, 1979).

48 See George A. Kennedy, *New Testament Interpretation Through Rhetorical Criticism*, 144–52; Stephen J. Kraftchick, "Ethos and Pathos in Galatians Five and Six: A Rhetorical Analysis," (Ph.D. Dissertation: Emory University, 1985); R. N. Longenecker, *Galatians*, see especially cix–cxix. Each of these writers points out the difficulty in finding in Betz's scheme a place for the paraenetic material of chs. 5–6 which, strictly speaking, has no place in the judicial speech. Longenecker (184–6) mounts a case for Galatians as evidencing mixed rhetorical genre. Judicial rhetoric dominates 1.6–3.7 and 4.8–11, Jewish argumentative strategies dominate in 3.6–4.7, and Greco-Roman deliberative rhetoric in 4.12–6.10.

49 *Rhetoric*, 1.3.3. Cf. Quintilian, *Institutes*, 3.8.

50 Aristotle, *Rhetoric*, 1.4. Religious ritual is specifically mentioned in *ad Alex.* 2. The opening chapters of 2 Maccabees contain a letter from Jerusalem to the Jews of Egypt arguing the case for the celebration in the Diaspora of the new festival of Hanukkah. The letter commences with a brief *narratio* of the destruction of Antiochus and his generals in Persia, and a notice concerning the imminent purification of the Jerusalem Temple (1.11–18). The letter seeks to persuade the addressees to keep the new festival coincidental with the purification by arguing that Antiochus' death was a direct result of divine intervention, an intervention the new festival celebrates, and that the purification is the harbinger of a re-gathering of all the people of God to Palestine (2.16–18). Scripture and tradition (see 1.19–2.12) point to the fact that this purification may usher in the long-awaited re-gathering of all the people of God. Far from being a merely Palestinian concern, therefore, the celebration of Hanukkah in the Diaspora is in the best interests of all and demonstrates solidarity with all the people.

51 *Rhetoric*, 3.14.11. Cf. Quintilian, *Institutes*, 3.8.6. An excellent example of a deliberative speech is Isocrates' *Panegyricus*. The speech is a plea to the Athenians

to prosecute war in Asia against the Persians whose overlordship of Greece has plunged the city-states into mutually destructive strife. Isocrates' intent is to persuade Athens and the other Greek city-states to mount a crusade against Persia under the leadership of Athens in the hope not only of ending Persian domination but of unifying all Greeks in a common cause. Alone of the Greek πόλεις, Athens has demonstrated the fortitude and ability to carry the fight to Persia. In the *proemium* (§§1–14) Isocrates heralds the greatness of this oratorical occasion, claiming that his ability as a rhetorician is more than adequate for the greatness of his theme. The *narratio* (§§15–159) focuses on the need for Sparta to be persuaded that Athens alone is fitted to lead the crusade against the Persians. In a sustained *encomium*, Isocrates rehearses the glories of Athens' past exercise of hegemony in turning back the threat from Persia, and lauds her contributions to the civilization of the world. He meets objections against his proposed Athenian hegemony by highlighting Spartan failures in the very matters in which the Athenians have excelled. He proceeds to furnish examples drawn from history of the success of small but purposeful forces over large armies, and draws attention to the inadequacies of the Persians as a fighting force. The epilogue (§§160–89) finds Isocrates arguing that the present opportunity provides excellent reason for going to war against Persia. It would be disgraceful (αἰσχρός) to neglect the opportunity since great advantage would accrue to the Greeks. Much stress is laid on the present shamefulness Greeks now endure in accepting Persian overlordship and the terms of the peace dictated by the Persians. Isocrates concludes by lamenting his unworthiness in speaking to his subject, namely, the greatness of Athens and the advantages of what would accrue should the undertaking succeed (§187, cf. §14).

52 1 Corinthians contains much paraenesis in this mode. See, e.g., the question of eating meat offered to idols (ch. 8), attendance at temple banquets (ch. 10), and conduct of worship (chs. 12–14).

53 *A Grammar of New Testament Greek* (Third Edition; Edinburgh: T. & T. Clark, 1908), 126. Normally prohibitions were expressed by μή with the subjunctive.

54 "The Letter of Paul to the Galatians: A Deliberative Speech," *NTS* 35 (1989), 1–26.

55 Smit, "The Letter of Paul to the Galatians," 23.

56 See *ad Alex.* 35: "We are not speaking to contest a case," the writer notes, "but for display" (ἀλλ' ἐπιδείξεως ἕνεκα λέγομεν).

57 *Rhetoric*, 1.3.3.

58 See the excellent discussion of epideictic oratory by T. C. Burgess, "Epideictic Literature," *Chicago Studies in Classical Literature* 3 (1902), 89–253.

59 See *Rhetoric*, 3.14.2–4. Isocrates' speech *Evagorus* is a typical example of an epideictic speech. Note particularly the amplification of Evagorus' achievements and the technique of comparison as a way of enlarging the accomplishments of the

subject (cf. 2 Cor. 10.12). In the *proemium* (§§1–11) Isocrates claims that though the filial public reverence of the memory of his father by Nicocles is indeed honorable how much more the dead Evagorus, the late King of Cyprus, would welcome the praises in speech of his principles exemplified in his life and his deeds. The *narratio* (§§12–72) deals first with Evagorus' descent from semi-divine heroes, and enumerates the portents and oracles that occurred at his birth. As a boy he was distinguished by his beauty, strength, and modesty. As a man, his excellence in body and mind were clearly evident. He conducted his campaign for the throne according to god-fearing principles. The perilous deeds he performed surpassed those of other famous claimants such as Cyrus, some of whose successes were achieved by impiety. As king Evagorus spent much time in deliberation with others. He ruled with justice, upholding the laws. He undertook to defend his capital, inaugurated Greek educational practices, and attracted a large number of Greeks to make their home in Cyprus. Isocrates praises his services to the majority of Greeks in counselling the Persians to equip a naval force to defeat the overweaning Spartans. Of all men, Isocrates concludes, Evagorus has earned the merit of immortality. In the epilogue (§§73–81) Isocrates confesses that as an orator he is well-passed his prime, otherwise the eulogy would have been better finished. Nevertheless, he claims to have adorned Evagorus' memory, concluding with an appeal to Nicocles, as one distantly descended from Zeus (§81), to live worthily of his father and of all his ancestors.

60 See Edwin A. Judge, "Paul's Boasting in Relation to Contemporary Professional Practice," *ABR* 16 (1968), 37–50; Christopher J. Forbes, "Comparison, Self-Praise and Irony: Paul's Boasting and the Conventions of Hellenistic Rhetoric," *NTS* 36 (1986), 1–30; Mark Harding, "The Classical Rhetoric of Praise and the New Testament," *RThR* 45 (1986), 73–82 (especially 77–81). For another example of satire on the conventions of the epideictic speech, see Lucian, *The Fly* (LCL edition Vol. 1).

61 Judge ("Paul's Boasting," 47) argues that Paul is deliberately turning on its head the Roman honor of the mural crown (*corona muralis*) awarded to the first soldier up and over the wall of a besieged city (see, e.g., Polybius, *The Histories*, 6.39.5; Livy, *History of Rome*, 6.20.8). See also Stephen H. Travis, "Paul's Boasting in 2 Corinthians 10–12," *SE* 6 (1973), 530; Furnish, *II Corinthians*, 541–2.

62 See his *Letters in Primitive Christianity*, 42.

63 *Letters in Primitive Christianity*, 42.

64 See his *The Language and Imagery of the Bible* (Philadelphia: Westminster, 1980), 32–36.

65 See Caird, *Language and Imagery*, 32.

66 Caird, *Language and Imagery*, 33. Thus, a quotation of scripture "may be the basis of an appeal to authority [i.e., on the part of the writer to sanction some moral code,

for example], but an allusion is always a reminder of what is held in common." Cf. MacDonald, *Pauline Churches*, 139–42, 146 with respect to the use of "cohesive language" in the hymns of Colossians and Ephesians.

67 Verner, *Household of God*, 110.

68 Lock, *A Critical and Exegetical Commentary on the Pastoral Epistles*, 42. Jeremias, *Die Briefe an Timotheus und Titus*, 23 also nominates the Christ hymn of 1 Tim. 3.16 as the high point of the letter.

69 See his *The Story of Christ in the Ethics of Paul: An Analysis of the Hymnic Material in the Pauline Corpus* (JSNTSS 36; Sheffield: JSOT Press, 1990), chs. 7 and 8.

70 See Fowl, *The Story of Christ*, 191. In his approach to 1 Tim. 3.16–4.5, has Fowl been too influenced by his interpretation of the purpose of Col. 1.15–20 with respect to the argument of that letter?

71 See *The Household of God*, 110–1. See also his comments on the similar function of 2 Tim. 2.11–13 noted in the text above.

72 Verner, *Household of God*, 111.

73 See Dibelius and Conzelmann, *Pastoral Epistles*, 61; Brox, *Pastoralbriefe*, 159–60; Jeremias, *Die Briefe an Timotheus und Titus*, 23.

74 So Fowl, *The Story of Christ*, 183.

75 See my unpublished M.A. (Hons.) thesis "The Terminology of Respecting and Serving the Gods," (Macquarie University; North Ryde, NSW, 1988), 153–4. Cf. Kidd, *Wealth and Beneficence*, 138. Kidd rightly notes the change in the meaning of εὐσέβεια in 1 Tim. 5.4 in which honoring one's parents is portrayed as "a fundamentally religious act."

76 The term πίστις has a three-fold meaning in Aristotle. It signifies (i) conviction or belief, (ii) the technical means, whether deductive (enthymeme) or inductive (example), employed to produce conviction in the hearer, and (iii) material for conviction to be found in the areas of logos, ethos, and pathos with respect to the subject at hand. See Grimaldi, *Commentary*, 1.19–20. When Aristotle speaks of logic, ethos, and pathos as πίστεις he is using the term in its third sense. The term πίστις has significant ramifications for the study of the NT. In the rhetorical tradition the term denotes both the "means of persuasion" and the resultant belief. See Kennedy, *Aristotle*, 30 n. 9. See also Kinneavy's extensive discussion of this issue in his *Greek Rhetorical Origins*. His thesis is that the concept of πίστις in the NT is heavily indebted to its use in the rhetorical tradition. Those who are πιστοί have been persuaded by the performative discourse of the Christian preaching about the Christ event. However, see Wilder, *Early Christian Rhetoric*, 29 for the view

that the persuasive force in early Christian preaching resides in the dynamic of the claim to be imparting revelation and not in argument.

77 Cf. *ad Alex.* 7. Cf. Cicero, *de Oratore*, 2.27.116. In addition to those extrinsic proofs cited by Aristotle and the *ad Alex.* Cicero mentions statutes, Senate decrees, judicial precedent, magisterial orders, and opinions of counsel as examples of extrinsic proof. Quintilian, *Institutes*, 5.11.42–44 mentions supernatural evidence among the categories of extrinsic proof.

78 See "Aristotelian Tradition," 315.

79 The Platonic dialogues deal exclusively with this kind of proof. In rhetoric, however, pathos and ethos make significant contributions to the persuasiveness of the speech. See also Grimaldi, *Commentary*, 1.40. He defines logical proof (he terms it "reason") as language "which sets forth for the mind of the auditor the logical structure of the subject matter so that his mind can grasp its inner coherence and meaning."

80 See also *Topics*, 1.1 for syllogisms, and 1.12 for inductive examples.

81 παυσώμεθα τῆς ἀρχῆς τῆς κατὰ θάλατταν ἐπιθυμοῦντες (§64).

82 *On the Peace*, 67–68.

83 LCL translation of *Areopagiticus*, 11.

84 LCL translation of *Areopagiticus*, 17.

85 See, e.g., *Letters*, 26 and 78.

86 See Donelson, *Pseudepigraphy*, 98–99. Examples have overtaken enthymetic argument in Seneca. Donelson also cites Cancik, *Untersuchungen zu Senecas Epistulae morales*, 24 in support.

87 For text see the LCL volume of Lysias' speeches.

88 See Kennedy's discussion of the "abbreviated syllogism" in his *Aristotle*, 42 n. 60, and in his Appendix 1 (#F, 297–8).

89 See Grimaldi, *Commentary*, 1.62, who gives this example of an εἰκός: "children love their parents." This statement is generally true; it is a probability. The "probability," Grimaldi concludes, "is grounded in the order of reality and consequently men (*sic*) accept it as a most likely statement of truth" (*Commentary*, 1.63).

90 Grimaldi, *Commentary*, 1.64. His examples of "necessary" and "unnecessary signs" are respectively "child points to parent" (i.e., every child must have been parented)

and "storm clouds point to storm" (i.e., storm clouds presage a storm [but occasionally the storm does not materialize]).

91 Grimaldi, *Commentary*, 1.65.

92 See *Aristotle*, 184 n. 145. Kennedy instances the sayings of Jesus reported in the Gospels. See also the study of the enthymemes of the Synoptic Gospels by R. B. Vinson, "A Comparative Study of the Use of Enthymemes in the Synoptic Gospels," in Watson (ed.), *Persuasive Artistry*, 119–41. Vinson, who adopts the definition of enthymeme as a truncated syllogism (i.e., one of the terms of the syllogism is "suppressed," 119), notes *inter alia* how in particular the Markan and Matthean Jesus uses enthymemes in support of his commands and pronouncements. These are noted in the text by the presence of causal particles such as ὅτι and γάρ.

93 In confrontations with the Jews, the Johannine Jesus persists in asserting that he is the Revealer without furnishing witnesses to his credentials (see John 8.12–20). In Gal. 1.11–12 Paul likewise asserts that his own grasp of the significance of the Christ-event and its implications for life are the product of revelation (ἀποκάλυψις). He was not taught by others. The Jerusalem apostles only confirmed the truth of what he asserted (2.2–3). See also Beker, *Paul the Apostle*, 10 for Paul's use of the language of prophetic call in Gal. 1.15–16. Cf. Wilder, *Early Christian Rhetoric*, 29: "The basic character of the Gospel . . . is revelation, not persuasion."

94 Aristotle, *Rhetoric*, 1.2.3–22. See discussion in Donelson, *Pseudepigraphy*, 69–90.

95 Donelson, *Pseudepigraphy*, 80–81.

96 Donelson, *Pseudepigraphy*, 81–85.

97 Donelson, *Pseudepigraphy*, 85–87.

98 Donelson, *Pseudepigraphy*, 88–90. However, he contends that the unexpressed major premise in this argument "establishes the place of these teachings in the plan of salvation" (88).

99 W. M. Sattler, "Conceptions of *Ethos* in Ancient Rhetoric," *Speech Monographs* 14 (1957), 55–65 (esp. 57–61), draws attention to Aristotle's understanding of ethos as both subjective (the speaker's ethos) and objective (the ethos of others). Quintilian, *Institutes*, 6.2.8–19 contends that pathos and ethos appeals are closely linked, differing only by degree. The former deal with stronger emotions, the latter with more gentle emotions, persuading and inducing a feeling of goodwill in the hearers. This point is also acknowledged by Sattler ("Conceptions of *Ethos*," 62–63).

100 Defenders of the Pauline authorship of the PE have habitually charged those who contend that the letters are pseudonymous with not being able to provide a credible reason for the existence of these notices. See, e.g., Kelly, *Pastoral Epistles*, 32–33.

Fiore, *Personal Example*, 101–63 and Donelson, *Pseudepigraphy*, 23–42 note the similar use of personal example in other pseudepigraphical letter collections. This practice is, of course, derived from the use of example for paraenesis in non-pseudepigraphic letters of exhortation. For the function of what is apparently trivial and anecdotal in Seneca's letters, see Cancik, *Untersuchungen*, 75–76.

101 Cf. Fitzgerald's analysis of the Greco-Roman background of the catalogues of suffering of 1 and 2 Corinthians in his *Cracks in an Earthen Vessel*, 47–116.

102 Donelson, *Pseudepigraphy*, 29.

103 Donelson, *Pseudepigraphy*, 104.

104 See Wisse, *Ethos and Pathos*, 5.

105 See the discussion in Kennedy, *Aristotle*, 163–4.

106 Cf. Pol. *Phil.* 5.3: "[I]t is good to be cut off from the lust of the things in the world" (ἀπὸ τῶν ἐπιθυμιῶν ἐν τῷ κόσμῳ).

107 1 Tim. 4.12: μηδείς σου τῆς νεότητος καταφρονείτω. Cf. *Rhetoric*, 2.15.2: καὶ καταφρονητικὸν καὶ τῶν ὁμοίων ἐστὶ τοῖς προγόνοις τοῖς αὐτῶν.

108 See *Rich Christian*, 149–82.

109 See Dibelius and Conzelmann, *Pastoral Epistles*, 21. For discussion of the contribution of Dibelius to the debate concerning the paraenetic materials in the Pauline literature, see the introduction of Robert J. Karris, "The Function and Sitz im Leben of the Paraenetic Elements in the Pastoral Epistles," (Th.D. Dissertation; Harvard University, 1971). For the classical, Hellenistic, and Greco-Roman background, see, especially, 1–44. Karris seeks to challenge Dibelius' view that the paraenesis of the PE has little to do with the distinctive ideas of Paul but is merely traditional "and employed out of didactic habit" (ix).

110 "The Polemic of the Pastoral Epistles," *JBL* 93 (1972), 549–64. For the virtue and vice-lists of the PE, see B. S. Easton, "New Testament Ethical Lists," *JBL* 51 (1932), especially 7–11; E. Kamlah, *Die Form der katalogen Paränese im Neuen Testament* (Tübingen: Mohr, 1964), 198–200; N. J. McEleney, "The Vice Lists of the Pastoral Epistles," *CBQ* 36 (1974), 203–19.

111 This is also noted in Luke T. Johnson, "II Timothy and the Polemic Against the False Teachers: A Re-examination," *JRelS* 6.2/7.1 (1978–79), 1–3.

112 See Karris, "Polemic," 552–5. The false teachers are greedy, deceivers, they do not practise what they preach, they indulge in verbal quibbles, and they have a subversive effect on women. Of course, as Karris acknowledges, this does not rule

out the fact that the false teachers may have been guilty of some of these shortcomings, but the fact is they can all be found in traditional polemic.

113 See F. H. Colson, "'Myths and Genealogies'," 265–71. Colson argues that the phrase "myths and genealogies" (1 Tim. 1.4; Tit. 3.9) refers to an excessive intellectualism in Hellenistic Jewish circles in which the Hebrew Bible was subjected to the same sort of rigorous study as Homer by which the personal details of the characters were reduced to lists and pedigrees.

114 Karris, "Polemic," 557 believes that the reference to unspecified "myths" in 1 Tim. 1.4 is a stock charge. However, in Tit. 1.14 the myths are specified as Jewish and, therefore, less likely to be part of stock polemic (see "Polemic," 562).

115 *Contra* Towner, *The Goal of our Instruction*, 40–44. Towner argues that the teaching ministry of women derives, not from the false teachers, but from an over-realized eschatology. However, in view of the fact that 2 Tim. 2.17–18 condemns the view of Hymenaeus and Philetus that the resurrection has already occurred, it would be natural to argue that there was indeed a link between the false teachers and the emancipation of women to which 1 Tim. 2.11–15 bears witness.

116 See, e.g., Karris, "Polemic," 563 n. 58; Towner, *The Goal of Our Instruction*, ch. 2 (21–45).

117 Quinn, "The Holy Spirit in the Pastoral Epistles," 346.

118 This tradition is apparent in late literature of the second century C.E., notably the *Prot. Jas.* 13.1. However, it is also encountered in earlier works. See 4 Macc. 18.7–9 (mid first century C.E.), *Apoc. Abr.* 23.1–5 (ca. 100 C.E.), and, perhaps, in the late first century C.E. *2 Enoch* 31.6. In 2 Cor. 11.3 Paul himself also seems to know the legend of the seduction of Eve. He uses the same compound as 1 Tim. 2.14, namely, ἐξαπατάω, to refer to the serpent "deceiving" Eve (ὁ ὄφις ἐξηπάτησεν Εὕαν), but, unlike the Pastor, does not make any anthropological point. For discussion of the Jewish tradition of the seduction of Eve, see A. T. Hanson, "Eve's Transgression," in *Studies in the Pastoral Epistles*, 64–77; Roloff, *Der erste Brief an Timotheus*, 139 n. 150; Houlden, *Pastoral Epistles*, 71–72; Max Küchler, *Schweigen, Schmuck und Schleier: Drei neutestamentliche Vorschriften zur Verdrängung der Frauen auf dem Hintergrund einer frauenfeindlichen Exegese des Alten Testaments im antiken Judentum* (NTOA 1; Freiburg/Göttingen: Universitätsverlag/Vandenhoeck & Ruprecht, 1986), 32–52. Not all scholars are convinced that the legend of the seduction of Eve is referred to in 1 Tim. 2. See, e.g., Towner, *1–2 Timothy & Titus*, 78; Easton, *Pastoral Epistles*, 129. What cannot be denied, however, is the reinforcement of conventional gender roles by the Pastor. On Greco-Roman expectations of the mastery of men over women see Aristotle, *Politics*, 1259a37ff. and the insightful discussion in Stanley K. Stowers, *A Rereading of Romans: Justice, Jews, and Gentiles* (New Haven: Yale University Press, 1994), 49–53, 93–95.

119 See Verner, *Household of God*, 170–1; Kelly, *Pastoral Epistles*, 68–70. However, Karris, "Function," 114–6 argues that 1 Tim. 2.13–15 and Tit. 2.5 are not formulated against the opponents' teaching, or that the opponents necessarily forbade marriage, or promoted emancipation of women. While this may be true with respect to the false teachers, 1 Tim. 2.13–15, at least, does indulge in polemic which is not stock, and which is probably directed to an actual situation in which women taught men, much to the outrage of the Pastor.

120 Karris, "Polemic," 563.

121 The virtue lists of the PE (1 Tim. 3.2–3, 8; Tit. 1.7–8; 3.1–2) serve the positive function of setting the true teachers and their followers over against the false. According to Karris, "Function," 121, true teachers are to vindicate the correctness of their teaching by their exemplary lives. This same reason is adduced with respect to the life of believers in public.

122 Karris, "Polemic," 559.

123 "II Timothy and the Polemic Against the False Teachers," 1–3.

124 See, e.g., Karris, "Function," 121. The false teachers' teaching is wrong because the teachers are immoral. Although Karris acknowledges that the polemic directed against them in the vice lists is stock, he does accept that they are immoral people.

125 See, e.g., Pseudo-Plato, *Letters*, 7 (the would-be king Dionysius); Seneca, *Letters*, 83 (the drunkard Lucius Piso); Jude 10–11 (Cain, Balaam, and Korah).

126 Donelson, *Pseudepigraphy*, 125.

127 Cf. Cicero, *de Oratore*, 2.185–216; Quintilian, *Institutes*, 6.2.2–7, 20–36. Both writers mention the necessity of the orator experiencing the emotions to which he desires his hearers to respond. Quintilian observes that while there are many who can construct logical arguments, there are few orators who have the ability to move the judge by pathos (6.2.3). Emotional power, he adds, dominates the courts. Crucial is the ability to cause judges to take personal interest in the case being presented. Pathos arguments, he notes, are almost entirely concerned with "anger, dislike, fear, hatred and pity" (6.2.20).

128 See Smit, "The Letter of Paul to the Galatians," 19–21. Smit draws attention to the function of the *indignatio* in the rhetorical handbooks (see 19 n. 1). Cf. Kraftchick, "Ethos and Pathos Appeals," 240–7.

129 Kennedy, *Aristotle*, 122.

130 Cf. the similar material in *ad Alex*. 34 and 36 (first half); Quintilian, *Institutes*, 6.2.

131 Not relevant to the PE are Aristotle's discussions of fear (2.5), shame (2.6), kindness (2.7), being indignant (2.9), envy (2.10), and zeal (2.11).

132 Note Demosthenes' introduction to his *Against Aphobus, 1*. The orator admits his youth (§2), affirms his expectation of receiving justice at the hands of the court, and promises to speak to the facts and to keep his speech short (§§2–3).

133 See also Ign. *Pol.* 2.1. For further discussion, see John T. Fitzgerald, "Paul, the Ancient Epistolary Theorists, and 2 Corinthians 10–13," in David L. Balch, Everett Ferguson and Wayne A. Meeks (eds.), *Greeks, Romans, and Christians: Essays in Honor of Abraham J. Malherbe* (Minneapolis: Fortress, 1990), 190–200. See especially 194 n. 26 in which Fitzgerald observes that πραότης and ἐπιείκεια create goodwill between author and addressee.

134 See discussion of this urgency in Abraham J. Malherbe, "'In Season and Out of Season'," *JBL* 103 (1984), 235–43. Choosing the right moment to engage in moral exhortation was considered desirable in the Greco-Roman world. However, Malherbe draws a distinction between those who are open to correction and the false teachers in view in 2 Tim. 4.2. The latter are beyond reclamation. Consequently, the exhortation to gentleness is waived with respect to them. Timothy should simply preach the word regardless of the appropriateness of the "time" or the heedless disposition of the false teachers. The καιρός of 4.3, when people will not heed the truth, has already arrived.

135 The crowning argument against Simon, the allegedly violent accuser in Lysias' *Against Simon*, concerns his quarrelsomeness in a military campaign against Corinth. The defendant, on the other hand, portrays himself as a model of rational and self-controlled behavior.

136 Examples are the defendant's plea in Lysias' *On the Murder of Eratosthenes* that the court uphold as justifiable the homicide of his wife's lover lest the outrage in society against adultery and adulterers be diluted; Demosthenes' impassioned appeal with respect to Meidias in his *Against Meidias* concerning the propriety of protecting Demosthenes and the state against people like him; and Aeschines' portrayal of the character of Timarchus in *Against Timarchus*, a man who has conspicuously offended the sexual mores of a whole society.

137 See, e.g., Dibelius and Conzelmann, *Pastoral Epistles*, 147 on Tit. 3.3–7. Cf. Quinn, *Titus*, 164, 200–01.

138 See Kennedy, *Aristotle*, 154 n. 76 for the pity-exciting potential of dress.

139 See Aristotle, *Rhetoric*, 2.8.15; cf. 2.9.1.

Conclusion

I have made a distinction in this book between the assumed epistolary situation and the actual situation of the PE. In the former, Paul writes to trusted associates, Timothy and Titus, with directives and reminders concerning the fulfilment of the charge he has given and bequeathed to them for the maintenance and propagation of the Pauline deposit. The assumed congregational audience is one step removed. They are the beneficiaries of the apostle's ministry via his trusted emissaries. The responsibilities of the emissaries are to maintain the order of the church (1 Timothy) or to set the church in order (Titus), to continue to instruct the believers in the faith by teaching and example, and to recall them to their commitment and obligation with its moral and social implications. The rhetoric of the PE as letters of moral exhortation takes this (assumed) situation seriously because it is only in so far as the PE are accepted as convincing and persuasive at the level of their assumed authorship that the Pastor is able to address the actual situation of the addressees.

I have observed that the Pastor utilizes persuasive strategies in support of his enterprise of actualizing and commending Pauline tradition in the interests of securing it not only for his generation but for generations to come. First among these strategies is his intention to write recognizably Pauline letters in form and content as actualizations of the apostle's teaching for a generation facing a grave threat to the Pauline heritage from false teachers. The Pastor also uses persuasive strategies derived from the tradition of classical rhetoric. These were intended in the first place to be applied to the craft of devising speeches. Letters of moral exhortation generated their own set of persuasive techniques, some of which were derived from and sympathetic with oratory. My intention in this book has been to shed light on these strategies in the PE from the point of view of the Greco-Roman tradition of writing letters of moral exhortation (chapter 2) and the speech tradition (chapter 3).

The four broadly conceived approaches to the PE surveyed in chapter one were not, in the main, cognizant of the persuasive strategies employed by the Pastor. However, the first of the approaches surveyed makes an indirect contribution to understanding the PE as letters which are rhetorically literate. In demonstrating the probability that Paul did not write the PE, Baur and Holtzmann and their "descendants" have invited attention to the rhetorical potential of the double pseudonymity of the PE and the manner in which the Pastor commends his message to his audience. Those scholars whose work I examined in the section on *Traditionsgeschichte* have demonstrated how much the PE are indebted to the received Pauline tradition, which, I surmise, may have been transmitted to the churches of the PE primarily through a corpus of ten letters. The Pastor's appeal to Pauline tradition forms a most important strategy for him, since it was his intention to write letters embodying that tradition and, moreover, the Pauline apostolic *persona* as it had been transmitted to (or even remembered by) him.

Why have the PE proven so influential right down to our own era? The reason can be assessed from the rhetorical point of view. The Pastor has sharpened Paul's authority in order to cement the Pastor's interpretation of the apostle's vision of the contours of Christian life and leadership. Some Christian traditions continue to place themselves under the authority of the Pastor's Paul in denying ordination and congregational leadership to women, and in maintaining patriarchal modes of church and family life. My study of the rhetoric of the PE has attempted to demonstrate that in their cultural situation the letters mounted a highly persuasive and literate campaign fought on two fronts: *against* the false teachers, and *for* a vision of church life and leadership sanctioned by the apostle himself.

The PE are best characterized as letters standing self-consciously in the Pauline tradition and in the Greco-Roman tradition of moral exhortation. Allowing for some differences between the PE and the Pauline corpus, I concluded in chapter two that for those who already accepted the authority of Paul in the tradition transmitted to them, the PE, both in form and as actualizations of Paul's theology and practice, might be received as convincingly Pauline in character. The PE can be situated within the epistolary tradition of Greco-Roman moral exhortation, though without minimizing the Pastor's own adaptation of this tradition as an author subscribing to the saving achievement of Christ and the implications of that achievement for present life and eschatological hope. In addition 2 Timothy presents features which derive from the genre of the testament, a species of moral exhortation found chiefly in early Jewish literature. Given the persuasive strategies peculiar to this genre, the Pastor grounds the exhortation of this letter even more effectively in the authoritative *persona* of the apostle. By their association with 2 Timothy in the corpus, the authority of the exhortation imparted by the assumed author of 1 Timothy and Titus is also augmented and enhanced.

However, the rhetorical strategies of the PE can be also assessed from the perspective of Greco-Roman oratory since the persuasive strategies appropriate for letters derive much of their dynamic from the medium of effective public speech. The deliberative and epideictic species of oratory have much in common with the PE. Judged from the perspective of deliberative rhetoric, the Pastor persuades and dissuades, affirming the benefits of loyalty to Pauline tradition (as he has actualized it) and the disadvantages of heeding the false teachers. From the aspect of epideictic rhetoric, the Pastor affirms the values and perceptions that he and the audience already endorse. He also has his own agenda to commend. The Pastor appeals for their support on the basis of what he and they hold in common, namely, respect for Paul's authority, commitment to certain social conventions, and shared possession of liturgical formulations and entrusted traditions.

The Pastor's use of polemic plays a significant role in the persuasive strategy of the letters. By its use he not only contrasts the model of the good teacher and the godly life which it engenders and enhances but seeks the audience's assent to his aversion of the false teachers and the moral and spiritual turmoil their teaching is already having and is bound to have on the lives of the believers in the future. The content of the false teaching does not accord with the Pastor's perception of what is permissible within the contours of the Pauline heritage.

The PE participate in the venerable tradition of rhetorical practice and theory. This is demonstrated by the author's use of rhetorical deduction and induction and by the use of arguments grounded in appeals to ethos and pathos. I have also sought to underscore the fact that the Pastor has quite intentionally assumed a disposition in his address to his audience, which, he trusts, they will find appealing. In this way continued loyalty to Paul and his legacy on the part of the addressees will be promoted. Thus, the appreciation of the PE's literateness and persuasive force is considerably enhanced.

The letters, as I have argued throughout this book, are meant to be read as actualizations of the Pauline heritage received by the communities, but given new voice for times radically discontinuous from those of the apostle. The author wrote, in effect, what might be termed "letters in character." The Pastor's message in all three letters can be summarized thus—the health and future prospect of the churches is integrally related to their faithfulness to the Pauline legacy.

The Pastor creates a powerful image of the apostle. He is the very embodiment of the authoritative psychagogue. He suffers yet endures. He nears death, yet still carries on his mission in good conscience and with undiminished confidence in the promises of God. In the fiction of the emissary addressees receiving reminders of their charge to order the household of God in accordance with *Kirchenordnungen* from the assumed author, the Pastor is appealing to a contemporary leadership which is exhorted to model itself on the image of Paul both for the present and the future. Dedication on the part of the leaders to this task will result in securing an eternal reward both for them and the beneficiaries of their ministry. He finds cause for commending and for warning them. In short, he summons them to perseverance through the fiction created by the technique of double pseudonymity.[1] Yet, in his use of liturgical materials and his evocation of Paul he speaks the language of his audience, seeking their goodwill and their assent to his exhortation in matters which may prove confrontational. In his polemic against the false teachers he endeavors to persuade the audience to underwrite his vision of the true teacher and the true believer.

Ultimately, the Pastor desires his message to be accepted as the audience would have accepted Paul's. While he no doubt perceived that his letters would not be universally well-received, he sought to actualize and translate the *persona* and teaching of Paul for their edification and continued security in the Pauline tradition. The right of the apostle to exhort, to prescribe, and to sanction was unquestioned. The Pastor therefore seeks to convey a credible image of the *persona* of the apostle. But that *persona* was also that of the *pastor pastorum dei*. This is why the Pastor lays such great stress on the fact that the assumed addressees are loyal, trusted, valued, and already well-equipped emissaries of the assumed author, who writes to them by way of reminder. If the Pauline heritage was to be secured for generations to come, the Pastor knew that he had to be persuasive at the point of demonstrating goodwill towards the actual addressees.

Assessment of the Pastor's achievement must take into account the insights to be gained from a study of rhetoric. The Pastor wrote letters which, judged by the rhetorical conventions of his own culture, amount to highly literate, effective, and persuasive affirmations of Paul and the Pauline tradition in a situation which threatened his heritage as the Pastor understood it. By the strategies adopted in the letters, the Pastor addressed the leaders directly and the believers in general, urging them (in Paul's name) to give the same unqualified endorsement of his vision of the proper shape of life in the church and the world as the assent they had already given to the *persona* of Paul received in the tradition and now actualized and brought to speech by the Pastor for their ongoing commitment to the apostle's legacy.

NEW DIRECTIONS IN THE STUDY OF THE PE

In the Epilogue of Robert Karris' 1971 dissertation, "Function and *Sitz im Leben* of the Paraenetic Elements in the Pastoral Epistles," the author expresses the conviction that the discussion of the authorship of the letters has become "petrified."[2] He expresses the hope that his own examination of the paraenesis of the PE will give new direction to the understanding of the PE. He trusts that the old arguments about authorship can be seen against a "different landscape," namely, that of the tradition of polemical address of the classical, Hellenistic, and Greco-Roman eras, which, Karris notes, experienced an upsurge after ca. 70 C.E. He anticipates, in part, the directions of my own analysis of the PE when he notes their affinity with paraenetic works like Isocrates' discourse *To Demonicus*.[3]

It is my conviction that my study of the PE demonstrates how readily susceptible these letters are to rhetorical analysis. However, such a study does not render obsolete the debate concerning authorship. The acceptance of the arguments for the double pseudonymity operating in the PE opens up new appreciations of the literary art of the Pastor. We encounter an author who is passionately committed to bringing Pauline tradition to speech for his generation. To do so he must write a Pauline letter; a letter in character. He must affirm Pauline tradition not only because his audience affirms it already but because out of that "treasure" comes the καινὰ καὶ παλαιά for securing the heritage of the apostle for generations to come (cf. Matt. 13.52). The "old things" are the Pauline traditions the Pastor and his audience both affirm. The "new things" comprise those applications of those traditions to congregational life by which the distinction between the Paul and the false teachers will be clearly demarcated. The Pastor, evoking the authority and pastoral care of the apostle Paul, aspires to the commendation of his hearers by their reception of his letters written in Paul's name as the faithful householder, the οἰκοδεσπότης, who with goodwill commends the old and urges the new.

NOTES

1 See MacDonald, *Pauline Churches*, 206.

2 See "Function," 133 n. 1.

3 Function," 134.

BIBLIOGRAPHY

A. Ancient Authors and Texts

Aeschines. *The Speeches*. Loeb Classical Library, 1919.

Amidon, Philip R. S.J. trans. and ed. *The Panarion of St. Epiphanius, Bishop of Salamis: Selected Passages*. New York: Oxford University Press, 1990.

Aristotle. *Topics*. Loeb Classical Library, 1960.

——— *The Politics*. Loeb Classical Library, 1950.

——— *The Art of Rhetoric*. Loeb Classical Library, 1926.

Bailey, C. ed. *Epicurus: The Extant Remains*. Reprint. Westport: Hyperion, 1979.

Barrett, Charles K. ed. *New Testament Background: Selected Documents*. Revised Edition. San Francisco: Harper & Row, 1989.

Charlesworth, James H. ed. *Old Testament Pseudepigrapha*. 2 vols. New York: Doubleday, 1983 and 1985.

Cicero. *De Inventione*. Loeb Classical Library, 1949.

——— *De Oratore*. Loeb Classical Library, 1942.

——— *Letters to his Friends*. Vol. 3. Loeb Classical Library, 1927–29.

——— *Letters to Atticus*. Loeb Classical Library, 1913–39.

Demetrius. *On Style*. Loeb Classical Library, 1927.

Demosthenes. *Private Orations*. Vol. 1. Loeb Classical Library, 1936.

——— *Against Meidias etc*. Loeb Classical Library, 1935.

Diogenes Laertius. *Lives of Eminent Philosophers*. Loeb Classical Library, 1925.

Düring, I. *Aristotle's Protrepticus: An Attempt at Reconstruction*. Göteborg: Elanders, 1961.

Epictetus. *The Discourses, the Manual, and the Fragments*. Loeb Classical Library, 1926–28.

Eusebius. *Ecclesiastical History*. Loeb Classical Library, 1926–32.

Grenfell, B. P., and A. S. Hunt, eds. *The Oxyrhynchus Papyri*. Vol. 3. London: Egypt Exploration Society, 1903.

Grenfell, B. P., A. S. Hunt, and E. J. Goodspeed, eds. *The Tebtunis Papyri*. Vol. 2. London: Henry Frowde, 1907.

Gutas, D. ed. *Greek Wisdom Literature in Arabic Translation: A Study of the Graeco-Arabic Gnomologia*. New Haven: American Oriental Society, 1975.

Hennecke, E., and W. Schneemelcher, eds. *New Testament Apocrypha*. Revised Edition. Vol. 2. Louisville: Westminster/John Knox, 1992.

Hesiod. *The Homeric Hymns, and Homerica.* Loeb Classical Library, 1929.
Homer. *Iliad.* Loeb Classical Library, 1924–25.
——— *Odyssey.* Loeb Classical Library, 1919–31.
Horst, P. W. van der. *The Sentences of Pseudo-Phocylides.* Leiden: Brill, 1978.
Hunt, A. S., and C. C. Edgar, eds. *Select Papyri.* Vol. 1. Loeb Classical Library, 1932.
Hunt, A. S., and J. Gilbart Smyly, eds. *Tebtunis Papyri.* Vol. 3. Part 1. London: Humphrey Milord, 1933: 66–102.
Jonge, M. de, ed. *Testamenta XII Patriarcharum.* Leiden: Brill, 1964.
Josephus. *Against Apion.* Loeb Classical Library, 1976.
Kennedy, George A. ed. *Aristotle: On Rhetoric.* New York/Oxford: Oxford University Press, 1991.
Lake, K. ed. *Apostolic Fathers.* Loeb Classical Library, 1935–36.
Livy. *History of Rome.* Vol. 3. Loeb Classical Library, 1924.
Lohse, E. *Die Texte aus Qumran Hebräisch und Deutsch.* 2nd Edition. Munich: Kösel Verlag, 1971.
Lucian. *Works.* Loeb Classical Library, 1913–67.
Lysias. *Speeches.* Loeb Classical Library, 1930.
Malherbe, Abraham J. *Ancient Epistolary Theorists.* Atlanta: Scholars Press, 1988.
——— ed. *The Cynic Epistles.* Reprint. Atlanta : Scholars Press, 1986.
Metzger, Bruce M., and Roland E. Murphy, eds. *The New Oxford Annotated Bible with the Apocrypha.* New York/Oxford: Oxford University Press, 1991.
Norlin, G., and L. van Hook, eds. *Isocrates.* Loeb Classical Library, 1928–45.
Parsons, P. J. ed. *The Oxyrhynchus Papyri.* Vol. 42. London: Egypt Exploration Society, 1974.
Plato. *Dialogues.* Loeb Classical Library, 1914–35.
Pliny. *Letters and Panegyricus.* Loeb Classical Library, 1969.
Plutarch. *Moralia.* Vol. 10. Loeb Classical Library, 1936.
Polybius. *The Histories.* Vol. 3. Loeb Classical Library, 1923.
Quintilian. *Institutio Oratorica.* 4 vols. Loeb Classical Library, 1920–22.
Rhetorica ad Alexandrum. Loeb Classical Library, 1937.
Rhetorica ad Herennium. Loeb Classical Library, 1954.
Roberts, A., and J. Donaldson, eds. *The Ante-Nicene Fathers.* Reprint. 10 Vols. Grand Rapids: Eerdmans, 1986.
Rose V. ed. *Aristoteles Fragmenta.* Reprint. Stuttgart: Teubner, 1966.
Schaff, P., and H. Wace, eds. *Nicene and Post-Nicene Fathers.* Second Series. *St Jerome: Letters and Select Works.* Revised Edition. Vol. 6. Grand Rapids: Eerdmans, 1989.
Seneca. *Moral Essays.* Loeb Classical Library, 1928–35.
——— *Epistulae Morales.* Loeb Classical Library, 1920.

Städele, A. *Die Briefe des Pythagoras und der Pythagoreer*. Meisenheim: Anton Hain, 1980.

Stevenson, J. ed. *A New Eusebius*. New ed. revised by W. H. C. Frend. London: SPCK, 1987.

Theognidis et Phocylidis fragmenta: et adespota quaedam gnomica. Berlin: De Gruyter, 1978.

Vermes, G. *The Dead Sea Scrolls in English*. 4th Edition. Penguin Books, 1995.

B. Modern Authors

A Committee of the Oxford Society of Historical Theology. *The New Testament in the Apostolic Fathers*. Oxford: Clarendon, 1905.

Alexander, P. S. "Epistolary Literature." In M. E. Stone, ed. *Jewish Writings of the Second Temple Period*. Philadelphia/Assen: Fortress/Van Gorcum, 1984: 579–96.

Aland, K. "The Problem of Anonymity and Pseudonymity in Christian Literature of the First Two Centuries." *JThS* 12 (1961): 39–49.

Aune, D. E. *The New Testament in Its Literary Environment*. Philadelphia: Westminster, 1987.

Balch, D. L. *Let Wives be Submissive: The Domestic Code in 1 Peter*. Atlanta: Scholars Press, 1981.

Barnett, A. E. *Paul Becomes a Literary Influence*. Chicago: University of Chicago Press, 1941.

Barrett, C. K. "Pauline Controversies in the Post-Pauline Period." *NTS* 20 (1973–74): 229–45.

——— *The Signs of an Apostle*. London: Epworth, 1970.

Bassler, Jouette M. "A Plethora of Epiphanies: Christology in the Pastoral Epistles." *PSB* 17 (1996): 310–25.

Bauckham. Richard J. "Pseudo-Apostolic Letters." *JBL* 107 (1988): 469–94.

Bauer, W. *Orthodoxy and Heresy*. Philadelphia: Fortress, 1971.

Baur, F. C. *Die sogennanten Pastoralbriefe des Apostels Paulus*. Stuttgart and Tübingen: J. G. Gotta'schen Verlagshandlung, 1835.

Beckwith, R. "The Ancient Attitude to Pseudonymity." In *The Old Testament Canon of the New Testament Church: and its Background in Early Judaism*. Grand Rapids: Eerdmans, 1985: 346–58.

Beker, J. Christiaan. *The New Testament: A Thematic Introduction*. Minneapolis: Fortress, 1994.

——— *Heirs of Paul*. Philadelphia: Fortress, 1991.

——— "Paul the Theologian: Major Motifs in Pauline Theology." *Int* 43 (1989): 352–65.

——— "Paul's Theology: Consistent or Inconsistent?" *NTS* 34 (1988): 364–77.

——— *Paul the Apostle*. Philadelphia: Fortress, 1980.

Berger, K. "Hellenistische Gattungen im Neuen Testament." In *Aufstieg und Niedergang der römischen Welt*. Part 2. Vol. 25. No. 2 (1984): 1034–1432, 1831–85.

——— *Formgeschichte des Neuen Testaments*. Heidelberg: Quelle & Meyer, 1984.

——— "Apostelbrief und apostolische Rede/Zum Formular frühchristlicher Briefe." *ZNW* 65 (1974): 190–231.

Betz, H. D. *Galatians*. Philadelphia: Fortress, 1979.

——— "The Literary Composition and Function of Paul's Letter to the Galatians." *NTS* 21 (1974–75): 353–79.

Boer, M. C. de. "Images of Paul in the Post-Apostolic Period." *CBQ* 42 (1980): 359–80.

Bradley, D. G. "The *Topos* as a Form in the Pauline Paraenesis." *JBL* 72 (1953): 238–46.

Branick, V. P. "Apocalyptic Paul?" *CBQ* 47 (1985): 664–75.

Brown, R. E. *The Churches the Apostles Left Behind*. New York/Ramsey: Paulist, 1984.

——— "The Unity and Diversity in New Testament Ecclesiology." *NovT* 6 (1963): 298–308.

Brox, N. *Die Pastoralbriefe*. Reprint. Regensburg: Pustet Verlag, 1989.

Buck C., and G. Taylor. *Saint Paul: A Study of the Development of his Thought*. New York: Scribners, 1969.

Bultmann, R. *Theology of the New Testament*. 2 Vols. New York: Scribners, 1951 and 1955.

——— "Pastoralbriefe." In H. Gunkel, and L. Zscharnak, eds. *Die Religion in Geschichte und Gegenwart*. Vol. 4. Tübingen: Mohr, 1927–31: 993–7.

Burgess, T. C. "Epideictic Literature." *Chicago Studies in Classical Literature* 3 (1902): 89–253.

Caird, G. B. *The Language and Imagery of the Bible*. Philadelphia: Westminster, 1980.

Cancik, H. *Untersuchungen zu Senecas Epistulae morales*. Hildesheim: Georg Olms Verlagsbuchhandlung, 1967.

Carroll, K. L. "The Expansion of the Pauline Corpus." *JBL* 72 (1953): 230–7.

Childs, Brevard S. *The New Testament as Canon: An Introduction*. London: SCM, 1984.

Clark, D. L. *Rhetoric in Greco-Roman Education*. New York: Columbia University Press, 1957.

Collins, J. J. "Testaments." In M. E. Stone, ed. *Jewish Writings of the Second Temple Period*. Philadelphia/Assen: Fortress/ Van Gorcum, 1984: 325–55.

Collins, R. F. *Letters That Paul Did Not Write: The Epistle to the Hebrews and the Pauline Pseudepigrapha.* Wilmington: Michael Glazier, 1988.

——— "The Image of Paul in the Pastorals." *LTP* 31 (1975): 147–73.

Colson, F. H. "'Myths and Genealogies'—A Note on the Polemic of the Pastoral Epistles." *JThS* o.s. 19 (1918): 265–71.

Conzelmann, H. *1 Corinthians.* Philadelphia: Fortress, 1975.

Countryman, L. W. *The Rich Christian in the Church of the Early Empire: Contradictions and Accommodations.* New York/Toronto: Edwin Mellen Press, 1980.

Culpepper, R. A. *The Johannine School.* Missoula: Scholars Press, 1975.

Dahl, N. A. "The Particularity of the Pauline Epistles as a Problem in the Ancient Church." In *Neotestamentica et Patristica.* Novum Testamentum Supplements, no. 6. Leiden: Brill, 1962: 261–71.

Dalton, W. J. "Pseudepigraphy in the New Testament." *Catholic Theological Review* 5 (1983): 29–35.

Daube, D. "Rabbinic Methods of Interpretation and Hellenistic Rhetoric." *HUCA* 22 (1949): 239–64.

Deissmann, A. *Light from the Ancient East.* Reprint. Grand Rapids: Baker, 1978.

——— *Paul: A Study in Social and Religious History.* 2nd Edition. London: Hodder & Stoughton, 1926.

——— *Bible Studies.* Edinburgh: T. & T. Clark, 1901.

Dibelius, M. *From Tradition to Gospel.* New York: Scribners, 1965.

Dibelius, M., and H. Conzelmann. *The Pastoral Epistles.* Philadelphia: Fortress, 1972.

Dodd, C. H. *New Testament Studies.* Manchester: Manchester University Press, 1953.

Donelson, L. R. *Pseudepigraphy and Ethical Argument in the Pastorals.* Tübingen: Mohr, 1986.

Doty, W. G. *Letters in Primitive Christianity.* Philadelphia: Fortress, 1973.

——— "The Classification of Epistolary Literature." *CBQ* 31 (1969): 183–99.

Dunn, James D. G. *Romans 9–16.* Waco: Word, 1988.

——— "The Problem of Pseudonymity." In *The Living Word.* Philadelphia: Fortress, 1988: 65–85.

Easton, B. S. *The Pastoral Epistles.* New York: Scribners, 1947.

——— "New Testament Ethical Lists." *JBL* 51 (1932): 1–12.

Eichhorn, J. G. *Einleitung in das Neuen Testament.* Leipzig: Weidmannischen Buchhandlung, 1812.

Elliott, J. H. "A Catholic Gospel: Reflections on 'Early Catholicism' in the New Testament." *CBQ* 31 (1969): 213–23.

Ellis, E. Earle. "Pseudonymity and Canonicity of New Testament Documents." In Michael J. Wilkins and Terence Paige, eds. *Worship, Theology and*

Ministry in the Early Church: Essays in Honour of Ralph P. Martin. Journal for the Study of the New Testament Supplement Series, no. 87. Sheffield: JSOT Press, 1992: 212–24.

Fiore, B. *The Function of Personal Example in the Socratic and Pastoral Epistles.* Analecta Biblica, no. 105. Rome: Biblical Institute Press, 1986.

Fitzgerald, J. T. "Paul, the Ancient Epistolary Theorists, and 2 Corinthians 10–13." In D. L. Balch, E. Ferguson, and W. A. Meeks, eds. *Greeks, Romans, and Christians: Essays in Honor of Abraham J. Malherbe.* Minneapolis: Fortress, 1990: 190–200.

——— *Cracks in an Earthen Vessel: An Examination of the Catalogues of Hardships in the Corinthian Correspondence.* Society of Biblical Literature Dissertation Series, no. 99. Atlanta: Scholars Press, 1988.

Fitzmyer, J. A. "Some Notes on Aramaic Epistolography." *JBL* 93 (1974): 201–25.

Forbes, C. "Comparison, Self-Praise and Irony: Paul's Boasting and the Conventions of Hellenistic Rhetoric." *NTS* 36 (1986): 1–30.

Fowl, S. E. "A Metaphor in Distress: A Reading of NHΠIOI in 1 Thessalonians 2.7." *NTS* 36 (1990): 469–74.

——— *The Story of Christ in the Ethics of Paul: An Analysis of the Hymnic Material in the Pauline Corpus.* Journal for the Study of the New Testament Supplement Series, no. 36. Sheffield: JSOT Press, 1990.

Friedrich, G. "Glaube und Verkündigung bei Paulus." In F. Hahn, and H. Klein, eds. *Glaube im Neuen Testament.* Neukirchen-Vluyn: Neukirchener Verlag, 1982: 93–113.

Fuller, R. H. *A Critical Introduction to the New Testament.* Reprint. London: Duckworth, 1974.

Funk, R. W. "The Apostolic *Parousia*: Form and Significance." In W. R. Farmer, C. F. D. Moule, and R. R. Niebuhr, eds. *Christian History and Interpretation: Studies Presented to John Knox.* Cambridge: University Press, 1967: 249–68.

——— "The Letter: Form and Style." In *Language, Hermeneutic and the Word of God: The Problem of Language in the New Testament and Contemporary Theology.* New York/Evanston/London: Harper & Row, 1966: 250–74.

Furnish, V. P. *II Corinthians.* Garden City: Doubleday, 1984.

——— "Development in Paul's Thought." *JAAR* 38 (1970): 289–303.

——— *Theology and Ethics in Paul.* Nashville/New York: Abingdon, 1968.

Gaventa, B. R. "The Maternity of Paul: An Exegetical Study of Galatians 4:19." In R. T. Fortna, and B. R. Gaventa, eds. *The Conversation Continues: Studies in Paul and John in Honor of J. Louis Martyn.* Nashville: Abingdon, 1990: 189–201.

Gitay, Y. "Rhetorical Criticism and the Prophetic Discourse." In D. F. Watson, ed. *Persuasive Artistry: Studies in New Testament Rhetoric in Honor of George A. Kennedy.* Journal for the Study of the New Testament Supplement Series, no. 36. Sheffield: JSOT Press, 1991: 13–24.

Goodspeed, E. J. *The Formation of the New Testament.* Chicago: University Press, 1926.

Grimaldi, W. M. A. *Aristotle, Rhetoric: A Commentary.* 2 Vols. New York: Fordham University Press, 1980 and 1988.

Hanson, A. T. Review of *Paul the Apostle*, by J. Christiaan Beker. *JSNT* 14 (1982): 123–5.

——— *The Pastoral Epistles.* London: Marshall, Morgan & Scott, 1982.

——— "The Domestication of Paul: A Study in the Development of Early Christian Theology." *BJRL* 63 (1981): 402–18.

——— "Eucharistic References in 1 and 2 Timothy." In *Studies in the Pastoral Epistles.* London: SPCK, 1968: 96–109.

——— "Elements of a Baptismal Liturgy in Titus." In *Studies in the Pastoral Epistles.* London: SPCK, 1968: 78–96.

——— "Eve's Transgression." In *Studies in the Pastoral Epistles.* London: SPCK, 1968: 64–77.

Harding, Mark. "The Terminology of Respecting and Serving the Gods." Unpublished M.A. (Hons.) Thesis, Macquarie University, North Ryde, NSW, 1988.

——— "The Classical Rhetoric of Praise and the New Testament." *RThR* 45 (1986): 73–82.

Harrison, P. N. *Problem of the Pastoral Epistles.* Oxford: University Press, 1921.

Hengel, M. *The 'Hellenization of Judaea' in the First Century after Christ.* Philadelphia: Trinity Press International, 1989.

——— *Judaism and Hellenism.* 2 Vols. Philadelphia: Fortress, 1974.

Hoffmann, R. Joseph. *Marcion: On the Restitution of Christianity.* Chico: Scholars Press, 1984.

Holtzmann, Heinrich Julius. *Die Pastoralbriefe.* Leipzig: Wilhelm Engelmann, 1880.

Houlden, J. L. *The Pastoral Epistles.* Philadelphia: Trinity Press International, 1989.

Hughes, F. W. *Early Christian Rhetoric and 2 Thessalonians.* Journal for the Study of the New Testament Supplement Series, no. 30. Sheffield: JSOT Press, 1989.

Jaeger, W. *Paideia: The Ideals of Greek Culture.* 3 Vols. New York: Oxford University Press, 1939.

Jeremias, J. *Die Pastoralbriefe.* 8th Edition. Göttingen: Vandenhoeck & Ruprecht, 1963.

Johnson, Luke T. *Letters to Paul's Delegates: 1 Timothy, 2 Timothy, Titus.* Valley Forge: Trinity Press International, 1996.

——— *The Writings of the New Testament.* Philadelphia: Fortress, 1986.
——— "II Timothy and the Polemic Against the False Teachers: A Re-examination." *JRelS* 6.2/7.1 (1978–79): 1–26.
Judge, E. A. "St. Paul and Classical Society." *JAC* 15 (1972): 19–36.
——— "Paul's Boasting in Relation to Contemporary Professional Practice." *ABR* 16 (1968): 37–50.
——— *The Social Pattern of Christian Groups in the First Century.* London: Tyndale Press, 1960.
Jülicher, A. *An Introduction to the New Testament.* New York: G. P. Putnam's Sons, 1904.
Kamlah, E. *Die Form der katalogen Paränese im Neuen Testament.* Tübingen: Mohr, 1964.
Karris, Robert J. "The Polemic of the Pastoral Epistles." *JBL* 93 (1972): 549–64.
——— "The Function and Sitz im Leben of the Paraenetic Elements in the Pastoral Epistles." Th.D. Dissertation, Harvard University, 1971.
Käsemann, Ernst. "Paul and Early Catholicism." In *New Testament Questions of Today.* Philadelphia: Fortress, 1969: 237–51.
——— "Ministry and Community in the New Testament." In *Essays on New Testament Themes.* Philadelphia: Fortress, 1964: 63–94.
Keck, L. E. *Paul and his Letters.* Revised Edition. Philadelphia: Fortress, 1988.
Kelly, J. N. D. *A Commentary on the Pastoral Epistles.* London: A. & C. Black, 1963.
Kennedy, G. A. *New Testament Interpretation Through Rhetorical Criticism.* Chapel Hill: University of North Carolina Press, 1984.
——— *Classical Rhetoric and its Christian and Secular Tradition from Ancient to Modern Times.* Chapel Hill: University of North Carolina Press, 1980.
——— *The Art of Persuasion in Greece.* Princeton: Princeton University Press, 1963.
Kidd, Reggie M. *Wealth and Beneficence in the Pastoral Epistles.* Society of Biblical Literature Dissertation Series, no. 122. Atlanta: Scholars Press, 1990.
Kiley, M. *Colossians as Pseudepigraphy.* Sheffield: JSOT Press, 1986.
Kinneavy, J. L. *Greek Rhetorical Origins of the Christian Faith: An Inquiry.* New York/Oxford: Oxford University Press, 1987.
Knight, G. W. III. *The Pastoral Epistles.* Grand Rapids: Eerdmans, 1992.
Knoch, O. *Die 'Testamente' des Petrus und Paulus.* Stuttgart: KBW Verlag, 1973.
Koester, Helmut. *Introduction to the New Testament.* 2 Vols. Philadelphia and Berlin and New York: Fortress/de Gruyter, 1982.
——— "I Thessalonians—Experiment in Christian Writing." In F. F. Church,

and T. George, eds. *Continuity and Discontinuity in Church History.* Leiden: Brill, 1979: 33–44.

Koskenniemi, H. *Studien zur Idee und Phraseologie des griechischen Briefes bis 400 n. Chr.* Helsinki/Wiesbaden: Suomalaien Tiedakatamie/Otto Harrassowitz, 1956.

Kraftchick, Stephen J. "Ethos and Pathos in Galatians Five and Six: A Rhetorical Analysis." Ph.D. Dissertation, Emory University, 1985.

Kretschmar, G. "Der paulinische Glaube in den Pastoralbriefen." In *Glaube im Neuen Testament.* Festschrift H. Binder. Biblisch-theologische Studien 7; Neukirchen-Vluyn: Neukirchener Verlag, 1982: 115–40.

Küchler, Max *Schweigen, Schmuck und Schleier: Drei neutestamentliche Vorschriften zur Verdrängung der Frauen auf dem Hintergrund einer frauenfeindlichen Exegese des Alten Testaments im antiken Judentum.* NTOA 1; Freiburg/Göttingen: Universitätsverlag/Vandenhoeck & Ruprecht, 1986.

Kümmel, W. G. *Introduction to the New Testament.* 17th rev. ed. London: SCM, 1975.

Küng, H. "'Early Catholicism' in the New Testament as a Problem in Controversial Theology." In *The Living Church.* London: Sheed & Ward, 1963: 233–93.

Layton, B. *The Gnostic Scriptures.* Garden City: Doubleday, 1987.

Levison, J. R. "Did the Spirit Inspire Rhetoric?: An Exploration of George Kennedy's Definition of Early Christian Rhetoric." In D. F. Watson, ed. *Persuasive Artistry: Studies in New Testament Rhetoric in Honor of George A. Kennedy.* Journal for the Study of the New Testament Supplement Series, no. 50. Sheffield: JSOT Press, 1991: 25–40.

Lieu, Judith M. "Grace to you and Peace." *BJRL* 104 (1985): 161–78.

Lips, H. von. *Glaube—Gemeinde—Amt.* Göttingen: Vandenhoeck & Ruprecht, 1979.

Lock, W. W. *A Critical and Exegetical Commentary on the Pastoral Epistles.* Edinburgh: T. & T. Clark, 1924.

Lohfink, N. "Paulinische Theologie in der Rezeption der Pastoralbriefe." In K. Kertelge, ed. *Paulus in den neutestamentlichen Spätschriften: Zur Paulusrezeption im Neuen Testament.* Freiburg: Herder, 1981: 70–121.

Longenecker, R. N. *Galatians.* Waco: Word Books, 1990.

Lüdemann, G. *Early Christianity according to the Traditions in Acts: A Commentary.* Minneapolis: Fortress, 1989.

Luz, U. "Rechtfertigung bei den Paulusschülern." In J. Friedrich, *et al.*, eds. *Rechtfertigung.* Festschrift E. Käsemann. Tübingen/Göttingen: Vandenhoeck & Ruprecht, 1976: 365–83.

MacDonald, Dennis R. *The Legend and the Apostle: The Battle for Paul in Story and Canon.* Philadelphia: Westminster, 1983.

MacDonald, Margaret Y. *The Pauline Churches: A socio-historical study of institutionalization in the Pauline and Deutero-Pauline writings.* Society for

New Testament Studies Monograph Series, no. 60. Cambridge: University Press, 1988.

Mack, Burton L. *Rhetoric and the New Testament.* Minneapolis: Fortress, 1990.

Malherbe, Abraham J. "Hellenistic Moralists and the New Testament." In *Aufstieg und Niedergang der römischen Welt.* Part 2. Vol. 25. No. 2 (1992): 267–333.

——— *Paul and the Popular Philosophers.* Minneapolis: Fortress, 1989.

——— *Paul and the Thessalonians: The Philosophical Tradition of Pastoral Care.* Philadelphia: Fortress, 1987.

——— *Moral Exhortation: A Greco-Roman Sourcebook.* Philadelphia: Westminster, 1986.

——— "'In Season and Out of Season.'" *JBL* 103 (1984): 235–43.

——— *Social Aspects of Early Christianity.* Philadelphia: Fortress, 1977.

——— "'Gentle as a Nurse': The Cynic Background to 1 Thessalonians 2." *NovT* 12 (1970): 203–17.

Marrou, H. -I. *Histoire de l'éducation dans l'Antiquité.* 2 Vols. Paris: Éditions de Seuil, 1948.

Martyn, J. Louis. Review of *Paul the Apostle*, by J. Christiaan Beker. *Word and World* 2 (1982): 194–8.

McEleney, N. J. "The Vice Lists of the Pastoral Epistles." *CBQ* 36 (1974): 203–19.

Meade, David G. *Pseudonymity and Canon.* Wissenschaftliche Untersuchungen zum Neuen Testament, no. 39. Tübingen: Mohr, 1986.

Meeks, Wayne A. *The Moral World of the First Christians.* Philadelphia: Westminster, 1986.

Metzger, Bruce M. "Literary Forgeries and Canonical Pseudepigrapha." *JBL* 91 (1972): 3–24.

Mitton, C. Leslie. *Ephesians.* Grand Rapids: Eerdmans, 1973.

Moule, C. F. D. *The Birth of the New Testament.* 3rd edition; London: A. & C. Black, 1981.

Moulton, James H. *A Grammar of New Testament Greek.* Vol. 1, *Prolegomena.* 3rd Edition. Edinburgh: T. & T. Clark, 1908.

Moulton, James H. and George Milligan, eds. *The Vocabulary of the Greek Testament.* Reprint. Grand Rapids: Eerdmans, 1980.

Mullins, T. Y. "Topos as a New Testament Form." *JBL* 99 (1980): 541–7.

Munck, J. "Discourses d'adieu dans le Nouveau Testament et dans la littérature biblique." In *Aux sources de la tradition chrétienne: Mélanges offerts à M. Maurice Goguel.* Neuchatel: Delachaux & Niestlé, 1950: 155–70.

Murphy-O'Connor, J. *Paul the Letter-Writer: His World, His Options, His Skills.* Collegeville: Liturgical Press, 1995.

——— "2 Timothy Contrasted with 1 Timothy and Titus." *RB* 98 (1991): 403–18.

Nickelsburg, G. W. E. *Jewish Literature Between the Bible and the Mishnah.* Philadelphia: Fortress, 1981.
Nock, A. D. *Conversion.* Oxford: University Press, 1933.
Nordheim, E. von. *Die Lehre der Alten.* 2 Vols. Leiden: Brill, 1980 and 1985.
O'Brien, Peter T. *Commentary on Philippians.* Grand Rapids: Eerdmans, 1991.
——— *Introductory Thanksgivings in the Letters of Paul.* Leiden: Brill, 1977.
Oepke, A. "παῖς." In G. Kittel, ed. *Theological Dictionary of the New Testament.* Vol. 5. Grand Rapids: Eerdmans, 1967: 636–54.
Ollrog, W. -H. *Paulus und seine Mitarbeiter.* Neukirchen-Vluyn: Neukirchener Verlag, 1979.
Pardee, D. "An Overview of Ancient Hebrew Epistolography." *JBL* 97 (1978): 321–46.
Patzia, A. G. "The Deutero-Pauline Hypothesis: An Attempt at Clarification." *EvQ* 52 (1980): 27–42.
Prior, M. *Paul the Letter-Writer.* Journal for the Study of the New Testament Supplement Series, no. 23. Sheffield: JSOT Press, 1989.
Quinn, Jerome D. *The Letter to Titus.* New York: Doubleday, 1990.
——— "Paraenesis and the Pastoral Epistles." In M. Carrez, J. Doré, and P. Grelot, eds. *De la Tôrah au Messie.* Paris: Desclée, 1981: 495–501.
——— "The Holy Spirit in the Pastoral Epistles." In D. Durken, ed. *Sin, Salvation, and the Holy Spirit.* Collegeville: Liturgical Press, 1979: 345–68.
——— "P^{46}—The Pauline Canon?" *CBQ* 36 (1974): 379–85.
Räisänen, H. *Paul and the Law.* Philadelphia: Fortress, 1986.
Roetzel, C. Review of *Paul the Apostle*, by J. Christiaan Beker. *JAAR* 50 (1982): 117–9.
Roller, O. *Das Formular der paulinischen Briefe.* Stuttgart: Kohlhammer, 1933.
Roloff, J. *Der erste Brief an Timotheus.* Zürich: Benziger Verlag, 1988.
——— *Apostolat—Verkündigung—Kirche: Ursprung, Inhalt und Funktion des kirchlichen Apostelamtes nach Paulus, Lukas und den Pastoralbriefen.* Gütersloh: Gütersloher Verlagshaus G. Mohn, 1965.
Rudolph, K. *Gnosis.* San Francisco: Harper & Row, 1987.
Sanders, J. T. "The Transition from Opening Epistolary Thanksgiving to Body in the Letters of the Pauline Corpus." *JBL* 82 (1963): 348–62.
Saß, G. "Zur Bedeutung von δοῦλος bei Paulus." *ZNW* 40 (1941): 24–32.
Sattler,W. M. "Conceptions of *Ethos* in Ancient Rhetoric." *Speech Monographs* 14 (1957): 55–65.
Schenke, H. -M. "Das Weiterwirken des Paulus und die Pflege seines Erbes durch die Paulus-Schule." *NTS* 21 (1975): 505–18.
Schleiermacher, F. E. D. *Über den ersten Brief Pauli an Timotheus.* Braunschweig/Leipzig: Gerhard Reuter, 1897.
Schneemelcher, W. (ed.). *New Testament Apocrypha: Volume Two: Writings*

Relating to the Apostles; Apocalypses and Related Subjects. Revised Edition. Louisville: Westminster/John Knox, 1992.

Schrage, W. *Die konkreten Einzelgebote in der paulinischen Paränese.* Gütersloh: Mohn, 1961.

Schubert, P. *Form and Function of the Pauline Thanksgivings.* Berlin: Töpelmann, 1939.

Schulz, S. *Die Mitte der Schrift.* Stuttgart/Berlin: Kreuz Verlag, 1976.

Schütz, John H. *Paul and the Anatomy of Apostolic Authority.* Society for New Testament Studies Monograph Series, no. 26. Cambridge: Cambridge University Press, 1975.

Schwarz, R. *Bürgerliches Christentum im Neuen Testament?: Eine Studie zu Ethik, Amt und Recht in den Pastoralbriefen.* Klosterneuberg: Verlag Österreichisches Katholisches Bibelwerk, 1983.

Scroggs, R. "'Apocalyptic' as the Center of Paul's Gospel." *Interpretation* 36 (1982): 74–77.

Smit, J. "The Letter of Paul to the Galatians: A Deliberative Speech." *NTS* 35 (1989): 1–26.

Smith, W. A. *Ancient Education.* New York: Philosophical Library, 1955.

Sohm, R. *Wesen und Ursprung des Katholizismus.* Leipzig: Teubner, 1909.

——— *Das Kirchenrecht.* Leipzig: Duncker & Humboldt, 1892.

Solmsen, F. "Aristotelian Tradition in Ancient Rhetoric." In R. Stark, ed. *Rhetorika: Schriften zur aristotelischen und hellenistischen Rhetorik.* Hildesheim: Georg Olms Verlagsbuchhandlung, 1968: 312–49.

Speyer, W. *Die literarische Fälschung im Altertum.* München: C. H. Beck'sche Verlagsbuchhandlung, 1971.

Spicq, C. *Les Épîtres Pastorales.* 2 Vols. Paris: Gabalda, 1969.

Stenger, W. "Timotheus und Titus als literarische Gestalten." *Kairos* 16 (1974): 252–67.

Stirewalt, M. Luther Jr. *Studies in Ancient Greek Epistolography.* Atlanta: Scholars Press, 1993.

Stowers, Stanley K. *A Rereading of Romans: Justice, Jews, and Gentiles.* New Haven: Yale University Press, 1994.

——— *Letter Writing in Antiquity.* Philadelphia: Westminster, 1986.

——— *The Diatribe and Paul's Letter to the Romans.* Society of Biblical Literature Dissertation Series, no. 57. Chico: Scholars Press, 1981.

Thraede, K. *Grunzüge griechisch-römischer Brieftopik.* München: Beck, 1970.

Thrall, M. E. Review of *Paul the Apostle*, by J. Christiaan Beker. *JThS* 33 (1982): 268–70.

Thurén, J. "Die Struktur der Schlußparänese 1. Tim. 6, 3–21." *ThZ* 26 (1970): 241–53.

Thyen, H. *Der Stil der Jüdisch-Hellenistischen Homilie.* Göttingen: Vandenhoeck & Ruprecht, 1955.

Towner, P. H. *1–2 Timothy & Titus*. IVP New Testament Commentary Series; Downers Grove: IVP, 1994.

——— *The Goal of Our Instruction*. Journal for the Study of the New Testament Supplement Series, no. 34; Sheffield: JSOT Press, 1989.

Travis, S. H. "Paul's Boasting in 2 Corinthians 10–12." *SE* 6 (1973): 527–32.

Trummer, P. *Die Paulustradition der Pastoralbriefe*. Frankfurt am Main/Bern/Las Vegas: Lang, 1978.

Turner, N. *A Grammar of New Testament Greek*. Vol. 3, *Syntax*. Edinburgh: T. & T. Clark, 1963.

Verner, David C. *The Household of God: The Social World of the Pastoral Epistles*. Society of Biblical Literature Dissertation Series, no. 71. Chico: Scholars Press, 1983.

Vetschera, R. *Zur griechischen Paränese*. Smichow: Rohlicek & Sievers, 1912.

Vinson, R. B. "A Comparative Study of the Use of Enthymemes in the Synoptic Gospels." In D. F. Watson, ed. *Persuasive Artistry: Studies in New Testament Rhetoric in Honor of George A. Kennedy*. Journal for the Study of the New Testament Supplement Series, no. 36. Sheffield: JSOT Press, 1991: 119–41.

Wanke, J. "Der verkündigte Paulus der Pastoralbriefe." In W. Ernst, *et al*, eds. *Dienst der Vermittlung*. Leipzig: St. Benno-Verlag, 1977: 165–89.

Ward, Richard F. "Pauline Voice and Presence as Strategic Communication." *Semeia* 65 (1994): 95–107.

Watson, Duane F. "The New Testament and Greco-Roman Rhetoric: A Bibliographical Update." *JEThS* 33 (1990): 513–24.

——— "The New Testament and Greco-Roman Rhetoric: A Bibliography." *JEThS* 31 (1988): 465–72.

——— *Invention, Arrangement, and Style: Rhetorical Criticism of Jude and 2 Peter*. Society of Biblical Literature Dissertation Series, no. 104. Atlanta: Scholars Press, 1988.

Watson, Duane F., and Hauser, A. J. *Rhetorical Criticism of the Bible: A Comprehensive Bibliography with Notes on History and Method*. Leiden: Brill, 1994.

Wegenast, K. *Das Verständnis der Tradition bei Paulus und in den Deuteropaulinen*. Neukirchen: Neukirchener Verlag, 1962.

Weiss, J. "Beiträge zur Paulinischen Rhetorik." In *Theologische Studien: Herrn Wirk. Oberkonsistorialrath Professor D. Bernhard Weiss zu seinem 70. Geburtstage dargebracht*. Göttingen: Vandenhoeck & Ruprecht, 1897: 165–247.

Westermann, C. *Praise and Lament in the Psalms*. Atlanta: John Knox, 1981.

White, John L. *Light From Ancient Letters*. Philadelphia: Fortress, 1986.

——— "New Testament Epistolary Literature." In *Aufstieg und Niedergang der römischen Welt*. Part 2. Vol. 25. No. 2 (1984): 1730–56.

——— "Saint Paul and the Apostolic Letter Tradition." *CBQ* 45 (1983): 433–44.

——— "The Ancient Epistolary Group in Retrospect." *Semeia* 22 (1981): 1–14.

Wilder, A. N. *Early Christian Rhetoric*. London: SCM, 1964.

Wiles, Maurice F. *The Divine Apostle: The Interpretation of St. Paul's Epistles in the Early Church.* Cambridge: University Press, 1967.

Wilke, C. G. *Die neutestamentliche Rhetorik: Ein Seitenstück zur Grammatik des neutestamentlichen Sprachidioms*. Leipzig: Arnold, 1843.

Wilson, S. G. *Luke and the Pastoral Epistles*. London: SPCK, 1979.

——— "The Portrait of Paul in Acts and the Pastorals." In G. MacRae, ed. *Society of Biblical Literature 1976 Seminar Papers*. Missoula: Scholars, 1976: 397–411.

Winter, B. "The Importance of the *'Captatio Benevolentiae'* in the Speeches of Tertullus and Paul in Acts 24:1–21." *JThS* 42 (1991): 505–31.

Wire, Antoinette Clark. *The Corinthian Women Prophets: A Reconstruction through Paul's Rhetoric*. Minneapolis: Fortress, 1990.

Wisse, J. *Ethos and Pathos from Aristotle to Cicero*. Amsterdam: A. M. Hakkert, 1989.

Wolter, M. *Die Pastoralbriefe als Paulustradition.* Göttingen: Vandenhoeck & Ruprecht, 1988.

Wrede, W. *Paul.* London: Philip Green, 1907.

Young, F. *The Theology of the Pastoral Epistles*. Cambridge; University Press, 1994.

Ziesler, J. A. *Pauline Christianity*. Revised Edition. New York/Oxford: University Press, 1990.

Zmijewski, J. "Die Pastoralbriefe als pseudepigraphische Schriften." *Studien zum Neuen Testament und seiner Umwelt* 4 (1979): 97–118.

INDEX

Studies in Biblical Literature

This series invites manuscripts from scholars in any area of biblical literature. Both established and innovative methodologies, covering general and particular areas in biblical study, are welcome. The series seeks to make available studies which will make a significant contribution to the ongoing biblical discourse. Scholars who have interests in gender and sociocultural hermeneutics are particularly encouraged to consider this series.

For further information about the series and for the submission of manuscripts, contact:

Hemchand Gossai
Department of Philosophy and Religion
Culver-Stockton College
Canton, MO 63435